Sex, Drugs,
&
The Twinkie
Murders

"Father of the Underground Press" — *People*

"The Dean of Countercultural Journalism" — *High Times*

"The FBI was right; this man is dangerous — and funny, and necessary." — George Carlin

Sex, Drugs, & The Twinkie Murders

PAUL KRASSNER

Loompanics Unlimited
Port Townsend, Washington

Neither the author nor the publisher assumes any responsibility for the use or misuse of information contained in this book. It is sold for entertainment purposes only. Be Warned!

Published by:
Loompanics Unlimited
PO Box 1197
Port Townsend, WA 98368
Loompanics Unlimited is a division of Loompanics Enterprises, Inc.
Phone: 360-385-2230
E-mail: service@loompanics.com
Web site: www.loompanics.com

Cover Design by James Koehnline

ISBN 1-55950-206-1
Library of Congress Card Catalog Number 00-103089

CONTENTS

Dedication

To the women in my life — my wife Nancy, my ex-wife Jeanne, our daughter Holly, my sister Marge and our mother Ida — they have all taught me about the meaning of love and laughter.

"Always stay in your own movie." — Ken Kesey

Also by the author:

How a Satirical Editor Became a Yippie Conspirator in Ten Easy Years

Tales of Tongue Fu

Best of The Realist

Confessions of a Raving, Unconfined Nut: Misadventures in the Counter-Culture

The Winner of the Slow Bicycle Race: The Satirical Writings of Paul Krassner

Pot Stories For the Soul

Impolite Interviews

"I Was an Abortionist For the FBI," "Allen Ginsberg's Last Laugh," "The Great Kurt Vonnegut Cyberhoax," "Fuck Sunscreen," "The Memoirs of Monica Lewinsky," "President Clinton's Private

Confession," "Rapture, Shmapture" and "Kenneth Starr Meets JonBenet Ramsey" were published in *The Realist*.

"The Persecution of Lenny Bruce," "The Disneyland Memorial Orgy," "Who Killed Bobby Kennedy?," "Charlie Manson's Image," "The Zen Bastard Goes to Ecuador," "Abbie Hoffman's Forehead," "Wavy Gravy's Rainbow Bridge," "Further Weirdness With Terence McKenna," "The Neo-Pagan Festival," "A Survey of Drug Comedy in the '90s," "An Interview With Chiquita Banana" and "See You in the Funny Papers" were published in *High Times*.

"John Lennon and the FBI" and "The Tabloidization of America" were published in *In These Times*. "The New Age Odd Couple" was published in the *Whole Earth Review*. "The Parts Left Out of the Patty Hearst Trial," "The Swinger's Convention" and "The Sexual Misadventures of Female Comedians" were published in *Playboy*. "How I Invented Soft-Core Pornography," "Condoms Are Us," "Speaking of Scumbags," "The Funny Hooker," "Oral Sex Is On the Rise," "The Missing Episode of Seinfeld" and "The World Pornography Conference" were published in *Penthouse Forum*. "The Case of the Twinkie Murders" and "Be There Then" were published in *The Nation*. "Anita and the Blow-Up Doll" and "The Love Song of Timothy Leary" were published in *Tikkun*. "Worship At the Celebrity of Your Choice" was published in the *Los Angeles Times Sunday Magazine*.

"Driving While Stoned" and "A Tale of Two Conspiracies" were published in the *New York Press*. "Psychedelic Relics at the Cannabis Cup" was published in the *L.A. Weekly*.

"Predictions for 2000" was published in *Metro News*.

‧■█■‧

Introduction

When *Life* published a favorable profile of me, the FBI sent a poison-pen letter to the editor, complaining, "To classify Krassner as a social rebel is far too cute. He's a nut, a raving, unconfined nut." That was true, of course. But when *People* labeled me "father of the underground press," I immediately demanded a blood test. They were referring to *The Realist*, a countercultural magazine that I launched in 1958, several years before the word "countercultural" was coined. We accepted no advertising, and in 1974, I ran out of money and had to cease publication. In 1985, I reincarnated *The Realist* as a newsletter.

"The taboos may have changed," I wrote, "but irreverence is still our only sacred cow."

"Now I've decided to cease publication — this time, voluntarily — in 2001. (For a subscription to the final six issues, send $12 to Box 1230, Venice CA 90294.) When I originally started publishing, *The Realist* was truly a lone voice, but irreverence has since become an industry.

Also, there are a few novels I'd like to work on. The first was inspired by my association with Lenny Bruce. The story began to evolve in my mind after his death. I kept wondering, what would a contemporaneous Lenny be saying and doing? So I've been developing material on stage that will end up in the mouth of my protagonist. I find myself resenting this imaginary character for stealing my material. It's a very schizophrenic process. And it's a challenge to write fiction because you have to make stuff up. Of course, I've been making stuff up all my life, but that was journalism.

Or, rather, it was *presented* as journalism. In fact, *The Realist* became most infamous for a hoax, "The Parts Left Out of the Kennedy Book" in 1967. Jackie Kennedy had authorized William Manchester to write *The Death of a President*, but now she wanted portions of the manuscript excised. Unaware that I was utilizing an established literary form, apocrypha, I tried to nurture the utterly incredible in a context of credibility.

Imitating Manchester's style, I began with a true item — during the 1960 primaries, Lyndon Johnson had attacked JFK on the grounds that his father, Joseph P. Kennedy, was a Nazi sympathizer while he was U.S. Ambassador to Great Britain. Then I improvised on stories — one involving Marilyn Monroe — that White House correspondents knew to be true but which had remained unpublished.

I continued peeling off layer after layer of verisimilitude, getting closer and closer with each new paragraph to the climactic scene on Air Force One where Jackie walks in on LBJ, who is leaning over a casket and fucking the throat wound in Kennedy's corpse. This was not merely casual necrophilia, though. It had a serious purpose — to change the entry wound from the Grassy Knoll into an exit wound from the Texas Book Depository in order to fool the Warren Commission.

Well, it fooled a lot of *Realist* readers too, if only for a moment, but a moment in which they believed that the leader of the western world who had been escalating the war in Vietnam was totally insane.

Recently, though, I met a 25-year-old who told me about the LBJ-JFK encounter — not knowing I had written it — and who believes that the act of neck-rophilia had actually occurred. What I had originally intended as a metaphorical truth remains, in her mind, as literal truth. Thanks to current realities, my notorious satire has become a myth.

2

However, everything in *this* book has been thoroughly fact-checked, documented and vetted — except, obviously, "The Missing Episode of Seinfeld," "The Memoirs of Monica Lewinsky," "President Clinton's Private Confession," "An Interview with Chiquita Banana," "Rapture, Shmapture" and "Kenneth Starr Meets JonBenet Ramsey."

In any case, *The Realist* has served its purpose, and publications like the *Onion* are following in the same tradition that I was part of, except that it's published in cyberspace. Indeed, the Internet has changed the nature of protest. Locally, in Los Angeles, the battle against the telephone overlay system was mounted on the Net. Nationally, the Million Man Marijuana March has been publicized online. And globally, the demonstrations against the WTO in Seattle were organized on the World Wide Web.

Causes are still fought by individuals (Granny D., the 89-year-old grandmother who has been walking across the country to gather support for campaign finance reform) and groups (campus branches of Students Against Slavery). In Philadelphia, 2,000 students from around the nation gathered to pledge that they would not work for corporations that are environmentally unfriendly or exploit children. That conference didn't get quite the media coverage that *Who Wants to Marry a Multi-Millionaire?* did.

As I write this, the presidential race is on — summed up by the title of my next CD, *Campaign in the Ass* — and the rhetoric is so awesomely superficial that the candidates can't even get their sound-bites straight. George W. Bush intended to say, "John McCain is riding the high horse by taking the low road." Instead, it came out, "He can't take the high horse and then claim the low road." And Bush is against abortion, except in the case of rape, incest, or his pregnant daughter.

The pundits analyze whether Al Gore and Bill Bradley display enough animation during their debates, as if we're voting for Daffy Duck and Goofy. On second thought, they *are* Daffy and Goofy. And so are their positions. They're *for* the death penalty and *against* decriminalization of marijuana.

When California Attorney General Bill Lockyer went to Washington to try and talk sense about the war on (some) drugs to

General Barry McCaffrey, the drug czar actually threatened to jail him. And when Lockyer convened a task force to draft legislation to provide for distribution of medical marijuana — a right that already existed under Proposition 215 — Governor Davis' staff warned that he would veto it, no questions asked.

Meanwhile, in Kingman, Arizona, a severely disabled woman with no arms or legs was just sentenced to a year in prison for possession. The same week, in Augusta, Georgia, a man who's been in a wheelchair for 35 years, unable to do more than raise his shoulders, began a seven-year prison sentence for possession.

Conversely, there's a devastating report in the *Journal of the American Medical Association* documenting the alarming rise in the prescription of stimulants and antidepressants to children under the age of five, but members of Congress in both parties have refused to speak out because the pharmaceutical companies are such huge contributors. It's true insanity in the guise of pragmatic career moves.

Fortunately, my spiritual path helps me to maintain perspective. And what exactly could the spiritual path of an atheist be? Attempting to avoid getting a headache whenever I contemplate the infinity of time and space. Viewing reality through a filter of absurdity. Being in awe of nature and technology and the human spirit. Marveling at the process of coincidence. Meditating on the concept of evolution in every aspect of civilization. Relishing the miracle of consciousness. Playing with my ego instead of attempting to get rid of it. Developing an intimate relationship with the deity I don't believe in.

According to a recent survey by the Barna Group, an independent market-research company, about one out of five self-described atheists and agnostics (19%) pray to God during a typical week. I know I do. For example, before I go on stage to perform, I always pray, "Please, God, help me do a good show." And then I always hear the voice of God, booming, "SHUT UP, YOU SUPERSTITIOUS FOOL!"

My favorite metaphor for God comes from Krishnamurti. A disciple asked him, "Why is there evil in the world?" And he replied, "To thicken the plot." My working philosophy comes from

the comic strip, *Mary Worth:* "When in doubt, do the kindest thing."
I believe that existence has no meaning, and I enjoy every moment
of it. That's my religion. Life is a mystery. If it's not a mystery,
what the fuck *is* it?

Paul Krassner
Venice Beach
February 2000

I Was an Abortionist
for the FBI

When I launched my irreverent, anti-censorship magazine, *The Realist,* in 1958, there were 18 states with laws forbidding the sale of contraceptives. Birth control had always been one of my biggest causes. I did what I could. I paid the rent for William Baird's free birth-control clinic in Queens, and I published articles by Leo Koch, a biology professor who was dismissed from the University of Illinois because he wrote, in a letter to the campus newspaper:

"With modern contraceptives and medical advice readily available at the nearest drugstore, or at least a family physician, there is no valid reason why sexual intercourse should not be condoned among those sufficiently mature to engage in it without social consequences and without violating their own codes of morality and ethics."

Every condom was stamped with the legend, SOLD IN DRUGSTORES ONLY FOR THE PREVENTION OF DISEASE. In Newark, New Jersey, a "detail man" (sales distributor) for the Youngs Rubber Corporation, manufacturer of Trojans, had been warning pharmacists to tell their clerks that if anyone asked for contraceptives, he should be told, "Oh, you mean prophylactics, don't you?"

I interviewed a Youngs Rubber representative.

Q. "What about the 'for the prevention of disease' legend?"
A. *"That is the traditional use to which prophylactics are put."*

7

Q. "Oh, come now."

A. *"Well, of course, if a couple doesn't have the will power to abstain from having sexual relations, and they wish to avoid a pregnancy, it can be used for that purpose."*

Q. "Are you saying that an unwanted pregnancy is a disease?"

A. *"Well, of course, if you use that terminology, then it would be true."*

The detail man never got around to the detail of warning employees at one particular drugstore to be sure and say prophylactics. Two clerks were arrested there — one for selling a pack of Trojans to an undercover cop, the other for selling Orthogynol contraceptive jelly to a female undercover cop. They had been found guilty and fined $100 each for selling contraceptives "without just cause." Now the verdict was being appealed on the grounds that the 90-year-old statute was unconstitutional.

I was the only reporter in court. At one point, the judge asked the prosecutor, "What *is* just cause?"

A. *"Health or other reasons. But just cause is not where you or I, any person, walks in and the druggist sells indiscriminately without any cause whatsoever — such a sale is without legal right."*

Q. "Only with a prescription, then?"

A. *"I wouldn't say that it is only confined to a doctor's prescription, because a doctor may not be the only one who can establish just cause."*

Ultimately the judge declared the law unconstitutional. Meanwhile, freelance journalist Harry Kursh gave *The Realist* an exclusive report. For the first time in medical history, experimentation with a birth control pill was taking place — and the human guinea pigs were women in Puerto Rico. He wrote: "When the birth control pill is finally reported on by scientists and made commercially available, it may prove to be the political and sociological A-bomb of this age."

· ■ ▌ ■ ·

When Robert Spencer was in high school, his father, a district attorney, had a case brought to him by a renowned minister whose daughter was getting bizarre threatening letters. The elder Spencer suggested that the minister get samples of her handwriting, and it was clear that she had written the letters to herself. An investigation brought out the fact that she was pregnant and didn't want to be. The minister blew his brains out.

Young Spencer never forgot that incident. He went to medical school and became a general physician in Ashland, Pennsylvania. Eventually he began performing abortions. His reputation spread across America by word-of-mouth. He charged as little as $5. When an article in *Look* magazine stated, "There is no such thing as a 'good' abortionist — all of them are in business strictly for the money." I decided to ask Dr. Spencer for an interview, promising him anonymity.

He was the cheerful personification of an old-fashioned family doctor. During the interview, he used folksy expressions like 'by golly.' He rarely said the word *pregnant*. Rather, he would say, "She was *that way* and she came to me for help." Over a few decades he had performed 27,006 illegal operations, including some for a couple of priests who "had their housekeepers in trouble."

Q. "You've violated the law 27,006 times — how have you gotten away with it?"

A. *"Well, I don't know how."*

Q. "I mean you're not in jail."

A. *"No, that's true. And I haven't any doubt the country's known about me because, heavens, I've had people from practically every state in the union."*

Q. "You mean you can't explain it to yourself, why you're free?"

A. *"No, I don't know exactly why that is at all."*

Q. "Have police come to you for professional services?"

A. *"Oh, yes, I've had police in here, too. I've helped them out. I've helped a hell of a lot of police out. I've helped a lot of FBI men out. They would be here, and they had me a little bit scared — I didn't know whether they were just in to get me or not."*

Q. "What would you say is the most significant lesson you've learned in all your years as a practicing abortionist?"

A. *"You've got to be careful. That's the most important thing. And you've got to be cocksure that everything's removed. And even the uterus speaks to you and tells you. I could be blind. You see, this is an operation no eye sees. You go by the sense of feel and touch. And hearing. The voice of the uterus..."*

The June 1962 issue of *The Realist* with Dr. Spencer's interview included a reprint of an article from the *London Observer*: "Three Roman Catholic theologians have expressed the opinion that, in times of revolution and violence, it is lawful for women, particularly for nuns, to take contraceptive pills and precautions against the danger of becoming pregnant through rape...."

On that same page was our Rumor of the Month: "So-called 'flying saucers' are actually diaphragms being dropped by nuns on their way to Heaven."

I also included a cartoon by Mort Gerberg in that issue, depicting a Mother Goose character (the old lady who lived in a shoe who had so many children she didn't know what to do) speaking on the phone: "Dr. Burnhill? — uh — you don't know me, but — uh—I've been told that you could — uh — perform a certain — uh — operation—." It turned out that there was an actual Dr. Burnhill, a gynecologist-obstetrician in New York City, who called me in distress when patients started bringing that issue of *The Realist* to his office. He accepted my apology, though he didn't want a retraction. Almost every succeeding Gerberg cartoon would have a character named Burnhill.

After my interview with "a humane abortionist" was published, I began to get phone calls from scared female voices. They were all in desperate search of a safe abortion. It was preposterous that they should have to seek out the editor of a satirical magazine, but their quest so far had been futile, and they simply didn't know where else to turn. With Dr. Spencer's permission, I referred them to him. At first there were only a few calls each week, then several every day. I had never intended to become an underground abortion referral service, but it wasn't going to stop just because in the next issue of *The Realist* I would be publishing an interview with somebody else.

On December 1, 1965, the American Medical Association voted, after a bitter convention debate, to defer action on a report by its Committee on Human Reproduction, which urged states to loosen their abortion laws. But loosening the laws would have been a compromise at best. In San Francisco, Patricia Maginnis and Rowena Gurner organized the Society for Humane Abortion, announcing that they did *not* support "legalized" abortion: "Does one ever speak of a legal tooth extraction, a legal appendectomy, a legal hysterectomy, a legal tonsillectomy?" Rather, they were for total *repeal* of the laws.

They pointed out the problem of getting "involved in the complexities of whether to allow abortion to protect the physical and/or mental health of the pregnant women for rape, incest and so on. As long as such emphasis is placed on these individual (and relatively rare) cases, progress will be frustrated simply because underlying every argument is the mistaken concept that abortion, in itself, is evil. It would be rather strange to hear surgery for ulcers described as evil rather than as a means of dealing with a condition which warrants change."

In January 1966, I flew to San Francisco for a conference on Abortion and Human Rights, sponsored by the Society for Humane Abortion. There had never been such an event before, except for an unofficial abortionists "convention" a few years before in Atlantic City, which was attended by three doctors, all of whom had retired. This conference was being held at the San Francisco Hilton Hotel, renamed the Hilton-Abortion by attendees.

I met Dr. Bryan Henrie, an elderly osteopath from Grove, Oklahoma. Although there had been two deaths of mothers out of 1200 babies he delivered, when there was one death of a mother out of 5000 abortions he had performed, he was arrested on a manslaughter charge. After his conviction, he was given a farewell picnic by hundreds of patients and friends from his community and the surrounding area. On previous occasions he had been publicly commended for donations to the local library and, two years before, he was named Father of the Year. The arresting officers apologized to Dr. Henrie for arresting him.

"I'm not ashamed for the things I did that had me sent to prison," he said. "I'm not ashamed that I listened to those pleading women. I'm ashamed of a law that must be broken to save the honor and dignity of women. The law should determine who shall *perform* an abortion, never on whom it shall be *done*."

He served 25 months of a four-year sentence. The prison guards treated him with the same respect that he had shown their wives and girlfriends in his capacity as an abortionist. Only one prisoner wouldn't talk to him — an inmate who had made his living by extorting money from doctors who performed abortions. When Dr. Henrie was released from prison — on his 68th birthday — 400 neighbors held a homecoming party for him on the town square. But his license had been revoked, and he was forced to retire. He started working on a book, dedicated "to those women who cry in the night for help and receive instead rebuke."

I also met Sherri Finkbine, former host of the children's TV program, *Romper Room*. We were having dinner at a Chinese restaurant. She had become the center of the Great Thalidomide Controversy a few years previously, when she wanted to terminate a pregnancy that would have resulted in a deformed baby.

On July 31, 1962, James Wechsler wrote in the *New York Post:* "There is apparently reason to believe that no prosecution will be initiated if the abortion occurs." That same day, Max Lerner wrote in that same newspaper: "The parents must now decide whether to risk an almost certain prosecution." Sherri wasn't prosecuted, but she was persecuted, by mail and phone calls.

"I was shocked," she recalled, "that so much hate could be spewed forth in the name of religion." Such as a letter that wished, *I hope God takes away your other four children!*

"But this baby," she said with a shudder, "it would have been a head and a torso. It's been three and a half years, and it's still hard to get it out of my mind. Before this happened to me, I never thought about abortion. I just had *babies*."

One summer, her husband and two other teachers took a large group of high school students to Europe. In England, a doctor prescribed some tranquilizers for him. Later, in her fifth pregnancy, Sherri had nausea and tried those pills.

"If a tranquilizer could calm you down, why couldn't it stop the queasiness of a pregnant tummy?"

A few weeks later, in her local paper, there was a tiny news item about a move in England to abort mothers-to-be who had taken a certain "sleeping pill," and to practice euthanasia on the grotesque babies that were being born as a result. The next day a follow-up story labeled the drug a tranquilizer. Sherri's doctor wired the London pharmacy that had dispensed the pills, got their answer and recommended that she terminate her pregnancy.

"I was even naive enough," she said, "to request the abortion at St. Joseph's Hospital, where my last baby had been born."

The operation was set for a Thursday. On the preceding Sunday, she had decided to warn others who might *unknowingly* be in her predicament. That past year, a contingent of the National Guard had been stationed in Germany where thalidomide was manufactured. She phoned the editor of the *Arizona Republic*. He promised not to use her name. On Monday, page one had a black-bordered article with a screaming headline: "Baby-Deforming Drug May Cost Woman Her Child Here." The wire services picked it up, and there were worldwide repercussions.

The doctors cancelled Sherri's operation. They were too busy performing emergency surgery to cover each other's ass. They were aware that any citizen — without even knowing Sherri's identity — could have gone to the district attorney, challenging the "therapeutic" nature of the operation, and they could *all* face criminal prosecution. The hospital petitioned the state Supreme Court for a declaratory judgment and, although the case was dismissed without a hearing, Sherri Finkbine's name became a matter of public record, and she became an instant public figure.

As a result, Sherri was inundated with methods for terminating her pregnancy. There was one sure cure, a pint of aqua ammonia, but take care to dilute it, as ammonia will loosen a rusty bolt in five minutes — "only he didn't say whether to drink it or sit in it" — and there were suggestions that ranged from smelling turpentine fumes to taking a ride on a roller coaster. One man claimed he could hypnotize her into an abortion over the telephone. A skydiver "offered me the thrill of my life and a miscarriage as well." A doctor was willing to perform the operation for $1500 in an airplane out of the state's jurisdiction.

Her own doctor recommended Japan as the least red-tape-bound place to go. Abortion was legal there, a routine matter that cost $8.40 or, if you were affiliated with a health plan, 83 cents. But in Japan there was fear of anti-Japanese demonstrations by Americans who opposed the Finkbines, and they were refused a visa. Eventually she traveled to Sweden and became the first woman in history to have an abortionist with his own press representative. Ironically, the relative ease of obtaining abortions in Poland had been drawing *Swedish* women who found it difficult to obtain them in their native country. It was an international game of Musical Abortions.

The Pope publicly called Sherri a murderer, and a newspaper editorial claimed she was doing the whole thing as a publicity stunt — each accuser projecting the subjectivity of his own occupational hazard.

Now, at the Chinese restaurant, I presented Sherri with the message from my fortune cookie, obviously intended for her: "Confucius say: Angel with wings not so hot as angel with arms."

Reporters hounded her with the question, "Do you think the fetus has a soul?" She admitted that she'd never thought about it before, but Dr. Bryan Henrie had indeed thought about it. He'd aborted many Catholic girls, and he knew they believed that if the fetus is destroyed without baptism, it is an unpardonable sin and they would go to Hell. So, whenever he aborted a Catholic girl, he always baptized the fetus as a matter of course.

Three plainclothesmen were taping the proceedings at the Hilton-Abortion, including Dr. Lucile Newman's revelations about police officers who tell a patient that she won't get any painkilling drugs unless she reveals the name of the abortionist whose incomplete or infection-causing work had brought her to a hospital, which automatically called the cops.

▪▪█▪▪

While the Society for Humane Abortion was holding that conference in San Francisco, state police raided Dr. Spencer's clinic in Ashland, and arrested him. He remained out of jail only by the grace of political pressure. He was ultimately forced to retire from his practice, but I continued mine, referring callers to other physicians that he had recommended.

Occasionally I would be offered money by a patient, but I never accepted any. And whenever a doctor offered me a kickback, I refused but I also insisted that he give a discount for the same amount to those patients referred by me. One doctor who had charged $350 was arrested and went back in business at $600. He was arrested again and started charging $1000. I complained that many women couldn't afford his rate.

"I realize I'm pricing myself out of the market," he explained, "but security procedures require..."

Another abortionist, Dr. Luis, had operated a clinic in Havana. He fled Cuba when Castro took over, but his relationship with law enforcement under Batista had conditioned him for the climate in Florida, where he paid off local police in order to stay in business. Another abortionist there was *not* paying off, and when the cops arrested him, they gave his surgical instruments to Dr. Luis.

The wife of the officer in charge heard about the arrest and asked him if it was true. "You fool," she said, "I had an appointment with him this afternoon." Not only that, but her husband wasn't the father of the child that she didn't want to bear.

Dr. Luis opened up a New York branch of his practice. His office was wiretapped by five detectives for several months before they finally raided the premises, but instead of arresting the doctor, they extorted an agreement from him to pay $3500 a month to continue operating. They also took a few hundred dollars, which had just been paid to him by a patient I'd referred, Mary. They told her that they would return it all, but they gave her back only $10 and threatened to book her for manslaughter if she refused to appear as a material witness.

"Oh, yeah?" she responded. "How do you know it was a boy?"

Dr. Luis moved to New Jersey, so a couple of New York cops crossed the state line. One tried to get a lump sum of $50,000 while his cohort in the waiting room kept one eye on the patients and the other on *Bullwinkle*. But Dr. Luis faked them out. On a long-distance call, he told his wife in Spanish to contact their attorney, who in turn told her to contact the police, who in turn told her to show up at the airport with cut-up newspapers instead of cash in the envelope. The extorters were arrested and demoted, while Dr. Luis fled once again. There was a 37-state alarm out for him. He hid out in one of the remaining, if not original, 13 states.

When Mary saw a report about Dr. Luis in the *New York Journal-American*, she phoned them, and two reporters pumped her for information. She mentioned that I had referred her to Dr. Luis, so they called me to find out where he was hiding. I was unable to help them. A few days passed, and the *Journal-American* didn't run anything on Mary's story, so I called up a reporter I trusted at the *World Telegram & Sun*, Selwyn Raab, and arranged for him to interview her.

Next day the *World Telegram* headlined the story. The reporters at the *Journal-American* were furious. Not only had they been scooped, but with a story that they already had in their possession. Raab was called by the district attorney's office. They knew who Mary was, although Raab hadn't identified her. Their information could only have come from the vengeful *Journal-American*, which had promised her total anonymity.

An editor at the *Journal-American* called and berated me for betraying them. However, he said, I could redeem myself by revealing where Dr. Luis was. I told him I didn't know. He said he didn't believe me. I said I didn't trust him.

"And," I added, "even if I *did* know where Dr. Luis is hiding, I wouldn't tell you."

"All right, Paulie boy, we're gonna throw you into the lion's cage. We're gonna tell the D.A.'s office all about you."

"What's my crime — withholding information from the D.A. or withholding information from the *Journal-American*?"

He gave me until 8 p.m. to think it over. Mary and I called the D.A.'s office and made an appointment to appear as voluntary witnesses the next morning. A female officer, Detective Heath, saw Mary, who didn't want to talk without me there, so she told Mary to wait, then served her with a subpoena to appear before the Grand Jury. The man at the desk told me that my request had been turned down by the district attorney.

For several months, Detective Heath's office had been investigating abortionists because telephone answering services in New York were involved. But the abortionists functioned in other cities, and that's where the arrests were made.

Detective Heath complained, "The boys in Philadelphia and Camden and Jersey City get all the credit."

She asked women questions like, "Did the doctor make any advances toward you?" If nothing else, maybe they could nab him on the Mann Act. She asked an African exchange student, "The man who impregnated you — was he white, black or colored?" She asked the white woman who had befriended the exchange student, "Why did you have to help this girl? She's not an American citizen — and she's black." Detective Heath advised women to keep away from me because I had "strange Greenwich Village friends." She told a graduate student working on a thesis about abortion that to interview me would compromise the Columbia School of Journalism.

Detective Heath justified her work: "This is the law. We have to follow it. Abortion is an illegal act, and we have to punish people who commit it."

The irony of her mission was posed by one patient, who said, "Look, by catching these doctors who are the best ones available, you're only forcing girls to go underground to less competent people. Your whole concern isn't to protect lives but to force girls to find better means to *destroy* their lives by going to unqualified people."

However, the only alternatives to abortion that Detective Heath would consider were abstinence and adoption. "Birth control is out of the question," she insisted. "It offends morality and religion." On the wall of her office was a crucifix. On her desk were three gospel cards carefully placed so that their messages could be easily read by women who were invited to her office because their names had been on the records of an abortionist's answering service.

I was subpoenaed by district attorneys in two cities to appear before Grand Juries investigating criminal charges against abortionists. On both occasions I refused to testify, and each time the D.A. tried to frighten me into cooperating, with the threat of arrest.

In Liberty, New York, my name had been extorted from a patient by threatening *her* with arrest. The D.A. told me that the doctor had confessed everything and they got it all on tape. He gave me until 2 o'clock that afternoon to change my mind about testifying, or else the police would come to take me away.

"I'd better call my lawyer."

I went outside to a public phone and called, not a lawyer, but the doctor.

"That never happened," he said.

I returned to the D.A.'s office and told him that my lawyer said to continue being uncooperative. Then I just sat there waiting for the cops.

"They're on their way," the D.A. kept warning me.

But at 2 o'clock, he simply said, "Okay, you can go home now."

Bronx District Attorney Burton Roberts took a different approach. He told me that his staff had found an abortionist's financial records, which showed all the money that I had received, but he would grant me immunity from prosecution if I cooperated with the Grand Jury. He offered his hand as a gesture of trust. If I *had* ever accepted any money, I'd have had no way of knowing that he was bluffing.

"That's not true," I said, refusing to shake hands with him.

He was angry, but he finally had to let me go.

In San Francisco, I had become friends with Paul Jacobs, a radical union organizer. It was he who first suggested to frustrated Berkeley protesters that they march to the local draft board and burn their draft cards. This was before the authorities decided that such a symbolic gesture ought to be in violation of the law, which they proceeded to enact.

Jacobs was commissioned by the Health, Education and Welfare Department to write a paper, "Keeping the Poor Poor," for presentation at a social workers conference and to be included in a book on poverty. His analysis was prefaced by a Portuguese quotation he got from Henry Miller: *Cuando merda tiver valor pobre nasce sem cu.* Translation: "If shit ever gets to have any value, the poor will be born without assholes."

In *The Realist*, I applied that proverb to the subject of abortion:

"A poor woman has to undergo an unsuccessful hassle to get permission for a therapeutic — that is, a legal — abortion, even though she contacted German measles from a syphilitic cousin who raped her and then stole all her money plus the second-hand toys of her 18 children, and then she was calmed down with tranquilizers containing thalidomide. Whereas, a wealthy woman can avoid having an unwanted offspring, under safe and sanitary conditions, *simply because she decided* not to have a baby. Why, she might conceivably go so far some day as to achieve the ultimate status symbol by obtaining an abortion when she isn't even pregnant."

I continued to carry on my underground abortion referral service. Each time, though, I would flash on the notion that this was my *own* mother asking for help, and that she was pregnant with *me*. I would try to identify with the fetus, which was going to be aborted even while I was serving as a conduit to the performance of that very abortion. Every day I would think about the possibility of having never existed, and I would only appreciate being alive all the more.

Pretending to be the fetus was just a way of focusing on my role as a referral service. I didn't want it to become so casual that I would grow unaware of the implications. By personalizing it, I had to accept my own responsibility for each soul whose potential I was helping to destroy. That was about as mystical as I got. Maybe I was simply projecting my own ego. In any case, by the time these women came to me for help, they had *already* made up their minds. This was not some abstract cause far away — these were actual people in real distress right now — and I just couldn't say no. So I made a choice to abort myself every time. For nearly a decade this became my fetal yoga.

The Persecution of Lenny Bruce

Lenny was in mock shock. "Do you realize," he asked rhetorically, "that they're busting kids for smoking *flowers*?" But Lenny was an optimist. It was in 1960 that he said, "Now let me tell you something about pot. Pot will be legal in ten years. Why? Because in this audience probably every other one of you knows a law student who smokes pot, who will become a senator, who will legalize it to protect himself."

A sense of optimism was the essence of Lenny Bruce's humor, especially at its most controversial. And so, when it was discovered that Nazi leaders from Germany had resettled in Argentina with false passports, he displayed from the stage a newspaper with a huge headline: "Six Million Jews Found Alive in Argentina!" Now, that was the ultimate extension of optimism.

Lenny poked fun at the ridiculously high fees of show business by comparing them with the absurdly low salaries of teachers. He explored the implications of pornography, masturbation and orgasms before they were trendy subjects and became the basis of an 8-billion-dollar industry.

He ventured into fields that were mined with taboos, breaking from a long tradition of mainstream stand-up comics who remained loyal to safe material. They spewed forth a bland plethora of stereotypical jokes about mothers-in-law, Chinese waiters, women drivers, Marilyn Monroe, airplane food, Elvis Presley, and the ever popular complaints about "my wife," whether it had to do with her cooking, her shopping, her nagging or her frigidity.

I first met Lenny in 1959 when he came to New York for a midnight show at Town Hall. He was a charter subscriber to my magazine, *The Realist*, and he invited me to his hotel, where he was staying with Eric Miller, a black musician who worked with Lenny in certain bits, such as "How to Relax Colored People at a Party." Lenny would portray a "first-plateau liberal" trying to make conversation with Miller, playing the part of an entertainer at an all-white party.

Lenny's satire was his way of responding to a culture wallowing in its own hypocrisy. If it was considered sick to have a photo of him on the cover of his first album, picnicking in a cemetery, he knew it was really sicker to enforce racial segregation of the bodies that were allowed to be buried in that cemetery.

At this point in his career, Lenny was still using the euphemism *frig* on stage. Although the mainstream media were already translating his irreverence into "sick comic," he had not yet been branded "filthy." I handed him the new issue of *The Realist* featuring my interview with Albert Ellis, which included a segment on the semantics of profanity.

"My premise," said Ellis, "is that sexual intercourse, copulation, fucking or whatever you wish to call it, is normally, under almost all circumstances, a damned good thing. Therefore, we should rarely use it in a negative, condemnatory manner. Instead of denouncing someone by calling him 'a fucking bastard,' we should say, of course, that he is 'an unfucking villain' (since *bastard*, too, is not necessarily a negative state and should not only be used pejoratively)."

Lenny was amazed that I could get away with publishing it without resorting to asterisks or dashes as other magazines did.

"Are you telling me that this is legal to sell on the newsstands?"

"Absolutely," I said. "The Supreme Court's definition of obscenity is that it has to be material which appeals to your prurient interest."

Lenny magically produced an unabridged dictionary from the suitcase on his bed, and he proceeded to look up the word *prurient*, which has its roots in the Latin *prurie*, to itch."

"To itch," he mused. "What does that *mean?* That they can bust a novelty store owner for selling itching powder along with the dribble glass and the whoopie cushion?"

"It's just their way of saying that something gets you horny."

He closed the dictionary, clenching his jaw and nodding his head in affirmation of a new discovery: "So it's against the law to get you horny...."

In September 1961, Lenny was busted, ostensibly for drugs (for which he had a prescription), but actually because he was making too much money and local officials wanted a piece of the action. He was appearing at the Red Hill Inn in Pennsauken, New Jersey, near Philadelphia. Cops broke into his hotel room to make the arrest, and that night an attorney and bail bondsman came backstage and told him that $10,000 was all it would take for the judge to dismiss the charges. Lenny refused. A lawyer friend happened to witness this attempted extortion. The others assumed he was a beatnik just hanging around the dressing room. That was on Friday. On Monday, Lenny went to court and pleaded not guilty. "Incidentally," he added, "I can only come up with $50." The case was dismissed.

Five days later, at the Jazz Workshop in San Francisco, Lenny was arrested for portraying a Broadway agent who used the word *cocksucker* to describe a drag queen. This was the first in a series of arrests, ostensibly for obscenity, but actually for choosing religious and political icons as targets in his stream-of-consciousness performances.

Lenny was writing an autobiography, *How to Talk Dirty and Influence People*, which *Playboy* magazine planned to serialize, then publish as a book, and they hired me as his editor. We hooked up in Atlantic City, where Lenny drove me around in a rented car. We passed a sign warning, "Criminals Must Register," and Lenny started thinking out loud:

"Criminals must register. Does that mean in the middle of the hold-up you have to go to the County Courthouse and register? Or does it mean that you *once* committed a criminal act? Somebody goes to jail and after 15 years' incarceration, you make sure you get them back in as soon as you can by shaming anyone who would forgive them, accept them, give them employment, by shaming them on television — 'The unions knowingly hired ex-convicts.'"

And so Lenny decided to dedicate his book, "To all the followers of Christ and his teachings — in particular, to a true Christian, Jimmy Hoffa — because he hired ex-convicts as, I assume, Christ would have."

Lenny was taking Delaudid for lethargy, and had sent a telegram to a New York City contact—referring to "DE LAWD IN DE SKY..." — as a code to send a doctor's prescription. Now, in Atlantic City, he got sick while waiting for that prescription to be filled. Later, while we were relaxing on the beach, I hesitatingly brought up the subject.

"Don't you think it's ironic that your whole style should be so free-form, and yet you can also be a slave to dope?"

"What does that mean, a slave to dope?"

"Well, if you need a fix, you've got to stop whatever you're doing, go somewhere and wrap a lamp cord around your arm..."

"Then other people are slaves to *food*. 'Oh, I'm so famished, stop the car, I must have lunch immediately or I'll pass out.'"

"You said yourself you're probably going to die before you reach 40."

"Yeah, but, I can't explain, it's like kissing God."

"Well, I ain't gonna argue with *that*."

Later, though, he began to get paranoid about my role. "You're gonna go to literary cocktail parties and say, 'Yeah, that's right, I found Lenny slobbering in an alley, he would've been nothin' without me.'"

Of course, I denied any such intention, but he demanded that I take a lie-detector test, and *I* was paranoid enough to take him literally. I told him that I couldn't work with him if he didn't trust me. We got into an argument, and I left for New York. I sent a letter of resignation to *Playboy* and a copy to Lenny. A few weeks later I got a telegram from him that sounded as if we had been on the verge of divorce — "WHY CAN'T IT BE THE WAY IT USED TO BE?" — and I agreed to try again.

·■■■·

In December 1962, I flew to Chicago to resume working with Lenny on his book. He was performing at the Gate of Horn. When I walked into the club, he was asking the whole *audience* to take a lie-detector test. He recognized my laugh.

Lenny had been reading a study of anti-Semitism by Jean-Paul Sartre, and he was intrigued by an item in *The Realist*, a statement by Adolf Eichmann that he would have been "not only a scoundrel, but a despicable pig" if he hadn't carried out Hitler's orders. Lenny wrote a piece for *The Realist*, "Letter From a Soldier's Wife" — namely, Mrs. Eichmann — pleading for compassion to spare her husband's life.

Now, on stage, he performed the most audacious piece I've ever seen by a comedian. Lenny was empathizing with an orchestrator of genocide. Reading Thomas Merton's poem about the Holocaust, Lenny requested that all the lights be turned off except one dim blue spot. He then began speaking with a German accent:

"My name is Adolf Eichmann. And the Jews came every day to what they thought would be fun in the showers. People say I should have been hung. *Nein.* Do you recognize the whore in the middle of you — that you would have done the same if you were there yourselves? My defense: I was a soldier. I saw the end of a conscientious day's effort. I watched through the portholes. I saw every Jew burned and turned into soap.

"Do you people think yourself better because you burned your enemies at long distance with missiles without ever seeing what you had done to them? Hiroshima *auf Wiedersehen [German accent ends.]* If we would have lost the war, they would have strung [President Harry] Truman up by the balls, Jim. Are you kidding with that? Not what kid told kid told kid. They would just schlep out all those Japanese mutants. 'Here they did; there they are.' And

Truman said they'd do it again. That's what they should have the same day as 'Remember Pearl Harbor.' Play them in unison...."

Lenny was busted for obscenity that night. One of the items in the Chicago police report complained, "Then talking about the war he stated, 'If we would have lost the war, they would have strung Truman up by the balls.' "

The cops broke open Lenny's candy bars, looking for drugs.

"I guess what happens," Lenny explained, "if you get arrested in Town A and then in Town B — with a lot of publicity — then when you get to Town C they *have* to arrest you or what kind of shithouse town are *they* running?"

Chicago was Town C. Lenny had been released on bail and was working again, but the head of the vice squad warned the manager, "If this man ever uses a four-letter word in this club again, I'm going to pinch you and every one in here. If he ever speaks against religion, I'm going to pinch you and everyone in here. Do you understand? You've had good people here, but he mocks the pope — and I'm speaking as a Catholic — I'm here to tell you your license is in danger. We're going to have someone here watching every show."

And indeed the Gate of Horn's liquor license was suspended. There were no previous allegations against the club, and the current charge involved neither violence nor drunken behavior. The only charge pressed by the city prosecutor was Lenny Bruce's allegedly obscene performance, and his trial had not yet been held.

Chicago had the largest membership in the Roman Catholic Church of any archdiocese in the country. Lenny's jury consisted entirely of Catholics. The judge was Catholic. The prosecutor and his assistant were Catholic. On Ash Wednesday, the judge removed the spot of ash from his forehead and told the bailiff to instruct the others to do likewise. The sight of a judge, two prosecutors and twelve jurors, every one with a spot of ash on their foreheads, would have had all the surrealistic flavor of a Bruce fantasy.

The jury found Lenny guilty. The judge gave him the maximum penalty — a year in jail and a $1,000 fine — "for telling dirty jokes," in the words of one network news anchor. A week later, the case against the Gate of Horn was dismissed, but it had become obvious that Lenny was now considered too hot to be booked in Chicago again, a fear that would spread to other cities.

"There seems to be a pattern," Lenny said, "that I'm a mad dog and they have to get me no matter what — the end justifies the means."

In less than two years, he was arrested 15 times. In fact, it became a news item in *Variety* when Lenny *didn't* get arrested one night. While the Chicago verdict was on appeal, he was working at the Off-Broadway in San Francisco. The club's newspaper ads made this offer: "No cover charge for patrolmen in uniform." Since Lenny had always talked on stage about his environment, and since police cars and courtrooms had *become* his environment, the content of his performances began to revolve more and more around the inequities of the legal system.

"In the halls of justice," he declared, "the only justice is in the halls."

It was fascinating to watch Lenny work. "I found this today," he would say, introducing his audience to a bizarre concept. Then, in each succeeding performance, he would sculpt and re-sculpt his findings into a mini-movie, playing all the parts, experimenting from show to show like a verbal jazz musician, with a throwaway line evolving from night to night into a set routine. All Lenny really wanted to do was talk on stage with the same freedom that he exercised in his living room.

Sometimes it was sharing an insight: "Alcohol has a medicinal justification. You can drink rock-and-rye for a cold, pernod for getting it up when you can't get it up, blackberry brandy for cramps.... But marijuana? The only reason could be — to serve the devil — pleasure! Pleasure, which is a dirty word in a Christian culture. Pleasure is Satan's word."

Other times it could be just plain silliness: "Eleanor Roosevelt had the prettiest tits I had ever seen or dreamed that I had seen. *In her voice* I've got the nicest tits that have ever been in this White

House, but because of protocol we're not allowed to wear bathing suits...."

That harmless bit of incongruity would show up in Lenny's act from time to time. One night he was arrested at the Cafe Au Go Go in Greenwich Village for giving an indecent performance, and at the top of the police complaint was "Eleanor Roosevelt and her display of tits." Lenny ended up firing all his lawyers and defending himself at his New York obscenity trial. He was found guilty — in a sophisticated city like New York. Lenny was heartbroken.

At his sentencing, he again acted as his own attorney. His most relevant argument concerned the obscenity statute he'd been accused of violating. As part of his legal homework, he had obtained the legislative history of that statute from Albany, and he discovered that back in 1931 there was an amendment proposed which *excluded from arrest* in an indecent performance: stagehands, spectators, musicians and — here was the fulcrum of his defense — *actors*. The law had been misapplied to Lenny. Despite opposition by the New York Society for the Suppression of Vice, the amendment had been signed into law by then-Governor Roosevelt.

Lenny had complained that District Attorney Richard Kuh tried to do his act in court. A friend of mine who dated Kuh swears that he took her back to his apartment and played Lenny Bruce albums for her. Maybe some day he would play for her the soundtrack from the movie *Lenny*, with Dustin Hoffman doing Lenny's act on stage where he complains about the district attorney doing his act in court. But now, before sentencing, Kuh recommended that no mercy be granted because Lenny had shown a "lack of remorse."

"I'm not here for remorse, but for justice," Lenny responded. "The issue is not obscenity, but that I spit in the face of authority."

The face of authority spat back at him that afternoon by sentencing him to four months in the workhouse.

"Ignoring the mandate of Franklin D. Roosevelt," Lenny observed, "is a great deal more offensive than saying Eleanor has lovely nay-nays."

▪■▣■▪

On October 2, 1965, Lenny visited the San Francisco FBI headquarters. Two days later, they sent a memo to the FBI Director in Washington, describing Lenny as "the nightclub and stage performer widely known for his obscenity." The memo stated:

"Bruce, who advised that he is scheduled to begin confinement, 10/13/65, in New York State as a result of a conviction for a lewd show, alleged that there is a conspiracy between the courts of the states of New York and California to violate his rights. Allegedly this violation of his rights takes place by these lower courts failing to abide by decisions of the U.S. Supreme Court with regard to obscenity...."

On October 13 (Lenny's 40th birthday), instead of surrendering to the authorities in New York, he filed suit at the U.S. District Court in San Francisco to keep him out of prison, and got himself officially declared a pauper. Since his first arrest for obscenity, his earnings had plummeted from $108,000 to $11,000, and he was $15,000 in debt.

On May 31, 1966, he wrote to me, "I'm still working on the bust of the government of New York State." And he sent his doodle of Jesus Christ nailed to the cross, with a speech balloon asking, "Where the hell is the ACLU?"

On August 3, while his New York obscenity conviction was still on appeal, he received a foreclosure notice on his home. Lenny died that day from an overdose of morphine, on the cusp between suicide and accident. In his kitchen, a kettle of water was still boiling. In his office, the electric typewriter was still humming. Lenny had stopped typing in mid-word: *Conspiracy to interfere with the 4th Amendment const*

At the funeral, his roommate and sound engineer, John Judnich, dropped Lenny's microphone into his grave before the dirt was piled on. Eighteen months later, the New York Court of Appeals upheld a lower court's reversal of his conviction.

Fortunately for his legacy, there is a documentary, *Lenny Bruce: Swear to Tell the Truth*, which was a dozen years in the making. It was nominated for an Academy Award in 1999. But, as producer Robert Weide told me, prophetically, "If there's a documentary about the Holocaust, it will win." And then he added, "The odds against *my* film winning are six million to one."

Lenny really would've appreciated that.

The Disneyland Memorial Orgy

When Walt Disney died in December 1966, I remembered a couple of his statements with peculiar affection.

"I love Mickey Mouse," he once said, "more than any woman I've ever known."

In 1945, Aldous Huxley went to work for Disney as a consultant on the filming of *Alice in Wonderland*. There were rumors that Huxley had turned him on with magic mushrooms.

"If people would think more of fairies," Disney said a year later, "they would forget the atom bomb."

After his death, I went to Disneyland with a few friends, one of whose dog jumped into the car as we were leaving his home. Dogs weren't allowed in Disneyland. Neither were male humans having long hair or beards, except for musicians, so neither the Beatles nor Jesus Christ would have been permitted to enter Disneyland unless they were performing there.

We bluffed our way in with the dog by convincing a ticket-taker that the manager had given us permission earlier on the phone inasmuch as the dog was needed to guide my friend with impaired eyesight. Inside, we continued to fake it by explaining that the dog had already been cleared by the ticket-taker. But a large man with a small walkie-talkie approached us, offering a choice of putting the dog in the Disneyland kennel or leaving altogether. My friend complained that this exception to their rule had been arranged *two weeks ago*, and he asked to speak to the chief of security.

"I *am* the chief of security."

"Just the man I want to see."

Of course, the canine in question was *not* a seeing-eye dog, not even a German Shepherd. There was no metal brace for the owner to hold, just a rotten, knotted, leather leash. And the dog was a bloodshot-eyed Basset Hound that kept stumbling all over the ground looking for a place to pee. Apparently no dog had ever previously peed in Disneyland, not even Pluto. We decided to leave. But we were entitled to a refund. So, while the others waited at the gate, I was escorted to a building called City Hall. Inside, a woman was requesting that her lost child be paged over the loudspeaker, but she was refused because this wasn't considered an emergency.

I asked, "Was there any special ceremony when Walt Disney died?"

"No, we kept the park open. We felt that Mr. Disney would have wanted it that way."

"Well, wasn't there *any* official recognition of his passing?"

"We did fly the flag at half-mast for the rest of the month."

Also, stock in the Disney Company rose one point the day after his death and continued to ascend. The studio earned $100,000,000 the next year. Walt Disney was gone, but Mickey Mouse would continue to bask in his own immortality. There was a rumor that Disney's body had been frozen, although it was actually cremated. Somehow I had expected Mickey and Donald Duck and all the rest of the gang to attend the funeral, with Goofy delivering the eulogy and the Seven Dwarfs serving as pallbearers.

Walt Disney's death occurred a few years after *Time* magazine's famous "God Is Dead" cover and it occurred to me that Disney had indeed served as God to Mickey Mouse, Donald Duck, Goofy — that whole stable of imaginary characters now mourning in a state of suspended animation. Disney had been *their* Creator and he had repressed all their baser instincts, but now that he had departed they could finally shed their cumulative inhibitions and participate together in an unspeakable Roman binge, to signify the crumbling of an empire.

I contacted Wally Wood — who had illustrated the first piece I sold to *Mad* magazine — and without mentioning any specific details, I told him my general notion of a memorial orgy at Disneyland. He accepted the assignment and presented me with a magnificently degenerate montage.

Pluto was pissing on a portrait of Mickey Mouse, while the real, bedraggled Mickey was shooting up heroin with a hypodermic. His nephews were jerking off as they watched Goofy fucking Minnie Mouse on a combination bed and cash register. The beams shining out from the Magic Castle were actually dollar signs. Dumbo was simultaneously flying and shitting on an infuriated Donald Duck. Huey, Dewey and Louie were peeking at Daisy Duck's asshole as she watched the Seven Dwarfs groping Snow White. The Prince was snatching a glance at Cinderella's snatch while trying a glass slipper on her foot. The Three Little Pigs were humping each other in a daisy chain. Jiminy Cricket leered as Tinker Bell did a strip-tease and Pinocchio's nose got longer.

Actually, Mickey Mouse had been a convict in a chain gang when he originally met Pluto. In World War II, his name was the password for the D-Day invasion. And Snow White warned military personnel about the dangers of venereal disease. Now, in the Disneyland Memorial Orgy, although none of the characters' genitalia were shown, Wally Wood had nonetheless unleashed their collective libido and demystified an entire genre in the process.

In Oakland, an anonymous group published a flyer with *The Realist* logo on top, reproducing the last few paragraphs of "The Parts Left Out of the Kennedy Book," along with a few sections of the Disneyland centerspread in that same issue — adding, "Now on sale at DeLauer's Book Store, Your East Bay Family News and Book Store." The flyer was distributed in churches and elsewhere. The police would have moved in for an arrest had it not been for my west coast distributor, Lou Swift, who asked them not to act until they got a *complete* issue of *The Realist* and could see the material in context.

In Baltimore, the Sherman News Agency distributed that issue with the Disneyland Memorial Orgy removed. One employee told me that the Maryland Board of Censors had ordered this — that it was the only way *The Realist* could be sold in the state — but no such agency existed. Sherman's had merely taken what they considered to be a precaution. I was able to secure the missing pages, and offered them free to any Baltimore reader who had purchased a partial magazine.

In Chicago, a bookstore owner and my distributor — Chuck Olin, who actually ran an ice cream company — were charged with selling and distributing obscene material. Specifically, the complaint was about the Disneyland Memorial Orgy, but local reporters told me that the charge was actually a smokescreen to attack *The Realist* for publishing the Kennedy piece. Theoretically the charges couldn't stick. The centerspread certainly didn't arouse prurient interest. I tried to imagine a prosecutor telling a jury how they might get horny because look at what Goofy and Minnie Mouse are doing. But even if it *did* arouse prurient interest, the rest of *The Realist* was certainly not *utterly* without redeeming social value.

However, a judge there found the issue to be "obscene."

The charge against the distributor was dismissed, based on his lack of knowledge of the contents. The ACLU sought a federal injunction restraining authorities from interfering in any way with local distribution of *The Realist*. Other dealers were afraid to sell that issue, and in fact were warned by police not to sell it. I went on a late-night Chicago radio program, inviting the police to arrest me. Unlike the bookseller and distributor, I would plead not guilty. Nothing happened, except that a woman who was listening to her car radio had pulled over to the side of the road, and a policeman questioned her.

"I thought you were a prostitute," he explained, "here for the Furniture Convention."

The Disneyland Memorial Orgy in *The Realist* became so popular that I decided to publish it as a poster. The Disney Corporation considered a lawsuit but realized that I functioned financially on a proverbial shoestring, and besides, why bother causing themselves further public embarrassment? They took no action against me, and the statute of limitations finally ran out.

Meanwhile, the poster was pirated — painted in Day-Glo colors, gratuitously copyrighted in my name (spelled wrong) and widely distributed — without paying Wally Wood any royalties. I didn't sue the pirate, but Disney did, and the case was settled out of court.

As artistic irreverence toward the Disney characters continued to grow, attorneys for Walt Disney Productions got busy filing lawsuits to stop the sale of such items, because their corporate client had worked "for many years to acquire the image of innocent delightfulness known and loved by people all over the world, particularly, but not only, by children" — and now these same characters were being shown in a "degrading, lewd, drug addictive, offensive and defaced" manner, some of them "in poses suggestive of a love-in." On one hand the lawyers complained that "Some of the cartoons portrayed by these people are pornographic" and on the other hand they complained of "copyright infringement and unfair competition."

In 1971, 60,000 copies of an underground comic book, *Air Pirate Funnies*, were distributed — an extension of the Disneyland Memorial Orgy into story form, complete with bawdy speech balloons. One panel showed Mickey Mouse explicitly giving head to Minnie Mouse. He was saying, "Slup Slup Slup Slup Slup, *Gulp!* Slup Slup," while she was responding, "Ahhh Ng Oh! Yas! Ohhh M!" The Disney empire sued Dan O'Neill and the other cartoonists. One courtroom artist told me he planned to draw all the jurors with Mickey Mouse ears. In 1972, I was asked to submit a sworn deposition in the case:

"I have been the editor and publisher since its inception in 1958 of *The Realist*, which has been described by *Library Journal* as 'the best satirical magazine now being published in America.' I have read volumes one and two of *Air Pirates*, and find that their contents remain loyal to the traditional values of legitimate parody. It is always a presumption in this form of humor that whatever institution is criticized is, by definition, strong enough to withstand being made fun of. If a myth could actually be harmed — in this case, Mickey Mouse and his imaginary friends — merely by suggesting imperfectability, well, that is the risk and the blessing of democracy.

"In order to communicate an irreverence toward the Walt Disney characters, the original form must be imitated to provide the most effective vehicle of reaching the consciousness of the audience and hopefully causing them to question the one-dimensional infallibility of Disney's fairy tale world. For any government to imply otherwise would be to foster brainwashing. In Sao Paulo, Brazil, a city official in charge of a campaign to exterminate rats said that public support for the program was adversely affected by the popularity of Mickey Mouse among children. It is in the highest tradition of a free society to encourage the testing of conflicting ideas in an open marketplace; the comic books in question, therefore, are classic examples of artistic responsibility in action."

In 1975, the defendants were found guilty of copyright infringement. The judge ruled in Disney's favor and assessed $190,000 in damages. In 1978, the U.S. Court of Appeals upheld that decision, denying the cartoonists' defense that their parodies were "fair use" of copyrighted material, and that they drew the Disney characters in more exact likenesses than necessary to get their point across. But the court stated that "The desire of a parodist to make the best parody must be balanced against the rights of the copyright owner and his original expression. The balance is struck at giving the parodist what is necessary to conjure up the original." In 1979, the Supreme Court let stand the lower court ruling. Yes, the highest court in the land had managed to uphold the honorable image of Goofy.

But the Disney folks weren't victorious in every case. The Center for Constitutional Rights represented the Chilean co-authors of *How to Read Donald Duck* in a battle with Customs, and won. There was a law stating that if material came in through Customs which officials thought violated an American copyright, they could freeze the material and force the importer to fight for its release. This book was a sociological analysis of the capitalist ethic in Disney comics, illustrated with hundreds of strips. The case was won by proving that the reprinting was necessary fair use in order to comment on them.

However, in 1983, Canadian artist Carl Chaplin created *Wishing On a Star* postcards for free distribution. They depicted Disneyland being blown up by a nuclear bomb. Disney lawyers threatened legal action, demanding possession of the postcards. Chaplin said that "If Uncle Walt were alive, he would know that I did the painting to point up the horror of what could happen to all of mankind in a nuclear war." Nevertheless, he turned over all the remaining postcards. The irony was that, as a result of the lawsuit, that image was sent over the UPI wire and seen by millions who would otherwise have remained unaware of its existence.

In 1989, on the same day that Disney stock jumped 6-3/8 points in active trading, their attorneys arranged to have white paint splashed over the "innocent delightfulness" of Disney characters on murals at three daycare centers in Florida. They were replaced by Yogi Bear, Fred Flintstone and Scooby Doo. Yet another Mickey Mouse decision.

And in 1992, Britain's official artist for the Persian Gulf war, John Keane, got in trouble for his painting in which Mickey Mouse appears on what looks like a toilet, with a shopping cart of anti-tank missiles nearby, and a background of shattered palm trees. A spokesperson for the Disney empire said they were considering possible copyright implications. The artist said that the idea came to him in Kuwait City, in a marina used by the Iraqis, where he found a Mickey Mouse amusement ride surrounded by feces.

Who Killed Bobby Kennedy?

In February 1968, a group of New York Yippies — leaders of the newly formed Youth International Party — attended a college newspaper editors conference in Washington, D.C. Senator Robert Kennedy happened to get off the same train that we were on. He had announced that he would not run against Lyndon Johnson for the Democratic nomination. Now Kennedy was talking to an aide in the train station. Abbie Hoffman, Jerry Rubin and I stood there, looking like the Psychedelic Three Stooges as we ogled Kennedy.

"Look how tan he is," said Rubin. "What an opportunity. We've gotta *do* something."

Hoffman, on the other hand, didn't hesitate a second to devise any tactic. He simply followed his impulse.

"Bobby," he roared, "you got no guts!"

The senator flinched ever so slightly.

Rubin was the left brain of the Yippies, and Hoffman was the right brain.

As for me, two years previously, I had sent reprints of an article from David Dellinger's *Liberation* magazine — "American Atrocities in Vietnam" by Eric Norden — to every senator and member of Congress. Kennedy was the only one who had at least responded. Now I was tempted to thank him, but I didn't feel comfortable approaching, especially on the heels of Abbie Hoffman's outburst.

And yet it was as if Abbie's epithet had gotten through to Kennedy, for in March, he announced that he would run for president after all. Furthermore, he said that he would have "great reservations" about supporting LBJ if he won the nomination and the Republicans nominated a candidate who wanted to reduce the American military in Vietnam.

As a byproduct of Kennedy entering the race, Yippie enthusiasm was replaced by doubt, and there was serious talk about calling off the protest at the upcoming convention in Chicago that summer. Were the Yippies being co-opted by Kennedy? He even met with Allen Ginsberg, Tom Hayden and Phil Ochs. Kennedy wanted to know if there could be an alliance between the counterculture and the black power movement.

In April, Martin Luther King was assassinated. As attorney general, Kennedy had approved the FBI's wiretapping of King's phone. Now, as senator, he provided an airplane for King's widow. And Tom Hayden received a telegram inviting him to King's funeral.

In June, on the night that Kennedy won the Democratic nomination at the California primary, he was assassinated in the kitchen of the Ambassador Hotel in Los Angeles. And Tom Hayden received a telegram inviting him to Kennedy's funeral.

Kennedy had been on the *Tonight* show, telling Johnny Carson that cigarettes kill more people than marijuana, and I was prepared to believe that Sirhan Sirhan was a hired gun for the cigarette manufacturers. But, when John Kennedy was slain, Malcolm X described it as "the chickens coming home to roost," and now, by extension, that description could also be applied to Robert Kennedy.

In 1967, Drew Pearson wrote in his syndicated column: "In 1963 the CIA hatched a plot to knock off Castro. It would have been impossible for this to reach the high levels it did, say insiders, without being taken up with the younger Kennedy. Indeed, one source insists that Bobby, eager to avenge the Bay of Pigs fiasco, played a key role in the planning. Robert Kennedy was plagued by the terrible thought that he had helped put into motion forces that indirectly may have brought about his brother's martyrdom."

Conspiracy researcher Mark Lane expanded on that theme in the *San Francisco Express Times:* "It has been suggested that the CIA, intimately familiar with the details of Robert Kennedy's Castro assassination plan, utilized that aborted program to kill John Kennedy. My source (a former CIA official) states that not only logic dictated that approach, but that the known facts, known to a severely limited number of participants, confirmed that it happened exactly that way.

"According to that information, one of the men chosen by Robert Kennedy to participate in the Castro assassination was later employed by the CIA for the assassination that actually did take place in Dallas. Confronted with the obligation of pretending to accept a false account of the circumstances of his brother's death or publicly revealing that his own hand-picked assassin fired some of the shots, Kennedy chose the former course...."

Everyone perceived the assassination of Robert Kennedy through the filter of their own agenda. "I feel horrible," said Jerry Rubin. "Really sick. It's such an ugly, ugly thing, to keep thinking about a bullet in the brain. I really wanted to see Bobby Kennedy lose in California. I was disappointed when he won, but I feel very strange now. I really identify with Bobby Kennedy now."

Nevertheless, Jerry soon had a different slant —"Sirhan Sirhan is a Yippie!" — because Kennedy's death served to re-energize the Yippies' plans for going to Chicago. The new frontrunner, Vice President Hubert Humphrey, would never disavow Lyndon Johnson's war in Vietnam the way Kennedy had. Humphrey would hang himself with his own umbilical cord.

"The shooting of Kennedy," said Tom Hayden, "seems to mean that there's no peaceful way to make change within the system, not even mild reform."

Although the notion of a second gunman in the slaying of Robert Kennedy — namely, a security guard standing behind him — was disproved, is it possible that Sirhan Sirhan had been programmed to kill Kennedy? (A tabloid published a photo identifying the security guard as the killer, but when he sued for libel they were unable to provide any evidence.)

While awaiting trial, Sirhan was given several psychological tests. In one test, he was unable to provide a simple yes or no response to only two specific statements: "At one or more times in my life, I felt that someone was making me do things by hypnotizing me." And, "Someone has been trying to influence my mind."

During the trial, psychiatrist Bernard Diamond used post-hypnotic suggestion to program Sirhan into climbing the bars of his cell. There were two different accounts of that experiment.

In *Psychology Today*, Dr. Diamond stated: "He went over toward the guards and climbed the bars like a monkey. I asked him why. He answered in that cool way he affected, 'I am getting exercise.' Then I played the tape to prove to him that he had been under hypnosis to do just that. But he denied it and complained that I was bugging him."

In the book *RFK Must Die*, Robert Kaiser — who was also there — wrote: "Sirhan had no idea what he was doing up on the top of the bars. When he finally discovered that climbing was not his own idea, but Dr. Diamond's, he was struck with the plausibility of the idea that perhaps he had been programmed by someone else, in like manner, to kill Kennedy...."

Meanwhile, those two telegrams, one inviting Tom Hayden to Martin Luther King's funeral and the other inviting him to Robert Kennedy's funeral, each in its own frame, would remain hanging on the wall of his bedroom in Berkeley, side by side.

Charlie Manson's Image

Proud to be a hippie and wearing my new yellow leather fringe jacket for the first time, I was on my way to the original Woodstock Festival along with half a million others on a musical pilgrimage. At the same time, newspapers were headlining the murder in Beverly Hills of Sharon Tate, the actress wife of director Roman Polanski, their unborn baby, and a few friends.

The killers turned out to be members of the Charles Manson family, the ultimate perversion of a hippie commune. Manson was portrayed by the media as a hippie cult leader, and the counterculture became a dangerous enemy. Hitchhikers were shunned. Communes were raided. In the public's mind, flower children had grown poisonous thorns.

But Manson was raised behind bars. His *real* family included con artists, pimps, drug dealers, thieves, muggers, rapists and murderers. He had known only power relationships in an army of control junkies. Charlie was America's own Frankenstein monster, a logical product of the prison system — racist, paranoid and violent — even if hippie astrologers thought his fate had been predetermined because he was a triple Scorpio.

In August 1969, he sent his brainwashed family off to slay whoever was at the Tate home: the pregnant Sharon; hair stylist and drug dealer to the stars Jay Sebring; would-be screenwriter Voytek Frykowski; and his girlfriend, coffee heiress Abigail Folger. The next night, Manson accompanied the killers to the home of supermarket mogul Leno LaBianca and his wife.

And what a well-programmed family they were. A prison psychiatrist at San Quentin told me of an incident he had observed during Manson's trial. An inmate had said to Manson, "Look, I don't wanna know about your theories on race, I don't wanna hear anything about religion, I just wanna know one thing. How'd you get them girls to obey you like that?"

"I got a knack," Charlie replied.

His "knack" was combining LSD and mescaline with sing-alongs and games accompanying his perversion of techniques he'd learned in prison — encounter sessions, Scientology auditing, post-hypnotic suggestion, geographical isolation, subliminal motivation, transactional analysis, verbal probing and the sexual longevity that he had practiced upon himself for all those years in the privacy of his cell.

Hal Lipset, San Francisco's renowned private investigator, informed me that not only did the Los Angeles Police Department seize pornographic films and videotapes they found in Roman Polanski's loft, but also that certain LAPD officers were *selling* them. Lipset had talked with one police source who told him exactly which porno flicks were available, a total of seven hours' worth for a quarter-million dollars.

Lipset began reciting a litany of those private porn flicks. There was Greg Bautzer, an attorney for Howard Hughes, with Jane Wyman, the ex-wife of Ronald Reagan, who was governor of California at the time of the murders. There was Cass Elliot in an orgy with Yul Brynner, Peter Sellers and Warren Beatty, the same trio who, with John Phillips, had offered a $25,000 reward for the capture of the killers. There was Sharon Tate with Dean Martin. There was Sharon with Steve McQueen. And there she was with two black bisexual men.

"The cops weren't too happy about *that* one," Lipset recalled.

The murders were intended to imply that the victims had been selected at random, but I had always felt that Manson and his killers had some connection with them before the murders took place. I finally tracked down a reporter who told me that when she was hanging around with Los Angeles police, they showed her a porn video of Susan Atkins, one of Charlie's devils, with Voytek Frykowski, one of the victims, even though, according to legend, the executioners and the victims had never met until the night of the massacre.

But apparently the reporter mentioned the wrong victim, because when I wrote to Manson and asked directly, "Did Susan sleep with Frykowski?" he answered, "You are ill advised and misled. Sebring done Susan's hair and I think he sucked one or two of her dicks. I'm not sure who she was walking out from her stars and cages, that girl *loves* dick, you know what I mean, hon. Yul Brynner, Peter Sellers."

I continued to correspond with Charlie. He has become a cultural icon, the personification of evil. There are songs about him. In surfer jargon, Manson means a crazy, reckless surfer. For comedians, Manson is a generic joke reference. In 1992, I asked him how he felt about that.

He replied, "I don't know what a generic joke is. I think I know what that means. That means you talk bad about Reagan or Bush. I've always ran poker games and whores and crime. I'm a crook. You make the reality in court and press. I just ride and play the cards that were pushed on me to play. Mass killer. It's a job, what can I say."

I interviewed Preston Guillory, a former deputy sheriff in Los Angeles. "A few weeks prior to the arrests at the Spahn Ranch raid," he said, "we were told that we were not to arrest Manson or any of his followers. The reason he was left on the street was because our department thought that he was going to launch an attack on the Black Panthers."

And so it was that racism in the Sheriff's Department inadvertently turned them into collaborators in a mass murder. Yet Charles Manson is the only face you'll see glaring at you from some rebellious teenager's T-shirt. Because the killers left clues to imply that the victims had been slain by black militants, the media continues to imply that Manson's only motive was to start a race war.

However, on the evening of Friday, August 9, 1969, just a few hours before the slaughter took place, Joel Rostau, the boyfriend of

Jay Sebring's receptionist and an intermediary in a cocaine ring, visited Sebring and Frykowski at the Tate house, to deliver mescaline and cocaine. During the Manson trial, several associates of Sebring were murdered, including Rostau, whose body was found in the trunk of a car in New York.

The media continue to perpetuate the myth that Manson's only motivation was to start a race war. Actually, his so-called family had unknowingly served as a hit squad for organized crime figures he'd met in prison. Three decades later, Manson continues to serve as a symbol for the end of the '60s. One thing remains certain, though. Charlie never was a hippie.

John Lennon and the FBI

No wonder Mae Brussell was so excited. The attempted burglary of Democratic headquarters at the Watergate Hotel in Washington, D.C., on June 17, 1972 had suddenly brought her 8½ years of dedicated conspiracy research to an astounding climax. She recognized names, *modus operandi*, patterns of cover-up. She could trace linear connections leading inevitably from the assassination of John F. Kennedy to the Watergate break-in.

Three weeks later — while Richard Nixon was pressing for the postponement of an investigation until after the election, and the mainstream press was still referring to the incident as a "caper" and a "third-rate burglary" — Mae completed a long article for my magazine, *The Realist*, revealing the conspiracy and delineating the players, from the burglars all the way up to FBI Director L. Patrick Gray, Attorney General John Mitchell and President Richard Nixon.

Mae documented the details of a plot so insidious and yet so logical that we naively believed her article could forestall Nixon's re-election. The typesetter even wrote "Bravo!" at the end of Mae's manuscript. However, instead of my usual credit arrangement, the printer insisted on $5,000 cash in advance before this issue could go to press. I didn't have the money, and I had no idea how I would get it, but as I left the printing plant, I was filled with an inexplicable sense of confidence.

When I got home, the phone rang. It was Yoko Ono. She and John Lennon were visiting San Francisco, and they invited me to lunch. The Nixon administration had been trying to deport Lennon, ostensibly for an old marijuana bust in England, but really because they wanted to prevent him from performing free for protesters at the Republican convention that summer, which would have attracted several thousand young people who were for the music and against the war.

I brought the galleys of Mae's article to the restaurant. Her account of the government's motivation and methodology provided a context for the harassment of John and Yoko. When I mentioned my printer's ultimatum, no persuasion was necessary; they immediately took me to a local branch of their bank and withdrew $5,000 cash.

This occurred so *precisely* when I needed the money that my personal boundaries of coincidence were stretched to infinity. I could rationalize my ass off — after all, John and Yoko had been driving across the country, and they just *happened* to arrive at the particular moment of my need — but the timing was so exquisite that, for me, coincidence and mysticism became the same process.

When Jon Wiener was writing a biography of John Lennon, *Come Together*, he tried to obtain Lennon's FBI files, but some 200 documents were withheld because, it was alleged, their release would endanger national security. What little Wiener managed to obtain included pages that were fully blacked out. After a 14-year legal battle all the way up to the Supreme Court, the FBI agreed to release all but ten documents and to pay $204,000 to the ACLU for court costs and attorney fees.

Now, Jon Wiener's *Gimme Some Truth* (University of California Press), tells the story of that struggle. His book — dedicated to Mark Rosenbaum and Dan Marmalefsky, the lawyers who paved the path to that victory — chronicles Lennon's legal commitment to test the political potential of rock music, and documents the government's illegal commitment to stop him.

Before he met with the ACLU attorneys, their main concern was Wiener's agenda. "Was I some kind of obsessed fan? Or perhaps a burned-out hippie, living in the past? Or a conspiracy buff, eager to prove Reagan had ordered Lennon's assassination?" They were relieved to find that he was a history professor seeking the Lennon files as part of his research on the American past.

The ACLU strategy would be to show that Lennon was subject to surveillance as part of an effort to monitor political opponents of the Nixon administration, rather than because he was the subject of a legitimate law enforcement investigation.

The government claimed they were investigating Lennon because of his involvement with the Election Year Strategy Information Center (EYSIC) — an organization dedicated to defeating Nixon, led by two members of the Chicago Seven, Jerry Rubin and Rennie Davis — to which Lennon had contributed $75,000. FBI files indicated that EYSIC disbanded on March 1, 1972, yet 27 documents postdated that event.

"So this has nothing to do with a continuing investigation of a relationship between John Lennon and EYSIC," argued the ACLU. In fact, those documents "don't concern themselves with enforcement of the Anti-Riot Act, they concern themselves with statements being made at INS hearings...and 'how can we get John Lennon out of the country before the Republican convention?' "

Vincent Schiano, the INS chief trial attorney in charge of deporting Lennon, had orchestrated the deportation cases of such biggies as mob boss Carlo Gambino, happy hooker Xavier Hollander, former Nazi Hermine Braunsteiner Ryan and IRA revolutionary Joe Cahill. *Rolling Stone* reported that, after the Lennon case, Schiano left the INS, protesting that he was given carte blanche in the Lennon case but was given no power to go after former Nazis.

Ten days after Lennon's visa was revoked, the New York FBI sent an urgent teletype to J. Edgar Hoover, reporting that Lennon had won a delay in his deportation, that he would "fight a narcotics conviction in England," and that if he "wins the overthrow of a British narcotic conviction, INS will reconsider their attempts to deport Lennon."

Hoover died in May 1972, a month after he sent a letter to H.R. Haldeman at the White House about this "former member of the Beatles singing group," warning of his "avowed intention to engage in disruptive activities surrounding the RNC (Republican National Convention in Miami)." The entire text was withheld, but since Haldeman was Nixon's chief of staff, this letter would have served as blatant proof that the investigation of Lennon was totally political.

For 14 years, the FBI withheld four lines of a document: "For information of Bureau, NYCPD [New York City Police Department] narcotics division is aware of subject's recent use of narcotics and are attempting to obtain enough information to arrest both subject and wife Yoko based on PD investigation." Lennon told me how strangers kept trying to give him drugs.

In July 1972, while I was getting stoned on pot with John and Yoko at my office in San Francisco, the Miami office of the FBI was contacted by the New York office: "Miami should note that Lennon is reportedly a 'heavy user of narcotics'. This information should be emphasized to local Law Enforcement Agencies covering MIREP [FBI code for the convention], with regards to subject being arrested if at all possible on possession of narcotics charges."

The FBI even printed a flyer for distribution to local law enforcement agencies in Miami to facilitate the arrest of Lennon. However, the flyer featured a photo of a Lower East Side musician, David Peel, with a speech balloon announcing his record, "The Pope Smokes Dope."

In September 1972, the government declassified secrets of H-bomb design, but still kept dozens of pages in the Lennon files confidential, stored in locked containers inside locked strong rooms within secure buildings in fenced facilities patrolled by armed guards.

In December 1972, a month after Nixon had been re-elected, the Lennon files ended. The FBI had inserted an asterisk adjacent to the symbol number on many documents whenever "the source of the information was not a person but an illegal investigative technique." This whole case was, in Jon Wiener's words, a "rock 'n' roll Watergate."

■■■■

Yoko Ono and John Lennon spent that weekend at my home — situated on a cliff overlooking an almost deserted beach — in Watsonville, south of San Francisco. They loved being so close to the ocean. In the afternoon I asked them to smoke their cigarettes outside, but in the evening we smoked a combination of marijuana and opium, sitting on pillows in front of the fireplace, sipping tea and munching cookies.

At one point, I referred to Mae Brussell as a saint.

"She's *not* a saint," John said. "*You're* not a saint. *I'm* not a saint. *Yoko's* not a saint. *Nobody's* a saint."

We talked about the Charles Manson case, which I had been investigating. Lennon was bemused by the way Manson had associated himself with Beatles' songs.

"Look," John said, "would you kindly inform Manson that it was *Paul* [McCartney] who wrote *Helter Skelter*, not me."

Yoko said, "No, please *don't* tell him. We don't want to have *any* communication with Manson."

"It's all right," John said, "he doesn't have to know the message came from *us*."

"It's getting chilly in here," Yoko said to me. "Would you put another cookie in the fireplace?"

We talked about Mae's theory that the deaths of musicians like Jimi Hendrix, Janis Joplin, Jim Morrison and Otis Redding had actually been political assassinations because those performers served as role models, surfing on the crest of youth rebellion.

"No, no," Lennon argued, "they were already headed in a self-destructive direction." A few months later, he would remind me of that conversation and add, "Listen, if anything happens to Yoko and me, it was *not* an accident." Such was the level of his understandable paranoia. For now, though, we were simply stoned in Watsonville, discussing conspiracy theory, safe at my oasis.

Lennon was absentmindedly holding on to the joint.

I asked, "Do the British use that expression, 'to *bogart* a joint,' or is that only an American term, you know, derived from the image of a cigarette dangling from Humphrey Bogart's lower lip?"

"In England," he replied, with an inimitable sly expression, "if you remind somebody else to pass a joint, you lose your own turn."

▪■█■▪

A few months previously — in early March 1972 — a paid FBI informant, Julie Maynard, traveled from Madison, Wisconsin, with a local activist, Jane Hopper, to meet with anti-war movement leaders in New York City. Here is an excerpt from Julie's FBI report on Jane:

"She went over to Rex Weiner's house. He is the editor of the *New York Ace,* which is an up and coming underground paper. He seems to be an old political hand. He was very glad to see us and proposed a party that night to welcome us to New York, at his newspaper office. The party started at about 9 p.m., so Hopper had time to go eat at Tom Forcade's house. He lives in a real dump.... He has no legitimate phone. To call out he taps into a Hungarian person's phone."

"There is a girl there named Linda who acts as a servant for Tom and [his roommate] Frank. Linda's parrot interjects 'Right on' whenever the conversation gets rousing. Tom is trying to train it to say 'Eat shit' whenever he argues with anyone, but the bird now says it to him whenever he sees him. The cage is surrounded by small objects that Tom has thrown in response. From there Hopper went to the party. She was introduced to the elite of the radical left...."

Presumably, this document had been blacked out in its entirety, not because Tom Forcade tried to teach a parrot to say 'Eat shit,' but rather because the report concluded with a crucial piece of information — Lennon had announced that he would come to the convention *only if it was peaceful* — thus contradicting the FBI's justification for investigating him.

This report from FBI informant Julie Maynard was filed ten days after Hoover's warning to Nixon of Lennon's "avowed intention to engage in disruptive activities."

Moreover, in May 1971, a confidential FBI document about Lennon's appearance on the *Dick Cavett* show reported that

"Lennon declared he would not participate in antiwar activities at the Republican National Convention."

Other released documents reveal such endangerments to national security as "Mike Drobenare is using his parents' car again," "Alex is still in NYC and is growing a full beard" and "Yoko can't even remain on key."

For the first time in 14 years, Yoko Ono commented publicly on the FBI files. "I was there," she told the *Minneapolis Star-Tribune.* "I knew all that, John was not being Communist or being violent or anything like that. It was obvious to all of us. It was kind of surprising, I think. We were being bugged, so we knew they were after us. I think it's nice that they're releasing [the files] now. It's due to the fact that the then-government and the now-government are totally different."

And now, if you'll excuse me, I have to put another cookie in the fireplace.

THE NEW AGE
ODD COUPLE

One afternoon in 1972 I sensed that there was something vaguely different about my *papier mâché* sculpture of Donald Duck with eight arms. There it stood on the mantel over the fireplace at my home in Watsonville, California. Then I realized what it was — he had *ten* arms now. The additional arms were actually two pairs of shoelaces. Later I found out that Ken Kesey had been around. He had bought a pair of shoelaces for himself, but they came in packages of three.

The year before, I had moved from New York to California when *Whole Earth Catalog* founder Stewart Brand hired Kesey and me to co-edit *The Last Supplement to the Whole Earth Catalog*. Kesey had been reading a book of African Koruba stories. The ecological moral of one parable was, "He who shits in the road will meet flies on his return." With that as a theme, we assigned R. Crumb to draw his version of the Last Supper for our cover of *The Last Supplement*.

One morning in the kitchen I couldn't help but notice that Kesey was pouring some white powder — from a box he found on the pantry shelf — into his crotch.

"I've used cornstarch on my balls for years," he explained.

It sounded like an organic commercial in the making. Our public service ad would appear with step-by-step photos on the inside back cover of *The Last Supplement* — which, after all, was about tools, information, ideas, visions — with Kesey giving this pitch:

"Y'know how it is when you're swarthy anyway and maybe nervous like on a long freeway drive or say you're in court where you can't unzip to air things out, and your clammy old nuts stick to your legs? Well, a little handful of plain old cornstarch in the morning will keep things dry and sliding the whole hot day long. Works better than talcum and you don't smell like a nursery. Also good for underarms, feet, pulling on neopreme wet suits and soothing babies' bottoms. And it's bio-degradable."

■■■

I continued to travel back and forth between Watsonville and my room in the basement of the lawyers' yellow-painted mansion in San Francisco. At the time, Stewart Brand's marriage was breaking up, and he moved to a room in the basement too. We shared a bathroom next to his room.

"During my first night in the room" Stewart confessed, "as I lay there awrithe with loneliness, three young girls came down from a party upstairs and started a party of their own in the toilet on the other side of my thin board wall. It was interrupt, eavesdrop or kill myself. They discussed their first lesbian encounters, and how they learned to get off sexually on water fountains in high school, and compared notes of the bed habits of their host, and then one said, 'You know who has a room in this basement?' 'No, who?' 'Paul Krassner.' *'Paul Krassner* — (ecstatic moan) — he's with the Jefferson *Air*plane!' "

I gave Stewart a key to my room so he could have access to the refrigerator, invited him to use my phone until he got his own, and offered my king-size waterbed for his use whenever I was in Watsonville. I hadn't intended for this to be bread cast upon the waterbed, but when the lawyers' yellow mansion was sold and everybody had to move out, Stewart found an apartment on Rose Street — there were actual roses imbedded in the tar along the street — and he agreed to let me rent the small room he used as a library for my San Francisco headquarters.

"It'll be on a trial basis," Stewart said, "as long as our lifestyles don't conflict."

Mae Brussell — whose conspiracy research I was publishing in *The Realist* — warned me against it. "I can smell a rat," she said. "And for sure, Stewart Brand is a government pig. Be really careful how much you tell him of yourself or your business. His kind can really hurt you in many ways. And do not put it past him. You are working in a dangerous area now and certain precautions are necessary."

"What are you saying? Am I in some kind of physical danger?"

"No, but he'll try to psych you out."

I defied my conspiracy guru and took the room anyway.

As you walked up the stairs to our apartment, you passed Stewart's styrofoam sailboat hanging on the wall. At the top of the stairway was a closet filled with his records. On the outside of the closet door there was a full-length mirror, so you could see yourself coming up the stairs. Stewart had taped onto the mirror a Christmas card with this message:

"Sanskrit means the Way-seeker, Kan-jizai Bosatu or Avalokitesvara Bodhisattva is said to observe human suffering and change Himself, whenever necessary, into 33, hence an infinite number of different guises to save mankind. Whenever He feels it best, He even appears as a harlot or a demon to truly save man. For this reason, anyone who appears before you should be regarded as the personification of Avalokitesvara Bodhisattva who has appeared to save you, namely, to guide you to spiritual enlightenment, in that appearance. Then you can, and must, be thankful to him no matter how harsh and unkind he may appear."

Three of the walls in my room were lined with bookshelves that Stewart had built for his library. One night the heaviest shelf collapsed, with its contents falling all over my little cot. Had I been there, I might've been killed by his double-volume set of *The Ancient Art of Warfare* alone. On the one available wall I taped a photo of my daughter, Holly, and a couple posters. One was an American Indian. The other was Richard Nixon, with a quote from his inaugural address:

"I think of what happened to Greece and Rome and you see what is left — only the pillars. What has happened, of course, is that great civilizations of the past, as they have become wealthy, as they have lost their will to live, to improve, they then have become subject to the decadence that eventually destroys the civilization. The United States is now reaching that point."

▪■█■▪

Stewart and I followed a hallowed tradition of brotherhood. Damon and Pythias. Simon and Garfunkel. Martin and Lewis. Lewis and Clark. Don Quixote and Sancho Panza. Huntley and Brinkley. Stanley and Livingston. Amos and Andy. Archie and Jughead. Brand and Krassner. Although we were both graduates of the Merry Pranksters acid test, we were opposites in appearance and style.

Stewart was tall. I was short. He had closely-trimmed straight blond hair. I had long curly brown hair. His craggy features were those of a Nordic god. I resembled a friendly gargoyle with battle scars. He wore a wristwatch even when he slept. I didn't even wear one when I was awake. He was neat, throwing things away all the time, and the stuff he kept was organized in file cabinets. I was a sloppy packrat, and had a file cabinet but it remained empty.

Stewart was carnivorous and ate meat. I was a vegetarian and ate meat, but only once a week, usually his leftovers while he was at the Zen Center a block away. He had a strange sweet tooth. In college, his favorite snack was a slice of white bread spread with butter and sugar. Now he liked chocolate chip yogurt and sesame graham cookies. He was a real cookie freak. He would even eat unbaked cookie dough, before it ever became a trendy ice-cream flavor. He occasionally smoked cigarettes and drank wine. I never did either, but he turned me on to hot buttered rum and gave me a jar of batter for Christmas.

We would each entertain our own guests. Once I was in my room interviewing Manson family member Squeaky Fromme, while he was in his room interviewing anthropologist Gregory Bateson. I would share with Stewart my latest conspiracy theory, and he in turn would give me a copy of *Scientific American* with an article on the mathematics of coincidence. Our conversations were brief and to the point.

Stewart: "The real immorality of body-count morality is inaccuracy."

Paul: "I assume you're putting me on."

Stewart: "Assume I'm not. It's the best defense against suspected put-on."

Or this one:

Stewart: "We should admit to everybody that both *The Realist* and *The Whole Earth Catalog* were started with CIA money."

Paul: "How are they gonna disprove it?"

Stewart: "Hire us. And then we can cause some international incidents."

Paul: "I've never thought about the Central Intelligence Agency as a way of working within the system."

Stewart: "Did you know I'm starting an organization called the Peripheral Intelligence Agency?"

Paul: "My knowledge of it is an example of it."

Stewart: "Precisely. You've been an agent for years. How can you prove that you're not working for *them*, once the kind of knowledge you have is the kind they seek?"

Or this:

Stewart: "What's wrong with being an elitist?"

Paul: "Well, it's not spiritual, I guess."

Stewart: "But all those spiritualist guys are elitists."

Paul: "Well, it's hypocritical then."

And, my own personal favorite:

Paul: "Do you think competition begins with the spermatozoa racing for the ovum?"

Stewart: "I think the sperm don't race, they *dance around* the ovum."

Stewart and I learned about each other's private idiosyncrasies. He noticed that I kept my *Playboy* Award for satire in my closet, and I noticed that he kept his National Book Award for *The Last Whole Earth Catalog* in his closet. He observed me absentmindedly turning over thumb tacks on the window sill so that nobody would accidentally prick a finger.

We even affected each other's sensibilities. Once I came home, looking forward to a relaxing Carrot Bubble Bath, but the tub was filled with Stewart's potted plants so that they could nourish themselves on water while he was away on a speaking tour, and I didn't have the heart to disturb them. Another time, we were driving somewhere, and he stopped to help a stranded motorist, but confessed that he wouldn't have done it if I hadn't been in the car.

Occasionally, we'd go to a movie. I remarked that even though people were expected to leave their popcorn containers or ice-cream wrappers on the floor to be swept up by a theater employee, I found it difficult to do so. Stewart told me of his trip to Mexico with Stephanie Mills, where the streets were paved with garbage, and there they were, this pair of renowned environmentalists, both getting off on littering the ground.

The closest we came to double-dating was when he cooked dinner for four. I had gotten a call from Anne Beatts, whom I'd met at the *National Lampoon* office in New York years ago, so I invited her over. She had curly hair when we met that one time, but now it was straightened and I didn't recognize her and thought she was Stewart's date, so I left her standing in the kitchen talking to him while I sat in my little bedroom watching the TV news. Only when Stewart's *real* date arrived did I realize how much need we had for a personal choreographer.

I had been enjoying THC, a white powder featuring the ingredient in marijuana which gets one high, so this was like super-pot. On the night that my favorite improv group, The Committee, was going to have its final performance, and while Walter Cronkite was concluding the news with his customary "That's the way it is," I snorted all the THC I had left, as preparation for my personal pilgrimage to The Committee for the end of a satirical era.

The last thing I remember was brushing my teeth, talking to Stewart, and being overwhelmed by the drone of his electric saw.

Since I was out at the time, here's how he described to me what had happened:

"I had been building a bed while you stood in the hall doorway reporting the latest turns in your hassle with Scientology. After a prolonged peculiar silence, I peeked in the hall to find that you were gone, replaced by a vacant-eyed robot which opened and closed its mouth, made a drifty gesture with a tube of toothpaste and said, 'Nn... Gn...' Terrifying. All I could think was that the Scientologists must've finally zapped you.

"After a while, the thing (you) toppled like a tree, *crash*, and commenced baying into my buffalo rug. I phoned a friendly shrink for consultation. He listened to symptoms — you were by now into a howly slow-motion laugh, 'Haaaaaa haaaaaa haaaaaa haaaaaa' — and the shrink suggested I take you to UC hospital for evaluation. I told the nurse, 'He's editor of *The Realist*.' 'Is that so?' she said politely. You spelled your name for her."

It was 11:30 that night when, as they say in comic books, I came to. I tried to fly so I could tell whether I was dreaming, but I couldn't flap my arms because I was attached to the bed by restraining devices. There were canvas straps tying down my wrists and ankles. I was definitely awake, but I had no idea where I was or how I had gotten there.

I would learn later that Stewart had brought me to this hospital with the aid of a couple of students from the Zen Center. I did remember a doctor asking me, "Okay, tiger, what'd you take?" I started to answer, "T-H..." I was tempted to spell out THE ULTIMATE DRUG but my motor control was not exactly a tightrope walker's prayer, and I had to struggle just to utter T-H-C.

"Affording us bedsiders enormous relief," Stewart recalled. "We didn't know what the hell you were down with. At the THC announcement, the doctor smiled and relaxed. 'Let him enjoy it.' On other subjects you had been equally loquacious. In answer to any question whatever — 'How you doin, Paul?' — you would intone, 'My name is Paul Krassner. I am editor of *The Realist*. P-A-U-L-K-uh-A-S-N-R-E.' "

Of course, I had assumed that I was in some secret laboratory, being debriefed by the CIA. A couple of friends were now leaning over my hospital bed. I managed to ask two questions: "Did they inject me with any drug?" And, "Have they been taping what I've been saying?" It was my paranoid way of trying to bring things back into focus. Stewart was gone, but he had left a note for me on the table beside my bed.

9:30 p.m.
Hello Paul — Since you're merely flipped out (stoned) and not dying, I'm gonna go meet my date. Background: you passed out in the hallway — at 7:30 p.m. I brought you to UC Emergency Hospital at 8. You started coming around at 8:30 and let us know you'd had some THC (and LSD?). Wavy [Gravy] or others may drop by later. I'll call in from time to time and I'll check by later.
Stewart
P.S. You promised to tell the American people the truth. You also remarked that "It's okay!" Hope you remember details.

All I could remember was that for a few hours I had been in a space beyond good and evil, yet clinging hard to the paradox of human subjectivity. Birds flew by with the faces of my loved ones. While my body was writhing with ecstasy — which is why they attached me to the hospital bed — my consciousness was in some other place that felt like pure energy, where everything was related to everything else simply because it existed. I'd had my first overdose and missed The Committee's last performance.

In our apartment the next day, Stewart said, "I would've put you to bed, but I thought you were having an epileptic fit."

"Did you stick a *TV Guide* in my mouth like you're supposed to?"

"You were doing fine with the buffalo rug."

Zodiac, an alternative news service, issued this report in September 1972:

"The conspiracy trial of six members of Vietnam Veterans Against the War in Gainesville, Florida, has been postponed until after the November election. Federal Judge David Middlebrook ruled in favor of the defense, which claimed that the Vietnam War would be a political issue in the upcoming election and that the war would also be a major issue in the conspiracy trial. Judge Middlebrook said that the trial would be postponed 'indefinitely' — until at least after the November election. Prior to the judge's decision, the trial had been scheduled to start early next month. The six VVAW members have been accused of plotting to use a variety of bizarre weapons — including fried marbles, sling shots, cross bows, cherry bombs and scuba divers — to violently invade Miami Beach and attack the Republican convention in August."

I immediately assumed it was a frame-up by government provocateurs. *Fried marbles*? Of course! My perception of the logic of those in power was that if they accused the veterans of having fried marbles as a weapon, the public would think it was too bizarre *not* to be true. When I first learned that Richard Nixon's favorite meal was cottage cheese with ketchup, I went and tried that. So it was only natural that I would now fry me up some marbles. Stewart was already accustomed to these little acts of weirdness.

"Just don't use my Teflon pan," he requested.

I went shopping and found a place that sold marbles. I asked for the kind that were best for frying. The clerk laughed at what she had to believe was my idea of a joke. I returned home and melted butter in my saucepan. Then I fried two marbles. Apparently the purpose in weaponry was that when a fried marble is catapulted from a sling shot it will shatter upon hitting the target. The poor person's cluster bomb.

"*Paul*," Stewart said in his best prissy Tony Randall voice. "You *sauteed* those marbles. A warm buttery marble is hardly an instrument of aggression. You should've added *sliced mushrooms*. At least follow the correct recipe: *Deep-fry* the marbles in fat hot enough to smoke slightly and then *plunge* them in cold water. *Zzzkk!* Ornamental little weapons."

A few months later, in a letter to *Harper's* magazine, Larry Rottman, past president of the National Executive Committee of the Vietnam Veterans Against the War, confirmed my original intuition:

"There have been hundreds of instances of known and attempted FBI infiltration into the [VVAW]. As early as 'Operation Dewey Canyon III,' the VVAW March on Washington in April 1971, at least six agents, wearing fatigues and trying to cause trouble, were discovered trying to pass as vets. Since that time, in nearly every state, FBI agents and informants have been attempting to destroy or discredit the VVAW by encouraging militant demonstrations, planting illegal drugs in veterans' homes and cars, offering VVAW members money for favors, for information, promising new cars in exchange for mailing lists, and even threatening blackmail over sexual encounters or traffic violations if cooperation wasn't given. An agent once told me he had the power to have me called back to active duty if I didn't answer certain 'non-self-incriminating' questions.

"Bureau involvement has now escalated into the condoning and encouragement of much more violent tactics. In Ohio, the ACLU has recently filed suit against an alleged informant, Reinhold Mohr — as well as the campus police chief — charging that Mohr tried to plant a machine gun and grenade launcher in the Kent State University VVAW chapter. And such insidious attempts have become almost commonplace. Yet, despite countless cases of provocation, harassment, assault and arrest, *no bona fide VVAW member has ever responded with force.* As our nation's agents of pain and suffering in Indochina, we (unlike our government) learned the horror and futility of violence. We leave violence to those who enjoy it and profit from it — whether at My Lai or Southern University. And no amount of federal indictments, grand juries or special investigations will stifle our rage against injustice or still our voices for truth. For when you awake, America (if you ever do), we will still be here."

No wonder the returning prisoners of war were serving as such a diversionary circus, milking the Vietnam drama dry of any possible plot. I carried that pair of fried marbles around for a long time, a cross-fertilization of Captain Queeg from *The Caine Mutiny* with his steel balls and little Linus from *Peanuts* with his security blanket.

I had a small black-and-white TV set in my room, but when Stewart wasn't home, I would watch the color set in his room. One night in his room I noticed a black-covered notebook which I assumed was a transcription of his interview with Gregory Bateson. As a lazy unbeliever's version of tossing the *I Ching*, I always used whatever was handy — a dictionary, a radio — to help crystallize a direction I might take. I opened Stewart's notebook at random, circled my index finger in the air and then landed on this — *Paul, you're studied and off!* — in Stewart's handwriting.

"*Yaaaggghhh*," I whispered.

This was positively weird. Stewart had written to himself what he couldn't tell me. My impulse was to confess this accidental discovery immediately, but I didn't know when he'd be back. Still, I had to tell somebody. But who? Our mutual friend, Wavy Gravy. He'd be sure to understand.

"Stewart's *diary?*" Wavy said. "Paul, a diary is *inviolate*. But I suppose that's your role, the Cosmic Yenta."

"But I didn't *know* it was his diary. So, does being inviolate mean that you don't want to hear what he wrote about *you?*"

"All right. What did he write about me?"

"He doesn't even mention you."

I finally apologized to Stewart. "I hope you won't consider this a conflict in our lifestyles," I told him. "I mean it's not as if I *fried* your diary."

"It's just your talent for condensation as well as trespass — at last you've compressed crime and punishment into a single act. You blundered into a notebook in which I occasionally exercise ideas and exorcise demons. The damning statement about you was a low mood of vile self-opinion which projected itself onto a gallery of friends and family. To dispel the demon I wrote out the charges, and you strayed into the line of fire. Fortunately you know better than to take such a thing personally. All is forgiven."

When the Vietnam War finally ended, it seemed as if the antiwar movement I had been part of was vindicated, but I also felt depressed about the countless lives that had been wasted. I flew to New York for the celebration in Central Park.

Phil Ochs wanted to have an official poster announce "The War Is Over!" with a blow-up of that classic photo from the end of World War II, which showed a sailor kissing and hugging a female stranger in the crowded street. However, organizers of the event were warned that women's liberationists might object to such legitimizing of sexist aggression as a reward for killing. Instead, the poster featured a blow-up of a photo of a smiling young Vietnamese woman whose outstretched arms were covered with doves, and there was also a dove on her head.

Ken Kesey had a speaking engagement in Wisconsin and flew on to New York to pick up a car he had left there before one of his trips to Egypt. He was staying in a room at the YMCA, watching James Cagney strut his patriotic stuff in *Yankee Doodle Dandy*. On Sunday he ventured into Central Park for the "War Is Over" celebration, and somehow, in the middle of a crowd of 50,000, we found each other.

Instead of flying back to San Francisco, I traveled across the country in the back seat of an open-top convertible, with Kesey and his wife, Faye, in front. It was an appropriate time for rediscovering America. We stayed at motels along the way, but one night we slept in a cemetery, and the next morning Kesey sprinkled a baggie of marijuana seeds onto a few deserving gravesites.

Back in Oregon, he got a speeding ticket from a game warden who had been added to the state police force for the Memorial Day weekend. Later on, Kesey made a citizen's arrest of a speeding policeman, explaining to the startled recipient of this role reversal that by endangering the lives of school children, the cop was giving sanction to their destruction, and if he, Kesey, didn't act on his impulse, he would in turn, by his silence, be giving sanction to the policeman's behavior.

One stoned night I was feeling restless, and at 2 a.m. I took a walk from Stewart's apartment all the way down Market Street. A bag lady sitting in a doorway beckoned me. I immediately convinced myself that *she* must be the Bodhisattva. We talked for ten minutes. Then, as I was about to leave, I gave her a $5 bill and bent down to kiss her on the cheek. She went *"Aauugghhh!"* — and put an arm up to shield herself from me.

It was a truly humbling experience to be rejected by a bag lady, and I felt a touch of *deja vu.*

Back in New York, I had once observed that I gave money only to those who asked for it, and I realized that I was rewarding assertiveness rather than exercising compassion, so I decided to give money only to street people who *didn't* ask for it. I saw my first opportunity on a hot summer day. A man was standing near a brick wall, his back to me, looking up at a leaking air conditioner to catch the drips. Now *that's* thirst, I thought.

"Excuse me," I said, "can you use some spare change?"

"Whattaya think, I'm a bum? I'm the manager of this building, and I'm trying to figure out how to repair this fuckin' air conditioner."

And I quickly swallowed my spiritual pride.

■ ■ █ ■ ■

Ever since my friend Margo St. James masturbated me while sitting in the audience of a pornographic movie theater and wearing her nun's habit, I knew that her secret weapon was faith in irreverence. So it was practically pre-ordained that she would arrange for the first National Hookers Convention to be held at a church.

Margo had founded a loose woman's organization, COYOTE — an acronym for Call Off Your Old Tired Ethics — which provided legal help for prostitutes, even clothes to wear to court, plus alternative means of survival. Due to pressure from COYOTE in San Francisco, there was a change in the situation whereby a woman charged with prostitution wasn't allowed to be released on her own recognizance, but the man who raped her was allowed to be released on *his* own recognizance.

That double standard was the underbelly of every easy laugh stand-up comedians got when they did hooker jokes.

But Margo turned the finest trick of her life when she turned this prurient interest back on itself to spread the message of the Hookers

Convention. The official poster featured an illustration of a woman fingering her clitoris, and the slogan, "Our convention is different — we want everybody to come!" At a crowded press conference on the steps of City Hall, Margo was busy handing out COYOTE buttons to reporters like wafers at communion.

"The enforcement of prostitution laws differs in every state," she explained, "depending on the climate of the community, but they are all discriminatory in that they make the woman the scapegoat. As a woman/whore, I feel equality will never be achieved until woman's sexuality ceases to be the source of our shame; until the men are forced to abandon their pussy patrols.

"This is an economic threat to the men who make their living entrapping women and homosexual men — a threat to their safe and titillating job which actually makes them victims along with the women. Playing a role of participant when they are really the observer/apprehender destroys their moral fiber and integrity, develops their sadistic tendencies and often contributes to their corruption."

That evening, in the lobby of Glide Memorial Church, T-shirts were on sale, flaunting a slogan, *'74 — Year of the Whore!* Reverend Cecil Williams greeted the overflow convention: "This church is open for everybody. It has always been concerned with people who are misused and oppressed. I am delighted to welcome you...."

A few days later, a lay group, United Methodists for Methodism, would demand the dismissal of the entire leadership at Glide for permitting its premises to serve as a sanctuary for prostitutes.

Margo had been politicized by Flo Kennedy, founder of the Feminist Party, who delivered her keynote speech in a plain brown wrapper, inspiring a congregation horny for justice. Her sermon was titled "What Is This Shit?" With a dignity strangely enhanced by her purple cape, Daisy Duck eyelashes and Moms Mabley stance, she felt entitled to ask publicly why the FBI was orchestrating "a national campaign of busting prostitutes while everyone else is sucking their way to success *any*way?"

The insightful, 58-year-old, African-American attorney provided her own answer: "It's a control mechanism — of hookers, of veterans — of all victims. The government must maintain guilt as a tool of oppression over those whom they niggerize. Migrant farmers are brought in illegally, then they're on the defensive and can't fight for their rights."

A byproduct of the Hookers Convention was a growing awareness of the linear connections in suffering, which COYOTE had recognized by the range of its actions, from successfully protesting the automatic forced treatment for undiagnosed venereal disease of women arrested for prostitution (their presumably also-infected male customers were left alone) to the hookers' boycott of crewmen off a ship docked in from torture-infested Chile.

As I was leaving the convention, a lovely dark-haired woman wearing a black dress came out of a door, stood in the corridor and let out a loud sigh. An organizer of the event, she was temporarily exasperated. As a gesture of empathy, I let out a loud sigh in return. She walked over, gave me a kiss on the cheek and said, "Tom Robbins says hello."

Her name was Georgia Wilkins, and it was love at first sigh.

Stewart had said I could use his bed whenever he was out of town, so when Georgia and I started sleeping together, we took him up on the offer. One night she was having her period and we got his sheets all bloody. In the morning we had granola for breakfast in bed. Now the sheets were all bloody *and* granoly. Stewart returned that day before I had a chance to get his linens to the laundry.

"I'm pissed," he said.

Understandably so. I had really violated his space. But a rousing battle with his boffers — foam rubber bats sold in *The Whole Earth Catalog* — straightened it out for us.

Sometimes Georgia worked as a prostitute to help support herself and her two children. I tried not to be resentful of her johns.

"Think of them as my clients," she advised.

One time she came to my apartment, quite upset. She told me about a client who had taken her to the back room of a grocery store where there were bottles of wine.

"He opened a bottle of Ripple," she told me, "poured it on his cock, and I was supposed to suck it off. It's the first time I was ever asked to swallow come, and I was so disgusted that when he wasn't looking, I spit it back out into the Ripple bottle."

Georgia was one of the speakers for COYOTE, which was trying to influence the public's attitudes and ultimately decriminalize prostitution. On one occasion, she was hired to speak by the Junior Chamber of Commerce in Waterloo, Iowa. She arrived wearing jeans, sandals and African beads. "The Jaycees seemed like rebellious children who were having a good time upsetting the Bible Belt," she told me. But she got booed that night for saying, "Some marriages are nothing but a legalized form of prostitution."

Eventually, Georgia and I broke up. I simply didn't nurture our relationship, and she began sleeping with another guy. *For free!* I had adjusted to her having clients, but I wasn't ready for her to go to bed with somebody else because she actually *liked* him. That was too much for me to handle.

While Stewart Brand and I were roommates, I began writing *Tongue Fu*, a story of a Japanese-American with a 15-inch tongue. He belonged to a modern *kamikaze* organization for those who planned to commit suicide but wanted to accomplish something that would benefit society in the process. It was called Better Your Exit, or BYE. I showed the first three chapters to Stewart, and he agreed to serialize it in his new magazine, *Co-Evolution Quarterly*.

The fable served as an allegory for my conspiracy research and as a catharsis for my previous freakout from information overload, but the exorcism must have reversed itself. Vice President Spiro Agnew had resigned in the face of a tax scandal, Gerald Ford was *appointed* vice president, then in the wake of Watergate, Nixon resigned, Ford became president, he *selected* Nelson Rockefeller as *his* vice president, and for the first time in American history, we had a pair of executives in the White House who had not been elected, and I had a slight relapse.

In keeping with the concept of trickle-down conspiracy, I then became unduly suspicious of Stewart. Specifically, I managed to convince myself, without the slightest rational basis, that he had changed the ending of *Tongue Fu*.

I decided to confront my paranoia. On an afternoon that Stewart was staying home, I took a bus to Sausalito. A man sat down next to me in the bus. Uh-oh. Was he a CIA operative? We both had copies of the *Berkeley Barb*. I was reading the articles, and he was reading the sex ads.

When the bus arrived in Sausalito, I walked to the houseboat where Stewart's office was, and I checked out the galleys of *Tongue Fu*. Nothing had been changed. I felt sheepish, but I had successfully called my own bluff, and now I was okay again.

Back in the apartment, I didn't mention my little journey to Stewart. But I sensed that there was something vaguely different in my room. Then I realized what it was — my Richard Nixon poster. His eyes, which were usually looking toward the right, were now looking toward the left. It had that eerie effect of the Jesus face in a novelty-shop window, whose eyes follow you as you pass. Except that Nixon' s eyes were frozen in this new position.

I examined the poster more closely and was able to discern that the original eyeballs had been whited out from the right side, and new eyeballs had been drawn in the left-hand corners. Then I checked to see whether the eyes in my daughter's photo had also been changed, but no, she was still looking directly at me. So was my Indian guide. Only Nixon's eyes had been altered.

It seemed out of character for Stewart to have done this, but I asked him anyway.

"No, it wasn't me," he said. "But Kesey was around for a while."

"Of course! I should've realized it was Kesey when I saw that telltale trail of cornstarch."

Wavy Gravy's Rainbow Bridge

I am in search of words to describe the look on Daniel Ellsberg's face at the moment of my epiphany.

Ellsberg, who released the Pentagon Papers to the *New York Times* and the *Washington Post*, and I were on a panel about the '60s at Town Hall in New York City. Since I've copyrighted "the '60s," my royalty payments mounted up that evening.

Ellsberg admitted that he'd kept secret Vietnam War documents in his safe for years and was therefore responsible for the loss of thousands of lives in Southeast Asia.

Later, I told him about Lori Fortier, who was a witness in the Oklahoma City terrorist trial. She had testified that she knew Timothy McVeigh was planning to bomb the Federal Building, and with one phone call she could have saved 168 lives.

"She's a microcosm of your situation," I remarked to Ellsberg.

"But why didn't she tell?"

"Well, she said she was afraid of losing her life."

Ellsberg's demeanor suddenly became a mixture of shame and anguish as he confessed, so simply, "I was afraid of losing my career." That was my epiphany. I had seen the face of evil, and it was merely a man who had wanted to keep his prestige job, enjoy the feeling of power, eat at fine restaurants, pay the mortgage and send the kids to college.

▪■█■▪

In May 1997, Ken Kesey and the Merry Pranksters were on their way to the opening of a special exhibit, "I Want to Take You Higher: The Psychedelic Era," at the Rock and Roll Hall of Fame in Cleveland.

The *Bowling Green* (Kentucky) *Daily News* published a photo of "a man who didn't want to be identified" licking the side of the Prankster bus, Further. He was apparently under the belief that LSD had been mixed in with the painted designs.

"We got bumped from the induction ceremonies," Kesey told me. "We were supposed to be honored on the 6th of May, but Michael Jackson's people contacted the museum. They didn't think it would be fitting if Michael Jackson was on the same list as the bus, so they moved us to the 10th."

"You mean they think psychedelic exploration is worse than child molestation?"

"Yes," he said. "We are lower than pedophiles."

"Words to live by."

"I remember this old saying my dad had: 'I'm so low the snail shit on the bottom of the ocean looks like shooting stars in the sky.'"

And there it is, a perfect description of the look on Daniel Ellsberg's face at the moment of my epiphany. The search has ended.

▪■█■▪

By the time the Psychedelic Era exhibit closed 9½ months later, some 475,000 individuals had attended. Wavy Gravy, the countercultural clown who became a Ben & Jerry ice cream flavor, was one of them. Now, as the exhibit was ending, he returned, this time walking a rubber fish named Saul Bass on a stiff leather dog leash. Wavy takes him everywhere.

"I don't know what this means," he confides. "It may be my latent Christianity. But walking this fish in New York City, nobody asks me for money. People either enjoy the fish or they pretend it's not happening."

This was not Wavy's first pet fish. Somebody had once given him one of those fish purses they sell at airports. It was a rainbow trout, which he christened Kilgore Trout. Wavy kept his phone book and his money in his fish. He would lose the fish, but it would come back to him every time. At musical events, he would ask musicians and writers to autograph his fish. It became covered with famous signatures.

In New Hope, Pennsylvania, waiting for a bus to New York, he left his fish in a shopping cart and some guy found it, containing $600. He took it to a bar, boasting that he had Wavy Gravy's fish. A record company producer overheard him and called Abbie Hoffman, who lived in town and immediately came to the bar and tried to get the guy to relinquish the fish. He wouldn't, so Abbie — who wasn't exactly a police lover — now had to call them.

Wavy finally heard from the New Hope police, who informed him, "We've got your fish in custody."

Wavy Gravy didn't bring a fish on his first visit to the Rock and Roll Hall of Fame. He had gone to see his stuff on official display. Each item had its own personal history.

There was his sleeping bag, called Home Plate because it had actually served as home plate in the Great Softball Game. Two communes had challenged Wavy's commune, the Hog Farm. They all ate a lot of green acid left over from the Woodstock festival, and they made up the rules of the game.

Second base was inside a cottage on the second floor looking out the window. Third base, you had to slide down a rope into a big barrel full of water. And to get to home plate, a player had to pick you up at third base and *carry* you home. And home, when you got there, was a foot rub, a cheeseburger and a line of coke.

"It was back in those nutty days," Wavy explains, "and we didn't know any better. These days I think cocaine is Nature's way of telling people to spend money and be mean to their kids. If you saw the *Woodstock* movie, there is a scene where I'm snorting a line before I hit the stage. My mother said, 'What are you doing there?' I told her I was clearing my sinuses. That's when I started calling cocaine the Thinking Man's Dristan."

Also on display was Wavy's beautifully patched and embroidered jump suit, with his cardboard head coming out of it, wearing his good old cowboy hat. But his teeth — the "rainbow bridge"— weren't there. Wavy was thoroughly bummed out. He complained in an interview with the *Cleveland Plain Dealer*. The story was picked up by the wire services while Wavy was on tour. He was staying at a deco hotel in South Beach when the phone rang. It was *Rolling Stone* publisher and Hall of Fame organizer Jann Wenner.

"All right," Wenner said, "call off your dogs, the teeth are up."

■ ■ ■ ■ ■

Winnarainbow — the circus and performing arts camp Wavy has run for over 25 years — had been an appropriate place for the original announcement to arrive, that his rainbow bridge was formally inducted into the Rock and Roll Hall of Fame.

At camp, Wavy always led an orientation, at the end of which he would turn out all the lights and tell the kids: "In ancient times I was a teenage beatnik and I used to brush my teeth with Snickers bars and gargle with Hoffman's Black Cherry Soda, and after a while I began to get these cavities, and my teeth would rot out...."

Indeed, when he began to work at The Committee, an improv theater in San Francisco, dentists would leave their cards for him at the box office. Eventually, the Pranksters dentist, Dick Smith, began to work on his teeth. He overheard Wavy mutter to Neal Cassady that, "After listening to a lot of Vietnam War body counts, the only flag I wanna salute is a rainbow," so Smith secretly made the original rainbow bridge, each tooth was a different color of the rainbow spectrum. Kids thought it was cool.

Wavy would continue, the lights still off, "it's *not* cool, because every one of those teeth that came out was painful. It hurt. Finally I ended up with only six sacred stumps and it looks something like *this*" — he would shine a flashlight in his mouth and all the campers would go, *"Eiuuuuuu!"* And they would run and grab their toothbrushes. Wavy would get letters from parents: "I don't know what you did to our little Bobby, we could never get him to brush his teeth, but he's worn out five toothbrushes this month."

So now, on his second trip to the Rock and Roll Hall of Fame, Wavy was on a mission. He got a private tour of the Psychedelic Era exhibit, walking through with his rubber fish, which acted like a dowsing rod and headed immediately for the left rear tire, also made of rubber, on Janis Joplin's Porsche, and started sucking on it.

Then the fish led Wavy to his own display and, yes, the teeth were now there. The file can finally be closed on the case of the missing rainbow bridge.

The Parts Left Out of the Patty Hearst Trial

Groucho Marx said during an interview with *Flash* magazine in 1971, "I think the only hope this country has is Nixon's assassination." Yet he was not subsequently arrested for threatening the life of a president. In view of the indictment against Black Panther David Hilliard for using similar rhetoric, I wrote to the San Francisco office of the Justice Department to find out the status of their case against Groucho. The response:

Dear Mr. Krassner:

Responding to your inquiry of July seventh, the United States Supreme Court has held that Title 18 U.S.C., Section 871, prohibits only "true" threats. It is one thing to say that "I (or *we)* will kill Richard Nixon" when you are the leader of an organization which advocates killing people and overthrowing the Government; it is quite another to utter the words which are attributed to Mr. Marx, an alleged comedian. It was the opinion of both myself and the United States Attorney in Los Angeles (where Marx's words were alleged to have been uttered) that the latter utterance did not constitute a "true" threat.

Very truly yours,

James L. Browning, Jr.
United States Attorney

Browning was so anxious in his pursuit of justice that he successfully fought for the dismissal of charges against federal narcotics officers who had shot an innocent hippie in the back from their helicopter in Humboldt County. In 1976, I found myself sitting in a federal courtroom every day, observing Browning as he prosecuted a bank robbery case that seemed more like a perverted version of a Marx Brothers movie.

Patricia Hearst had been kidnapped by the Symbionese Liberation Army — led by Donald "Cinque" DeFreeze. She was kept in a closet, then she joined them, changed her name to Tania, adopted radical rhetoric and robbed a bank with them. Now the philosophical paradox which has plagued the history of human consciousness — *Is there or is there ain't free will?* — was finally going to be decided by a jury.

The abduction occurred in February 1974. One of the SLA's demands was a free food program. Patty's father, Randolph Hearst, publisher of the *San Francisco Examiner*, arranged for such a project in Oakland. Governor Ronald Reagan responded to the long line of people waiting for free food: "I hope they all get botulism."

In June, I mentioned in the *Berkeley Barb* the non-fact that I had been brought to meet Patty underground. I wrote: "Since there is nothing of investigatory value in the interview, I will not speak with the FBI. Nor am I able to supply any information that might earn me a $50,000 reward. Tania insisted that she had not been brainwashed. My impression is that she was."

In view of Mae Brussell's track record with the Watergate story, I decided to devote an entire issue of *The Realist* to her documented analysis, "Why Was Patricia Hearst Kidnapped?" — the thrust of which was that the SLA was essentially an espionage plot orchestrated by our secret Government in order to distort the message of idealism.

A year after the kidnapping, Patty Hearst was still on the lam, and *Crawdaddy*, a music magazine for which I wrote a column, wanted an article on the case. I wrote an imaginary interview, and *Crawdaddy* published it in their April 1975 issue. An excerpt:

Q. There was a pornographic novel, Black Abductor, *published a couple of years ago, which seems to parallel your case on several counts, although in the book the kidnap victim is raped —*

A. That didn't happen to me. I wasn't raped, but I have made love — of my own free will — with each and every one of my comrades. Male and female. And it's been extremely liberating, I'll tell you. I've learned more about my own sensuality in the past weeks than in my whole previous life.

Q. There's been a rumor that you used to visit Donald DeFreeze in prison —

A. That's impossible. It's a lie. I never did.

Q. And also that you knew [SLA member] Willie Wolfe before you were abducted?

A. That's another lie. I mean I feel as if I've known him all my life, but that's a false rumor.

Q. How have you been affected by the bisexuality?

A. I think it was an extension of sexuality. I had never been physically close to a black man like I've been with Cinque. I always thought nappy hair was tough — like Brillo, you know? — but it's really soft. And so then to become intimate with another woman — I could feel my inhibitions peeling off like layers of onion skin. And I became acquainted with my clitoris. My poor little neglected clitoris, ignored all these years. What a waste.

Q. What about the evidence that DeFreeze has been an informer for the Los Angeles Police Department?

A. That was his survival game. If he were still working for the pigs, we wouldn't be in danger now. I mean you can't confuse somebody like Cinque with — I met the Shah of Iran once and he was absolutely charming — but he's actually a vicious executioner. But I just hope some of those Watergate bastards go to prison, just so they get even a little taste of it and perhaps understand the lengths that a prisoner will go to — the deals and all — to escape legally, if that's really legal.

Q. What about music? What have you been listening to?

A. Well, we only have a radio here. At a previous safe-house there was a stereo, but we didn't have a variety of records. Joy of Cooking, we played them a lot. Pink Floyd, too. And there's a group called The Last Poets, and there's one cut on their album where they give their interpretation of all the symbolism on a dollar bill, and we just sat around, wiped out on some really excellent grass, looking at a dollar bill while they were reciting that. It's very powerful. I remember how I used to think, when I was a little girl, that real money was just official play money.

Q. *I feel silly asking this, but have you been brainwashed?*

A. No, I've been *coerced,* obviously, at the beginning, but I haven't been brainwashed. You have to understand what it's been like from my point of view. Instant introspection. The moment I was taken away, underneath the tremendous fright I was still aware that it was because I was the daughter of a wealthy family whose comfort depends on the suffering of others. I've always been vaguely aware of that but, you know, you try to repress that kind of thing so you can go on living comfortably yourself....

Q. *Did your family know you were getting stoned?*

A. Oh, sure. Listen, there was almost a pound of marijuana at our apartment when I, you know, went on this little involuntary vacation trip, but I'll bet my father and the FBI made some kind of agreement to keep it quiet. They couldn't very well pretend that Steven smoked and I didn't.

Q. *You were real close to Steven Weed. How do you view that relationship now?*

A. It seems like a previous incarnation. He had been my math teacher at Crystal Springs, but I was the aggressive one — in fact, that made me have sort of a vested interest in him — like he was an emotional *investment,* you know? And there was something, an adolescent romantic fantasy, about making out with your *tutor.* You got status for being independent.

But we ended up leading a very middle-class life in Berkeley. Listening to records, dinner parties — always with *his* friends, couples — and shopping for antiques, that was fun. But it was like a couple of children playing house, with my father helping out — with an MG here and a $1500 Persian rug there — he was saving that for a wedding present. God!

Sex was okay with us, but not really anything passionate. The only affection I got was foreplay. It was always a means to an end. It was always *functional*....

Q. You said on one of the communiques that the FBI wants you dead. Why is that?

A. Because I *know* too much, obviously. The FBI, and also my father's corporation advisors. I remember the way I used to hate hippies — who were in my own *age* bracket. I had to justify that hatred by bringing in the puritan ethic. Hippies were unproductive, right?

Anybody who cooperates with the FBI is signing their own death warrant. And it's the same with the pig corporate structure. Their whole existence is devoted to perverting innocent children into consumers.

Why do you think my mother wanted me to go to Stanford instead of Berkeley even though she's a goddam *regent* for the University? What kind of hypocrisy is *that?* She helps control a school that's not good enough for her own *daughter* to go to?

Well, *I'm* a hippie now. *I'm* a white nigger now.

Q. What exactly is it that you know too much about?

A. Well, that my whole kidnapping was *scripted* by the Government....

Earth News Service had called the FBI in San Francisco to find out why they didn't investigate when I originally announced in the *Barb* that I had met with Patty Hearst in captivity. An agent checked the files and found a notation that I had also announced I would never cooperate with the FBI, so they didn't bother. However, a week after C*rawdaddy* came out, a pair of FBI agents from the Santa Cruz office visited me in Watsonville, wanting to talk about the interview.

"I'm sorry, but I have nothing to tell you."

They repeated their request, still friendly and low-key.

"Everything I had to say about that has already been published," I explained. "There's nothing further to discuss."

They tried to peer in my window.

"Patty isn't here, is she?"

"If you get a search warrant, I'll let you look."

In the middle of a *Doonesbury* strip, Garry Trudeau spelled out the word Canaan, which was where a friend of his lived, but federal authorities were convinced it was really a reference to Patty Hearst's supposed hideout in Pennsylvania. William F. Buckley wrote that Patty should be sacrificed "in the name of Christ." And Catherine Hearst said that she would rather her daughter be dead than join the Communists. She also commented that if only Clark Gable had been at the apartment in Berkeley instead of Steven Weed, then Patty would never have been kidnapped. Probably true.

Patty Hearst was finally captured after 18 months. Although her own cousin, Will, said that he would not have recognized her, the arresting officer immediately said, "Patty, what are *you* doing here?" She was so surprised that she peed in her pants, an accident acknowledged in the *Chronicle*, but not in the *Examiner*. She was permitted to change in the bathroom.

The FBI inventory did not include "pants, wet, one pair," but there was on their list a two-foot marijuana plant — as compared with almost a pound of grass *not* reported by the FBI that was found at the apartment from which she had originally been kidnapped. There was also a bottle of Gallo wine in the SLA safe-house, not exactly a loyal gesture to the United Farm Workers whom they purported to support. And there was an unidentified "rock" found in Patty's purse.

A KGO newscaster reported breathlessly: "Patti Page has been captured!"

I had a lunch appointment with Will Hearst, assistant to the editor at the *Examiner* and grandson of Citizen Kane's prototype, William Randolph Hearst. Although Will claimed that his status as Patty's favorite cousin was a media creation, he was the very first one she requested to see after her arrest. Now he walked into the lobby.

"It's a bad day," he told me. "San Simeon has been bombed."

"Well, at least I have an alibi."

We postponed the lunch, and on the way home I stopped at the federal court building, where Patty's trial was in a preliminary stage. Originally, she was going to be defended by the radical team of Vincent Hallinan and his son, Kayo. The elder Hallinan was in Honolulu when the FBI captured Patty, and he assigned Kayo to visit her in jail. Although as Tania she had called Vincent Hallinan a "clown" in a taped conmmunique, now, as Patty, she said of Kayo, "He's good. Like, I really trust him politically and personally, and I can tell him just about anything I want and he's cool." It was, however, a lawyer-client relationship that would not be permitted to mature.

When Patty described her physical reaction to having her blindfold removed in captivity, Kayo recognized a similarity to reactions to LSD. Patty agreed there had been something reminiscent of her acid trips with Steven Weed in the old Hearst mansion. Besides, there was circumstantial evidence that the SLA could have dosed her with LSD. The brother of SLA member Mizmoon reported that she and fellow member Camilla Hall had taken acid; in *TV Guide*, reporter Marilyn Baker claimed that drugs had been found at the SLA safe-house in Concord; and on the very first taped communique, Patty herself had said, "I caught a cold, but they're giving me pills for it and stuff."

Her defense was going to be involuntary intoxication, a side effect of which is amnesia. So Patty would neither have to snitch on others nor invoke the 5th Amendment for her own protection. In response to any questions about that missing chunk of her life, she was simply going to assert, "I have no recollection." The Hallinans instructed her not to talk to anybody — especially psychiatrists — about that period.

But her uncle, William Randolph Hearst, Jr., editor-in-chief of the Hearst newspaper chain, flew in from the East Coast to warn his family that the entire corporate image of the Hearst empire was at stake and they'd better hire an establishment attorney — fast. Enter F. Lee Bailey. He had defended a serial killer, the Boston Strangler, and a war criminal, Captain Harold Medina from the My Lai massacre, but he said he would not defend Patty Hearst if she were a revolutionary. You've gotta have standards.

Bailey and his partner, Albert Johnson, visited with Patty for a couple of hours at San Mateo County Jail in order to encourage her to tell the psychiatrists everything and *not* say "I have no recollection." She could trust these doctors, they assured her, and nothing she said could be used against her in any way. Now her defense would be based on the Stockholm Hostage Syndrome. Patty had been kidnapped again.

Brainwashing does exist. Built into the process is the certainty that one has *not* been brainwashed. Patty's obedience to her defense team paralleled her obedience to the SLA. The survival syndrome had simply changed hands. F. Lee Bailey was Cinque in whiteface. Instead of a machine-gun, he owned a helicopter company — Enstrom, an anagram for Monster. Instead of taping underground communiques, he held press conferences. It was all show biz.

There had been a rumor that Patty was pregnant by Cinque. Indeed, one of the first questions that Randolph Hearst asked when he met sports figure Jack Scott — who had supposedly seen Patty on the lam — was to ascertain if that rumor was true. I wrote in the *Berkeley Barb*: "Now, with their daughter on trial, the Hearsts have hired a lawyer who wears pancake make-up to press conferences, the better to transform a racist fear into a Caucasian alibi."

I received this letter by certified mail:

Dear Sir:

You undoubtedly did not realize that the name "Pan-Cake Make-Up" is the registered trademark (U.S. Patent Office No. 350,402) of Max Factor & Co., and is not a synonym for cake make-up. The correct usage is "Pan-Cake Make-Up, capitalized and written in just that manner, or, under circumstances such as these, where you obviously did not intend to mention a particular brand, simply cake make-up.

We are sure that you are aware of the legal importance of protecting a trademark and trust that you will use ours properly in any future reference to our product, or, in the alternative, will use the proper generic term rather than our brand name. So that our records will be complete, we would appreciate an acknowledgment of this letter.

Very truly yours,
Max Factor & Co.
D. James Pekin
Corporate Counsel

In response, I explained that there had been a slight misunderstanding — what F. Lee Bailey had been wearing to all those press conferences was actually Aunt Jemima Pancake Mix — and I hoped that cleared up the matter.

It was not an easy task for Stephen Cook to report about the trial of his boss' daughter, what with the boss sitting right there in the front row of the courtroom to oversee him, but he didn't spare his employer from embarrassing testimony, and, to the *Examiner's* credit, he was not censored. However, Dick Alexander, who was writing feature material on the trial for the *Examiner,* had his copy changed so drastically that he requested his byline be dropped.

On the first day of the trial, he wore a tie with the legendary *Fuck You* emblazoning the design. Randolph Hearst chastized him for this, but Alexander continued to wear the tie. Perhaps it reminded Hearst of the time Patty screamed "Fuck you, Daddy!" in his office. A syndicated cartoon by Lichty — with the caption, "I don't know whether she was brainwashed, but she should certainly have her mouth washed out with soap!" — appeared only in the first edition of the *Examiner.*

The trial was also grist for the TV entertainment mill. On the *Merv Griffin* show, the audience voted 70-30 that Patty was guilty as charged. On *Maude,* the British maid studying for her citizenship test had to answer the question, "Who said, 'Give me liberty or give me death'?" She was given a hint that the initials were P.H. She did not guess Patrick Henry, but Patty Hearst. And Johnny Carson in his opening monologue wondered whether F. Lee Bailey would get Lockheed off "for kidnapping our money."

Soap-opera actress Ruth Warrick, who starred in *Citizen Kane*, revealed, "My name was not printed in any Hearst paper for five years after that film was released. I could be the star of a movie and my name couldn't even be mentioned in the ads in Hearst papers."

Patty had never seen *Citizen Kane*, particularly not while on the run, because it would've been too embarrassing to be caught there. Throughout her trial, there was a screen set up in the court, but instead of Orson Welles, over and over and over again, like some recurring nightmare, Patty would view footage of herself helping to rob the Hibernia Bank. One witness at the bank had been convinced that it was merely an episode for *Streets of San Francisco* and that Patty was just an actress.

Nancy Faber of *People* magazine became the unofficial courtroom fashion advisor. If you wanted to find out exactly what color Patty's pantsuit was, Faber would know that it was Iranian Rust. But while Patty was wearing light-brown eye shadow, or pearl-gray nail polish to indicate that she didn't have the hands of a criminal, the San Quentin Six were appearing before *their* jury each day in shackles and leg irons. Shana Alexander was the only journalist who skipped a day at the Patty Hearst trial to attend the San Quentin Six trial.

A rhetorical question had been asked of the press: "How can you justify extensive coverage of Patty Hearst and say little, if anything, about the San Quentin Six, in which the state has admitted not having any real evidence?" KQED interviewed media folks, who rationalized that they were only giving the public what it wanted. But when you had a TV program like *Mowgli's Brothers*, an animated cartoon based on Rudyard Kipling's *Jungle Books*, in which an abandoned baby is adopted by a couple of compassionate wolves who talk to him — and right there in the middle there's a commercial with Tony the Tiger telling young viewers that they should eat Frosted Flakes — was that not a form of brainwashing?

The San Quentin Six were to Patty Hearst as ginseng root was to Frosted Flakes.

John Lester of KPIX became the media advisor for the Hearst family when Patty was abducted. He warned Randolph Hearst that when he stepped through his front door he would be appearing on international television and therefore it would be important not to pick his nose. So, just before he opened the door, Hearst would call out, "Hey, John — look!" Lester would look and Hearst would proceed to stick his index finger up his right nostril, eliciting a horrified laugh from his media advisor. Then Hearst would walk out with black-dressed Catherine and mournfully greet the press. On the inside of the door, there was a sign that warned, "Don't Pick Your Nose!"

Patty's parents were there on view when the jury was selected, although the press was excluded. But how could the judge be sure that Randolph Hearst wouldn't leak the story to his own paper? And so they sat in the front row of the courtroom each day, that protective image of media royalty continuing to lurk behind Princess Patty in the subconscious memory of the jurors.

What was really on trial was the royal nuclear family — floor sample of a consumer unit that also serves as the original source of authority. If Patty had not "belonged" to her parents, why would anybody want to kidnap her? And if the princess had lived her pre-kidnap life inside the safety of the castle, then how could any nasty old SLA get her?

The message of this trial was clear: Destroy the seeds of rebellion in your children or we shall have it done *for* you. In the courtroom, spectators with binoculars focused on Patty and her parents, who were busy pretending that they weren't being watched for reactions. They had become a captive audience by being forced to listen in public to a tape-recorded communique from their princess, abdicating her right to the throne:

> Mom, Dad, I would like to comment on your efforts to supposedly secure my safety. The [food] giveaway was a sham.... You were playing games — stalling for time — which the FBI was using in their attempts to assassinate me and the SLA elements which guarded me....

I have been given the choice of, one, being released in a safe area or, two, joining the forces of the Symbionese Liberation Army.... I have chosen to stay and fight....

I want you to tell the people the truth. Tell them how the law-and-order programs are just a means to remove so-called violent — meaning aware — individuals from the community in order to facilitate the controlled removal of unneeded labor forces in this country, in the same way that Hitler controlled the removal of the Jews from Germany.

I should have known that if you and the rest of the corporate state were willing to do this to millions of people to maintain power and to serve your needs, you would also kill me if necessary to serve those same needs. How long will it take before white people in this country understand that whatever happens to a black child happens sooner or later to a white child? How long will it be before we all understand that we must fight for our freedom?

At the end of the tape, Donald "Cinque" DeFreeze came on with a triple death threat, especially to one Colston Westbrook, whom he accused of being "a Government agent now working for military intelligence while giving assistance to the FBI." This communique was originally sent to San Francisco radio station KSAN. News director David McQueen checked with a Justice Department source, who confirmed Westbrook's employment by the CIA.

Conspiracy researcher Mae Brussell traced his activities from 1962, when he was CIA advisor to the South Korean CIA, through 1969, when he provided logistical support in Vietnam for the CIA's Phoenix program. His job was the indoctrination of assassination and terrorist cadres. After seven years in Asia, he was brought home in 1970, along with the war, and assigned to run the Black Cultural Association at Vacaville Prison, where he became the control officer for DeFreeze, who had worked as a police informer from 1967 to 1969 for the Public Disorder Intelligence Unit of the Los Angeles Police Department.

If DeFreeze was a double agent, then the SLA was a Frankenstein monster, turning against its creator by becoming in reality what had been orchestrated only as a media image. When he finked on his keepers, he signed the death warrant of the SLA. They were burned alive in a Los Angeles safe-house during a shootout with police. When Cinque's charred remains were sent to his family in Cleveland, they couldn't help but notice that he had been decapitated. It was as if the CIA had said, literally, "Bring me the head of Donald DeFreeze!"

Consider the revelations of Wayne Lewis in August 1975. He claimed to have been an undercover agent for the FBI, a fact verified by FBI director Clarence Kelley. Surfacing at a press conference in Los Angeles, Lewis spewed forth a veritable conveyor belt of conspiratorial charges: that DeFreeze was an FBI informer; that he was killed not by the SWAT team but by an FBI agent because he had become "uncontrollable;" that the FBI then wanted Lewis to infiltrate the SLA; that the FBI had undercover agents in other underground guerrilla groups; that the FBI knew where Patty Hearst was but let her remain free so it could build up its files of potential subversives.

At one point, the FBI declared itself to have made 27,000 checks into the whereabouts of Patty Hearst. It was simultaneously proclaimed by the FDA that there were 25,000 brands of laxative on the market. That meant one catharsis for each FBI investigation, with a couple of thousand potential loose shits remaining to smear across "No Left Turn" signs. Patty had become a vehicle for repressive action on the right and for wishful thinking on the left.

A three-month-old baby, whose mother wanted to expose her to the process of justice, was being breast-fed in the back of the courtroom while Patty Hearst testified that she had been raped in a closet by the lover she had once described as "the gentlest, most beautiful man I've ever known."

Now, prosecutor James Browning was cross-examining her.

"Did you, in fact, have a strong feeling for Willie Wolfe?"

"In a way, yes."

"As a matter of fact, were you in love with him?"

"No."

"A little later, he asked if it had been 'forcible rape.'"

"Excuse me?"

"Did you struggle or submit?"

"I didn't resist. I was afraid."

Browning walked into the trap: "I thought you said you had strong feelings for him?"

"I did," Patty replied triumphantly. "I couldn't *stand* him."

It sure seemed fake. And yet, there was this letter to the *Berkeley Barb*:

Only a woman knows that the sex act, no matter how gentle, becomes rape if she is an unwilling partner. Her soul, as well as her body, is scarred. The gentleness of Willie Wolfe does not preclude rape. Rape, in this instance, was dependent upon Patricia Hearst's state of mind, not Willie Wolfe's. We must all remember that *only* Patty knows what *she* felt; and if we refuse to believe her, there can be no justice.

Patty also said that her intercourse with Cinque was "without affection."

The SLA women insisted they were not "mindless cunts enslaved by big black penises."

"You need seven inches," a reporter was explaining, "for a byline in *Newsweek*."

"Patty Frigid After DeFreeze," stated a headline that was set in type but not used in the *Daily Californian*, the Berkeley campus newspaper.

"Hearst Blows Weed," stated a later headline that *was* used in the *Daily Californian*.

"Is the Government saying," objected Bailey, "that everyone who smokes grass is a bank robber?"

Oh, that's right, this *was* a bank-robbery trial, wasn't it?

"Were you *acting* the part of a bank robber?" Browning asked Patty.

"I was doing exactly what I had to do. I just wanted to get *out* of that bank. I was just supposed to be in there to get my picture taken mostly."

Ulysses Hall testified that after the robbery, he managed to speak on the phone with his former prison mate, Cinque, who told him that the SLA members didn't trust Patty's decision to join them. Conversely, *she* didn't trust *their* offer of a "choice," since they all realized she'd be able to identify them if she went free — and so they made her prove herself by "fronting her off" at the bank with Cinque's gun pointed at her head. Out of the closet, into the bank!

Patty testified that Patricia Soltysik kicked her because she wasn't enthusiastic enough at a dress rehearsal, and Cinque warned her that if she messed up in any way, she'd be killed. Before the trial, prosecutor Browning had admitted that it was "clear from the photographs she may have been acting under duress." And during the trial, Bailey, with only 15 minutes to go before weekend recess, brought out the Government's suppression of photos showing Camilla Hall also pointing her gun at Patty in the bank.

Moreover, in a scene right out of *Blow-Up* or an aspirin commercial, a "scientific laboratory" had used a digital computer "to filter out the grain without changing the content," then scanned the photos with a laser beam, all to indicate that Patty had opened her mouth in surprise and recoiled in horror at the firing of shots in the bank, and that it was merely a shadow that made her look as if she were smiling during the robbery, although Cinque had given her strict orders to smile whenever she met anyone who was supposed to know she was Tania, because the original image of Patty, the one that was disseminated around the world, showed her smiling broadly.

No wonder KQED's courtroom artist Rosalie Ritz was approached by a promoter willing to pay her to design a Patty doll with a complete change of clothes so it could be turned into a Tania doll.

It did not come out in the testimony of Louis "Jolly" West that he once killed an elephant with an overdose of LSD — which UPI's Don Thackrey called "pachydermicide" — nor that Dr. West once spent eight straight hours in John Lilly's sensory deprivation tank. According to Kayo Hallinan, Patty "hated" West because she was aware of the fascistic implications of his proposed UCLA Center for the Study and Reduction of Violence, which would practice what it preached against — violence — in the form of electrode implantation and aversion therapy. Obviously, then, some kind of coercive persuasion must have been used to get her to talk to him. Perhaps she had been reduced to a state of infantile helplessness — once again.

A letter from a prisoner in the San Mateo County Jail: "I was coming out of the doctor's office when I saw Tania being taken out the front door. The guards had cleared the hallways of all prisoners and it was by mistake that I was let out at that time by the jail nurse. Tania was taken out by one female and three males. When I called to her I was dragged out of the hallway. Our comrade was exhausted and frightened, lethargic in her movements and appeared drugged. While I was in the doctor's office, I had noticed a 3-by-5 manila envelope — the type used to hold medications given to prisoners — which had written on it, 'Hearst.' There is little doubt she is being drugged."

Associated Press reported that "a source close to the specialists conducting the examination... said that the dosages of 'antipsychotic drugs' listed on Miss Hearst's medical report would themselves cause lethargy and disorientation." Would she eventually emerge from the psychiatric kidnapping only to proclaim, as she had previously done on an SLA communique, "I have not been brainwashed, drugged, tortured or hypnotized in any way"?

F. Lee Bailey put Patty on the witness stand. He asked her what Cinque had done on one occasion to show his disapproval.

"He pinched me."

"Where?"

"My breasts" — pause — "and down —"

"Your private parts as well?"

"Yes."

Then Browning cross-examined Patty:

"Did he pinch one or both of your breasts?"

"I really don't remember."

"Was it under your clothing?"

"Yes."

"In both places?"

"Pardon me, I don't think that the other was under my clothing."

"All right, your breasts he pinched by touching your skin. The pubic area, he did not touch your skin. Is that true?"

"That's right."

Good Lord, this was supposed to be the Trial of the Century, and the Government was trying to find out whether Cinque got bare tit.

Bailey fought unsuccessfully to have Patty testify about the bombing of the Hearst castle, so that the jury would know she was still, indirectly, afraid of SLA members Bill and Emily Harris. But, once more, Patty tricked Browning during cross-examination. He was asking why she hadn't taken advantage of opportunities to phone for help.

"It wasn't possible for me to call," she explained, "because I couldn't do it, and I was afraid of the FBI."

Browning was certainly not going to disagree with Bailey's contention that Patty suffered from "a misperception about the viciousness of the FBI," so he asked Patty if it had occurred to her to turn the Harrises in.

"I was afraid. They aren't the only people like that running around.... There were many others who could've picked up right where they left off."

Browning wondered if they really had such "power over your life."

"They did. It's happening right now."

"Has somebody been killed?"

Suddenly, Patty switched from her usual monotone to a hurried delineation of the latest terrorist acts, threats and broken promises, including this:

"San Simeon was bombed. My parents received a communique demanding $250,000 —"

Your Honor, please, the witness is leading the prosecutor. But it was too late. The jury had heard her.

Browning countered weakly: "Was anybody killed?"

"No."

Before the trial, Bailey's associate, Albert Johnson, had protested that, "contrary to what Sheriff McDonald says, [Patty Hearst and Sara Jane Moore, attempted assassin of President Gerald Ford] have not exchanged cordialities.... I don't want any inferences drawn from any conduct of the two of them simply because they are in the same institution, because there is absolutely no connection between the two cases."

But there *was* a missing link — the murder of Wilbert "Popeye" Jackson, leader of the United Prisoners Union. He had been killed, together with a companion, Sally Voye, while they sat in a parked car at two o'clock in the morning. I learned from impeccable sources that the hit *was known in advance* within the California Department of Corrections, the FBI, the San Jose and San Francisco police departments. But now — in mid-February 1976, while the Patty Hearst trial was in process — a similar charge was made in the company of some unusual accusations when a Berkeley underground group called Tribal Thumb prepared this statement:

> It has become known to the Tribal Thumb orbit that the CIA, FBI and CCS [Criminal Conspiracy Section] have made undercurrent moves to establish a basis for the total eradication of the Tribal Thumb Community.... [They] are involved in working overtime to unravel the mystery of Popeye Jackson's execution in an effort to plant Tribal Thumb in a web of conspiracy in that execution....
>
> The FBI's heavy involvement in the case of Popeye's death largely is due to the death of Sally Voye, who in actuality was moonlighting (outside her employment as a teacher) as a narcotics agent for police forces. Moreover, she was Popeye's control agent. Popeye was an informer on the movement.
>
> Several days ago, Patty Hearst was slipped out of her jail cell by the FBI and Mr. Randolph Hearst and taken to a nearby jail to identify a man being held there (we're withholding his name for now) who was allegedly closely associated with Tribal Thumb, to make an identification of this man's alleged trafficking of large quantities of arms to Tribal Thumb and the Symbionese Liberation Army. The result is that Miss Hearst pointed the comrade out as the trafficker of such weapons....
>
> Donald DeFreeze escaped from the California prison system with help from the FBI and California prison officials. His mission was to establish an armed revolutionary organization, controlled by the FBI, specifically to either make contact with or undermine the surfacing and development of the August Seventh Guerrilla Movement.
>
> We make note of the fact that the first communique issued by the SLA under the leadership of Donald DeFreeze was in part a duplicate of a communique issued by the ASGM. Further examination of those communiques establishes that the ASGM had surfaced and was in the process of developing some kind of operational format, when the SLA hastily moved, hard pressed for

something spectacular to cut off this thrust by the ASGM. The result was the incorrect and unfounded death of (school superintendent) Marcus Foster.

It is evident that the FBI through its sources of information knew of the underground existence of the ASGM and that the movement was obviously making plans to become public knowledge via armed actions against the imperialist state. Having had their attempts to infiltrate agents into the ASGM's mainstream frustrated, they sought the diverse method of establishing an organization they could control. So they made three approaches: Donald DeFreeze, who was in contact with Nancy Ling Perry, who worked at Rudy's Fruit Stand, from whom Patty Hearst often bought bagels and fruit juice.

DeFreeze was let loose and given a safe plan to surface as an armed guerrilla unit. That plan was to kidnap Patty Hearst — strategized by the FBI, Randolph Hearst, Patty Hearst and Nancy Ling Perry. The format of that plan of kidnapping Patty Hearst was extracted from a book, published by a publishing company named Nova owned by the Hearst Corporation, entitled *Vanished* (Tribal Thumb may have meant *Black Abductor*, by Harrison James, pseudonym for James Rusk, Jr., published by Regency Press, not affiliated with Hearst).

On April 8, after Patty was found guilty, there was a front page story in the *San Franciso Examiner*:

> Would-be presidential assassin Sara Jane Moore and the Patricia Hearst case are intricately linked in the web of evidence that led to yesterday's arrest of the accused murderer of militant prison-reform leader Wilbert "Popeye" Jackson, authorities have told the *Examiner.*
>
> These sources said Ms. Moore, now in custody in a Federal prison in San Diego, will be a star witness in the trial of the accused slayer.... And it was the arrest last September of Miss Hearst... that led to the break in the case, according to the primary investigators in the case....
>
> Booked into the San Francisco County Jail yesterday afternoon was Richard Alan London, 26, an ex-convict who has been in the Santa Clara County Jail in San Jose since last summer on an armed-robbery charge.... London is a member of a revolutionary band called the United Prisoners Union....
>
> Federal and local authorities flatly denied a report circulated by Tribal Thumb sources that Miss Hearst, convicted of bank robbery on March 20, was taken to the Santa Clara jail to identify London last week....

Last week? Why this change in chronology? The original Tribal Thumb statement alleged that Patty had identified London as a gunrunner for the SLA and Tribal Thumb more than a *month-and-a-half* previously. The truth is that she secretly began to turn state's evidence *early in her trial.* Usually, defendants tell what they know *before* trial, so the prosecution can decide whether or not to plea-bargain and avoid a trial. But this particular trial *had* to be held, if only to avoid giving any impression of plea-bargaining. Patty Hearst had been gang-banged behind the tent at the Hearstling Brothers Browning & Bailey Bread and Circus by both teams, prosecution and defense, while they were adversaries in a trial that was more carefully staged than a TV wrestling match.

Judge Oliver Carter had once sentenced Hedy Sarney to two-and-a-half years for bank robbery. She claimed at her sentencing that Tribal Thumb had made her do it. Now F. Lee Bailey reminded the judge that he had commented that her claim of coercion came too late and that she had refused to testify against the people she accused of forcing her to commit the crime, whereas, in the case of Patty Hearst, Bailey said cryptically, "Your Honor has been made aware of some facts which are relevant to him."

It was considered likely that Popeye Jackson could have been killed by police agents — to neutralize yet another black leader, rather than because he was supposed to be an informer. The United Prisoners Union reasoned that "if Popeye had been interested in snitching, he would have made all efforts to keep up his contacts with the NWLF (New World Liberation Front) rather than be 'cold and distant' or allow for any misunderstanding."

But was it possible, as Tribal Thumb pointed out, that Patty Hearst had participated in the planning of her own kidnapping while ostensibly *buying bagels*? An SLA manuscript stated that they had expected more trouble from their intended victim, "since we were planning on carrying her away, but she turned out to be real cooperative. She just lay down on the floor while one of the comrades tied her hands and blindfolded her."

When Patty was being interviewed in jail by prosecution psychiatrist Harry Kozol, she pulled a Raskolnikov (the character in Dostoievesky's *Crime and Punishment* who cannot repress the force of his own guilt) by darting from the room and complaining that Kozol had accused her of arranging her own kidnapping. Bailey asked him on the witness stand:

"Did you suggest that she got herself kidnapped?" He answered, "No."

In their first session, Kozol questioned Patty about Willie Wolfe. "I told her," he testified, "that I'd heard her speak tenderly of him [on the final taped communique] and I asked her this question: 'Is that the way you felt about him?' She seemed to get upset and deeply moved. I felt she was almost sobbing inside... but no tears ran down her face.... She said, 'I don't *know* how I feel about him.' I said, 'I'm not asking you how you feel. Is that how you *felt*?' She became very much upset, began to shake and quiver, obviously suffering. And she answered, 'I don't know why I got into this goddamn thing — shit!' And then got up and left the room, terribly upset."

Got into *what* goddamn thing? Patty could have been referring to her agreement to talk with psychiatrists, or to her decision to join the SLA, or to the kidnapping itself. In their second session, when she described the kidnapping scene, Kozol asked if there was anything else. He testified:

"There was some delay. She was sort of thinking. She began to look very uncomfortable and I told her, 'Never mind.' And she said, 'I don't want to tell you.' And I said, 'That's okay, if it makes you uncomfortable,' and then she blurted out that she was going to tell me anyway. She told me that four days before the kidnapping, while she was sitting in class, she was suddenly struck with a terrible fear that she was going to be kidnapped. This was an overwhelming sensation. It stayed with her. I said, 'What's so surprising about a girl from a well-to-do family worrying about kidnapping?' She brushed it aside and said, 'It wasn't anything of the sort. It was different.' For four solid days, she couldn't shake the fear. She finally thought in terror of running home to her parents, where she would be safe. She somehow fought that. Then the thing she dreaded occurred."

∎▪◼▪∎

The family of slain SLA member Willie Wolfe hired Lake Headley — an ex-police intelligence officer who was chief investigator at Wounded Knee — to find out what had really happened. What he discovered, with fellow researchers Donald Freed and Rusty Rhodes, was that the SLA was part of the CIA's CHAOS program. In that context, they were planning to kill Black Panther leader Huey Newton and succeeded in killing black school superintendent Marcus Foster *after* he agreed to meet Panther demands for educational reforms.

At Vacaville Prison, DeFreeze was permitted to set up Unisight, a program by which convicts could get laid by visiting females. According to investigator Headley, DeFreeze's visitors included kidnappers-to-be Nancy Ling Perry and Patricia Soltysik — *and* Patty Hearst, then 18, not going under her own name but using the ID of Mary Alice Siems, a student at Berkeley.

Headley's affidavit stated: "That Patricia Campbell Hearst and her parents disagreed bitterly over Patricia's political and personal relations. That a love affair between a black man and Patricia Hearst did take place prior to her relationship with her fiance Steven Weed. That Mrs. Randolph A. Hearst subjected her daughter to extreme pressure to change her personal and political relationships."

Patty began living with Weed in Berkeley later that year, in the fall of 1972. DeFreeze was transferred to Soledad in December 1972, where he was given the special privilege of using the trailers ordinarily reserved for married trustees. DeFreeze became a leader of the SLA and, according to Headley, renewed his affair with Patty for a brief time. The affidavit continued: "Discussions were held between Patricia Campbell Hearst and the Symbionese Liberation Army concerning a kidnapping — not her own."

Whose, then? Her sisters, Anne and Vicki. The idea of kidnapping Patty, too, was brought up — this was a year before it actually took place — but she didn't think it was such a great notion. But, if true, this would explain Patty's outburst at the moment of kidnapping: "Oh, no! Not *me!* Oh, God! Please let me go!"

The investigators presented their findings to the Los Angeles City Council, charging that the intelligence unit of the police department

— the Criminal Conspiracy Section — knew of the SLA's presence but *wanted* the shootout for test purposes. Headley acquired official film footage of the massacre, showing that the FBI used a pair of German Shepherds to sniff out Patty's presence so she wouldn't be inside the safe-house. Steven Weed was told by a cop at the shootout, "Don't worry, Patty's not in there."

On the tape of April 3, 1974, Patty said, "I have been given the name Tania after a comrade who fought alongside Che in Bolivia for the people." And on the tape of June 6, she said, "I renounced my class privilege when Cin [DeFreeze] and Cujo [Wolfe] gave me the name Tania." But in a *New Times* interview, Bill Harris said, "She chose the name Tania herself." According to Weed, her reading matter had ranged from the Marquis de Sade to *Do It* by Jerry Rubin. And, according to my Berkeley source, Patty and a former roommate had both read the book *Tania, the Unforgettable Guerrilla* a year prior to the kidnapping.

Further, I was told, the roommate had been subpoenaed to testify for the prosecution in Patty's trial, but the subpoena was withdrawn. I wrote about that in the *Berkeley Barb*. The FBI's liaison to the U.S. Attorney's office, Parks Stearns, Jr., denied this vehemently, shouting at me in the press room, "You're wrong!"

It could've been just a coincidence, but after that incident, the head marshal began hassling me for identification, even though I had been coming to the trial every day. One time he asked for my driver's license. I told him I didn't drive a car. Another time he asked for my Social Security card. I told him I never carried that around. I would present only my press credentials, which he accepted because there were too many media people around and he didn't want the attention that a scene would automatically create.

While Patty's trial was in progress, *Sundaz*, a Santa Cruz weekly, reported that Research West — the private right-wing spy organization that maintained files supplied by confessed burglar Jerome Ducote — "was purchased in October of 1969 with funds provided by Catherine Hearst," and that "after the Hearst connection became known to employees...at least one *Examiner* reporter was told to drop any further investigation into the Ducote case."

The *Sundaz* story stated not only that Catherine Hearst gave or lent most of the $60,000-$70,000 purchase price for the company, but also that prior to that purchase, the foundation supported itself through "contributions" averaging $1000, provided by Pacific Telephone, Pacific Gas & Electric, railroads, steamship lines, banks and the *Examiner*. In return, the files were available to those companies, as well as to local police and sheriff departments, the FBI, the CIA and the IRS. The *Examiner* paid $1500 a year through 1975 to retain the services of Research West.

In another case, a member of the Santa Clara district attorney's office testified that FBI agent Charles Bates had "categorically denied" having any of the stolen documents sought by the Santa Clara district attorney for an investigation of FBI-sponsored political burglaries. After being confronted with the testimony of one of his own subordinates, Bates ultimately turned over the documents. Some of the stolen documents, according to *Sundaz*, ended up with Catherine Hearst's pet project, Research West.

In 1969, Charles Bates was Special Agent at the Chicago office of the FBI when police killed Black Panthers Fred Hampton and Mark Clark while they were sleeping. Ex-FBI informer Maria Fischer told the *Chicago Daily News* that the then-chief of the FBI's Chicago office, Marlon Johnson, personally asked her to slip a drug to Hampton; she had infiltrated the Panther Party at the FBI's request a month before. The drug was a tasteless, colorless liquid that would put him to sleep. She refused. Hampton was killed a week later. An autopsy showed "a near fatal dose" of secobarbital in his system.

In 1971, Bates was transferred to Washington. According to Watergate burglar James McCord's book, *A Piece of Tape*, on June 21, 1972, White House attorney John Dean checked with acting FBI Director L. Patrick Gray as to who was in charge of handling the Watergate investigation. The answer: Charles Bates — the same FBI official who in 1974 would be in charge of handling the SLA investigation and the search for Patty Hearst. When she was arrested, Bates became instantly ubiquitous on radio and TV, boasting of her capture.

And, in the middle of her trial — on a Saturday afternoon, when reporters and technicians were hoping to be off duty — the FBI called a press conference. At five o'clock that morning, they had raided the New Dawn collective — supposedly the aboveground support group of the Berkeley underground Emiliano Zapata Unit — and accompanying a press release about the evidence seized were photographs still wet with developing fluid. Charles Bates held the photos up.

"Mr. Bates," a photographer requested, " real close to your head, please."

Bates proceeded to pose with the photos like Henry Fonda doing a camera commercial. Was there a search warrant? No, but they had a "consent to search" signed by the owner of the house, Judy Stevenson, who later admitted to being a paid FBI informant.

Not only did the raid seem timed to break into print simultaneously with the Sunday funnies, but the investigative technique also smacked of comic-strip morality. In *Dick Tracy* the next day, the "Crimestoppers Textbook" depicted a trio of stereotypical hippie terrorists preparing a time bomb, underscored by the question, "Would you deny police access to knowledge of persons planning your demise?"

Almost six weeks after that Saturday morning raid, I received a letter by registered mail on Department of Justice stationery:

Dear Mr. Krassner:

Subsequent to the search of a residence in connection with the arrest of six members of the Emiliano Zapata Unit, the Federal Bureau of Investigation, San Francisco, has been attempting to contact you to advise you of the following information:

During the above indicated arrest of six individuals of the Emiliano Zapata Unit, an untitled list of names and addresses of individuals was seized. A corroborative source described the above list as an Emiliano Zapata Unit "hit list," but stated that no action will be taken, since all of those who could carry it out are in custody.

Further, if any of the apprehended individuals should make bail, they would only act upon the "hit list" at the instructions of their leader, who is not and will not be in a position to give such instructions.

The above information is furnished for your personal use and it is requested it be kept confidential. At your discretion, you may desire to contact the local police department responsible for the area of your residence.

Very truly yours,

Charles W. Bates
Special Agent in Charge

But I was more logically a target of the Government than of the Emiliano Zapata Unit — unless, of course they happened to be the same. Was the right wing of the FBI warning me about the left wing of the FBI? Did the handwriting on the wall read *Co-Intelpro Lives?* Questions about the authenticity of the Zapata Unit had been raised by its first public statement in August 1975, which included the unprecedented threat of violence against the left.

When a Safeway supermarket in Oakland was bombed by the Zapata Unit, they claimed to have called radio station KPFA and instructed them to notify police, so they could evacuate the area, but KPFA staffers insisted they never received such a call. Now *The Urban Guerrilla*, aboveground organ of the underground NWLF, commented:

> Without offering any proof, the FBI has claimed that [those arrested] were members of the Emiliano Zapata Unit and mistakenly claimed that the Zapata Unit was part of the New World Liberation Front. These FBI claims and lies have been widely repeated by the media.
>
> As soon as they were arrested, Greg Adornetto, whom we knew as Chepito, was separated from the others and disappeared....
>
> A close analysis of all the actions and statements... by Chepito leads [us] to the inescapable conclusion that he is not just a weak informer, he is a Government infiltrator/provocateur. No other conclusion is possible when one considers that he led our comrades to a house he *knew* was under surveillance... carrying along things like explosives and half-completed communiques....
>
> He recruited sincere and committed revolutionaries who wanted to participate in being a medium for dialogue with the underground, got a bunch of them in the same room with guns, communiques and explosives, or even got some of them involved in armed actions, and then had...Bates move in with his SWAT team and bust everybody....

In addition, a communique from the central command of the NWLF charged that "the pigs led and organized" the Zapata Unit. "We were reasonably sure that it was a set-up from the beginning and we *never* sent one communique to New Dawn because of our suspicions."

After publishing the FBI's warning letter to me in the *Berkeley Barb*, I received letters from a couple of members of the Emiliano Zapata Unit in prison. One stated:

> I was involved in the aboveground support group of the Zapata Unit. Greg Adornetto led myself and several others to believe we were joining a cell of the Weather Underground, which had a new surge of life when it published *Prairie Fire*. I knew nothing about a hit list or your being on one, and can't imagine why you would have been. When we were arrested, FBI agent provocateur Adornetto immediately turned against the rest of us and provided evidence to the Government. We were basically caught with stolen explosives.

Another advised:

> You shouldn't have believed the boys in the black shiny shoes (FBI) about being on a Zapata hit list. They just found some addresses and Bates and his running partner Hearst wanted to build up some sensationalism to take the heat off of Patty's trial. They had over 75 people (politicians and corporate execs) under protection, thinking all of us didn't get arrested.

Jacques Rogiers, aboveground courier for the underground New World Liberation Front, told me that the reason I was on the hit list was because I had written that Donald DeFreeze was a police informer.

"But that was true," I said. "It's a matter of record. Doesn't that make any difference?"

It didn't.

"If the NWLF asked me to kill you," Rogiers admitted, "I would."

"Jacques," I replied, "I think this puts a slight damper on our relationship."

-■■■-

After Patty Hearst was arrested, she had a jailhouse conversation with her best friend since childhood, Trish Tobin — whose family, incidentally, controlled the Hibernia Bank that Patty had helped rob. Several times throughout the trial, prosecutor James Browning attempted to have the tape of that dialogue played for the jury, but Judge Carter kept refusing — until the end of the trial, when the impact of its giddiness would be especially astonishing.

Trish: "I had a lot of fights at Stanford."

Patty: "Oh, yeah? About what?"

Trish: "You."

Patty: "Oh — what were they saying? I can just imagine —"

Trish: "Oh, well, 'that fucking little rich bitch' — you know, on and on — and they said, 'She planned her own kidnapping,' and I said, 'Fuck you, you don't know what the fuck you're talking about, I don't even care if she plans her kidnapping and everyone's in the world, so you know something, I don't wanna hear *shit* out of you!" *(Laughter)*

The gossip was that Patty had arranged her own kidnapping in order to get out of her engagement to Steven Weed in as adventurous a way as possible—"I guess I was having second thoughts," she admitted, "I wasn't sure he was somebody I could stay married to" — but that she was then double-crossed and manipulated into becoming an informer.

In any event, Patty's jailhouse tape appeared to reveal a change in her outlook: "I'm not making any statements until I know that I can get out on bail, and then if I find out that I can't for sure, then I'll issue a statement, but I'd just as soon give it myself, in person, and then it'll be a revolutionary feminist perspective totally. I mean I never got really... I guess I'll just tell you, like, my politics are real different from, uh — way back when *(laughter)* — obviously! And so this creates all kinds of problems for me in terms of a defense."

An accurate forecast. So Patty testified that she was influenced to say that because captured SLA member Emily Harris was in the visiting room at the time Patty was talking to Trish Tobin.

Bailey asked, "Was she a party to your conversation?"

"Not by any intention of ours, no."

On cross-examination, Patty continued: "Emily was also on a phone." Prisoners and visitors had to converse over telephones while they looked at each other through a thick bulletproof-glass window. Patty said she knew that Emily could hear her talking simply because "I could've heard her if I'd stopped and listened." But jail records showed that Emily was *not* in the visiting room then.

While psychiatrist Harry Kozol was testifying in court, Patty was writing notes to Albert Johnson on a yellow legal pad. And while I diverted the head marshal's attention by acting suspiciously during recess, reporter Steve Rubinstein copied those notes, but wasn't allowed to include them in his story for the *Los Angeles Herald Examiner*, a Hearst paper.

In one of the notes, Patty described life in Berkeley with Weed: "I paid the rent, bought the furniture, bought the groceries, cooked all the meals (even while working eight hours a day and carrying a full course load), and if I wasn't there to cook, Steve didn't eat."

In another note, she clearly and concisely described where her mindset really was at in the San Mateo County Jail when she couldn't blame Emily Harris' eavesdropping as her motivation: "Dr. Kozol kept trying to equate the women's movement with violence. I repeatedly told him: 1. Violence has no place in the women's movement. 2. I didn't feel it was possible to make lasting changes in our society unless the issue of women's rights was resolved. Kozol kept trying to say things like, 'Isn't it more important to solve the poverty problem?' Any reform measures taken by the Government will only be temporary."

Although news items about the trial were clipped out of the daily papers by U.S. marshals, the sequestered jurors were not immune to media influence. During the trial, they all went out to see a few films, which they voted on.

They saw *One Flew Over the Cuckoo's Nest*, which, Ken Kesey complained, made Big Nurse the target and omitted the central theme of his book, that people go crazy in this country precisely because they can't handle the gap between the American Dream and the American Nightmare as orchestrated by the same combination that Patty was forced to experience, where organized crime and organized crime-fighting are merely different sides of the same corporate coin.

The jury also saw *Swept Away...*, reinforcing the theme that one does not transcend one's class unless one is already heading in that direction before circumstances temporarily shatter all those arbitrary rules that distinguish the classes.

And the jury saw *Taxi Driver* — once again perpetuating the myth of the lone nut assassin, played by Robert DeNiro, who, in this case, attempts to kill a political candidate, not because he has been hired by an intelligence agency, but rather because Cybil Shepherd won't stay and hold his hand at a porno movie.

Bill and Emily Harris let it be known that, if called to testify, they would take the 5th Amendment, but Emily testified, in effect, through the media. After Patty told the jury that Willie Wolfe had raped her, Emily was quoted in *New Times*: "Once Willie gave her a stone relic in the shape of a monkey face [and] Patty wore it all the time around her neck. After the shootout, she stopped wearing it and carried it in her purse instead, but she always had it with her."

Prosecutor James Browning read this in the magazine and he had an *Aha!* experience, remembering that "rock" in Patty's purse from the inventory list when she was originally captured. He presented it as his final piece of evidence in the trial, slowly swinging the necklace back and forth in front of the jurors, as if to hypnotize them.

Patty Hearst had once told a nun to go to Hell, but during the trial her monkey face necklace was replaced by a religious symbol. It didn't help. The jury found her guilty of being a bank robber — that is, a *virtual* bank robber.

They also found her guilty of fucking when she was fifteen-years-old — or why else would such information have been admissible as evidence during the trial? They don't allow that kind of testimony in a rape trial, but for a bank robbery it was considered relevant.

Judge Carter sentenced her to 35 years, pending the results of 90 days of psychiatric testing. He announced, "I intend to reduce the sentence. How much I am not now prepared to say."

If you were Patty, would you have answered True or False to the following statements:

* "My way of doing things is apt to be misunderstood by others."
* "I am always disgusted with the law when a criminal is freed through the arguments of a smart lawyer."
* "I feel that it is certainly best to keep my mouth shut when I'm in trouble."

Those are samples from the MMPI, a psychological test Patty had to take. In order to have her sentence reduced, she was required to undergo a psychiatric debriefing extended to six months. Kidnapped again. While Patty was still being probed by the shrinks, Judge Carter died, and the joke was that his replacement would sentence Patty to working as a teller at the Hibernia Bank for rehabilitative purposes.

(Eventually she faced seven years in prison, but after serving 23 months, her sentence was commuted by President Jimmy Carter.)

Graffiti remained mute testaments to the whole misadventure. With the same passion that some had previously spray-painted *Free Squeaky* and *Gravity Is the 4th Dimension*, others left messages like *Jail Rocky and Nixon, Not Tania* and *SLA LIVES*, which was long hidden in the enigmatic made-over *COLE SLAW LIVES* slogan that baffled tourists and convinced one visiting ex-Berkeleyite that a political activist named Cole Slaw was dead because there were graffiti saying he was alive.

Finally, although James Browning had once informed me that the Black Panthers were "an organization which advocates killing people" and that Groucho Marx's "utterance did not constitute a 'true' threat," it had since come out that the FBI itself published pamphlets in the name of the Panthers advocating the killing of cops and that an FBI file on Groucho was indeed begun and he actually *was* labeled a "national security risk." I called Groucho to tell him the good news.

"I deny everything," he said, "because I lie about everything." He paused, then added, "And everything I *deny* is a lie."

How I Invented Soft-Core Pornography

When I was a kid growing up in the 1940s, my older brother was selling nude photos of Hollywood stars like Rita Hayworth and Burt Lancaster for 75 cents apiece.

"But what's it *for*?" I asked.

"To give you a hard-on," he said. "But it's against the law."

I instinctively understood that the government should have no right to interfere with anybody's pleasure where nobody got hurt.

In 1958, pornography was on its way to becoming legal gradually, but at that stage of the game, the Supreme Court was unwilling to allow 1st Amendment protection of 'hard-core pornography' — as opposed, I assumed, to "soft-core pornography" — a term I made up.

Soft-core was obviously more respectable than hard-core, but it seemed sort of sneaky, *pretending* to be squeaky clean. So I decided to satirize the concept with a new feature in *The Realist*: "Soft-Core Pornography of the Month."

Phallic symbolism in magazines was a key ingredient of soft-core porn. A close-up of a stickshift in a Volkswagen ad was accompanied by the question, "Does the stickshift scare your wife?"

Another ad showed the face of a woman with an ecstatic expression. Her eyes were closed and her mouth was open. In her hand was a penis-shaped bottle of Lavoris Oral Spray which she was spraying into her mouth. It sure *appeared* that she was giving somebody a blow job.

A blatant example of soft-core porn was an ad for the MG, a British sports car, performing 69 with the owner underneath, and the warning, "Please don't drink the suspension system."

Another ad depicted one car mounted on another car — a vivid example of auto-eroticism — and the agency's art director told me that he had done it on purpose.

Folks in the advertising business often tried to see what they could get away with. An ad for 3M featured a photo of gooey white stuff leaking from an ice cream sundae onto somebody's knee. One account executive approved an ad where, if you looked carefully, you'd notice that a male model had an erection under his trousers.

Soft-core porn could also be found in comic strips. In *Batman*, Robin angrily shouts, "Girls?!? What fun is *this* case going to be!?!" In *Mary Worth*, a beautiful woman's face, eyes closed, mouthing a peeled banana, says, "He doesn't know it yet, but he's my new boyfriend." And in *Smilin' Jack*, our hero is strapped to a vibrating lounge chair. The sultry villainess kisses him, sits on his vibrating lap and says, "See, just agree to help the Chinese Reds develop their atomic bomb and life will be beautiful!"

Just to add to the confusion of such cold-war hysteria, I published and distributed a popular poster with red-white-and-blue lettering that screamed, *FUCK COMMUNISM!* Post Office officials tried to prevent me from sending it through the mails, but backed off when I accused them of being Commie sympathizers.

My patriotic slogan soon began to take on a life of its own. In a book by former congresswoman Pat Schroeder, *24 Years of House Work... and the Place Is Still a Mess: My Life in Politics*, she writes that conservative actor John Wayne once offered her a cigarette lighter engraved with the inscription, "Fuck Communism — John Wayne." She declined the gift.

Merely by reprinting certain publicity photos in *The Realist*, I robbed them of their innocence: Lady Bird Johnson with Lassie's snout burrowed in her crotch; Ronald Reagan clutching a young boy's head to *his* crotch; Jack Benny giving a funny look behind him to Ed Sullivan as they both ride on the same merry-go-round horse; Jimmy Durante standing behind a disabled little girl, apparently dry-humping her.

I was taken to task for *that* one by Joe Pyne, whose syndicated TV show was the forerunner of in-your-face interviewers. A transcript of our dialogue was included in my CIA file.

Pyne: I won't give this man's [Durante's] name, but he's probably one of the most beloved stars in all of the history of entertainment, and some time ago he posed for what obviously was an Easter Seal picture with a crippled child on crutches. Whatever information there was about that picture has been cropped, and Krassner has put on the top, "Soft-Core Pornography of the Month," and below indicates that the man is a child molester. How this man can take everything that is decent and worthwhile and twist it into something — Marquis de Sade looked like a Boy Scout compared to you.

Krassner: Well, let me just explain that. The beloved movie star you're talking about is —

Pyne: Don't mention his name, please!

Krassner: — obviously not a child molester, we all know that. The point of this whole feature called "Soft-Core Pornography of the Month" is simply to point out that obscenity exists only in the mind of the beholder, and that people can take a tender scene like that and find something dirty in it, if they wish.

Pyne: Where do you say all that? All you say is "Soft-Core Pornography of the Month" on the top, and then you say "Peterofilia in the Reader's Digest" *on the bottom.*

Krassner: It's pedophilia, Joe. Well, do you think for a moment that anybody's going to take that seriously, and think we're actually accusing that beloved movie star —

Pyne: Well, I have such respect for this man that I take it seriously....

Although readers of *The Realist* continue to send me examples of soft-core pornography, that TV appearance was the only time I've ever been publicly credited for inventing the term. It has since become part of the language, but it now refers to limited sexuality — from daytime soap operas to hotel-room videos that feature jiggling tits but no open vaginas, fucking scenes but no visible penetration — that's soft-core.

"But what's it *for*?"

"To give you a *soft*-on. And it's not against the law."

The Zen Bastard Goes to Ecuador

"Some patients decide that only the proper herb can heal while others put childlike faith in the power of the pill; still others insist that salvation can be achieved by mastering a particular yoga position or by repeating a mantra. Whatever you put your trust in can be the precipitating agent for your cure." — Irving Oyle, M.D.

"Laughter is one of the strongest medicines on the planet. If it's strong enough to kill an orgasm, surely it's strong enough to kill cancer." — Lotus Weinstock

In the summer of 1977 I got a magazine assignment to cover the trial of Roman Polanski. My daughter, Holly, was then 13 — the same age as the girl Polanski was accused of seducing — and she had decided to come to Santa Monica with me, sit in the front row of the courtroom and just stare at Polanski. She also planned to write an article about the trial from *her* point of view. However, Polanski fled the country.

I told Holly, "I'm gonna write about the trial anyway."

"How can you do that?"

"I'll just make it up as if it actually occurred. Roman Polanski's defense will be that the statutory rape laws are unconstitutional because they discriminate against kids."

"How would you feel if the kid was *me*?"

"Well, I'm a liberal father, but...you're right. I'm not gonna write the article."

When she was 14, Holly went to Mexico to learn Spanish at a school where no English was spoken. The next year, in the summer of 1979, she served as my translator on a three-week expedition to Ecuador, focusing on shamans and healers.

Fellow explorers included six males (two trip leaders, a physician, a harmonica player and a pair of psychiatrists) and five females (a poet, a cook, a therapist and a printer studying to be an anthropologist). Holly was the only adolescent among a dozen adults, so this trek would have elements of an archetypal rite of passage for her.

Our journey would climax with a group ingestion of *ayahuasca*, a hallucinogenic vine similar to *yage*, used by shamans throughout the Amazon basin to have visions and communicate with jungle spirits during their healing ceremonies.

Holly hoped to participate in that experience. Wanting to be a responsible parent, I gave her some literature to read, including an article by Dr. Andrew Weil, author of *The Natural Mind*.

"Vomiting is the first stage of the effect of *yage*," he wrote. "It is not fun, and I say that as someone who likes to vomit in certain circumstances."

This did not discourage Holly in the slightest.

Our starting point is Quito, the capital city of Ecuador, known as the Shrine of America. It is 9,000 feet above sea level, and in one day you can go through the weather of all four seasons.

In Ecuador they jest about how the ancient power of the water spirit people was invoked to flood the land when it was seized by the colonists. In more recent years, oil exploration resulted in this bittersweet joke among the Indians: "Maybe we will be like the *gringos* and have canned sardines flown in from the coast." In fact, one shaman we would visit actually had taped to his wall the wrappers from a can of sardines and a bar of Lux soap.

The unholy trinity in Ecuador consists of the missionaries, the military and the oil companies. The international oil companies first invaded Ecuador in the late '60s. Within a few years, what had once been a subsistence economy was injected with a strong dose of technological dependence.

On September 15, 1972, then-President Guillermo Lara flew to Shell Airport with a group of captains and colonels, each the head of a national agency. The flight, which took 20 minutes from Quito, was timed to correspond with sunrise. The plane, *La Cucuracha*, touched down at 6 a.m. Paratroopers wearing red berets, who had been trained in Panama for commando warfare, flaunted their Czech-made automatic rifles at buses and cars. Fixed bayonets lined the route.

The Aucas — there were only an estimated 500 left of this tribe who survive in unpopulated areas of the jungle — once killed several employees of Texaco. There are crossed wooden swords on any path leading to an Aucan village. They are a symbolic warning to keep away. We shall not be visiting the Aucas.

But gasoline still costs as little as 15 cents a gallon, and the shell Military Camp carries on.

While we are there, however, the military government is preparing to transfer power to the newly elected liberal, Jaime Roldos. He has beaten one opponent who got a million dollars from the oil people for his campaign. There were full-page ads:

"Vote Against Roldos If You're Catholic."

The president-elect announced, "I want to show that democracy can be imposed in an orderly manner and that social justice can be achieved. This might sound Utopian and may even be a source of amusement to some, but if we ignore the possibility of achieving social change through the institutional framework of the country, it's the same as saying that democracy isn't the most just and perfect form of government."

The culture is a strange blend of tradition and technology.

In Quito, I acquire an advertising poster — they call it *propaganda* — featuring a man wearing an apron and holding up a bottle of cleansing powder called *El Macho*.

We visit Leaves of Grass, a vegetarian restaurant that has a customary bulletin board. "Free room and board for one female," reads one message—"dig this experiment in international living." To a poster offering courses in acupuncture, the *I Ching* and midwifery has been added, "Hashish for sale." In the bathroom, a graffito promises, "Legalize pot and cure the world!"

I had been told that possession of marijuana could result in six months' imprisonment and $50,000 worth of legalized shakedowns in the form of fines, lawyers' fees and judges' bribes.

I was able to verify a few details of one horror case in which an individual was arrested because he was accused of having used cocaine. It was Christmas and his wife was 7½ months pregnant. He has seen her only once since his arrest and hasn't even met their baby. He was put in a clinic that charged him $600 a month, plus he had to pay for his own armed guard. He was fingered by a hippie who had been busted in the U.S. and was then brought to Ecuador to work illegally as an informer for the DEA.

There are, of course, legal drugs. Coca-Cola is everywhere. So are cigarettes, coffee, booze and Ataka, which, claims a TV commercial during the Miss America competition, "eliminates all pain."

The most popular song goes, "Let's just get blasted on tobacco and rum." Number two on the hit parade is "In the Navy" by the Village People. And an automobile horn honks out the first five notes of "Strangers in the Night."

Playing in movie theaters are dubbed versions of *Superman, Death on the Nile, Julia* and *Pretty Baby*. The film *Grease* was immensely popular, as evidenced by the glut of John Travolta and Olivia Newton-John T-shirts for sale.

Westernization has crept in among the authentic Indian goods for sale. On market day, one booth on a side street features a monkey that picks your horoscope from a drawer, and a selection of Viewfinder cassettes including *The Flying Nun, Project Apollo, SWAT, Bonanza, Mickey Mouse, Powerful Puss* and *Lassie*.

And, among all the bare feet, an occasional pair of Adidas.

∙■■■∙

Ibarra, north of Quito, is the territory of the Otovalan Indians, living in the shadow of snow-capped volcanoes. Every Saturday, rows of bland gray beach-umbrella-sized cement mushrooms (a gift of the Dutch government) sprouting from an otherwise barren city block, are temporarily reincarnated into a crowded, buzzing marketplace, the sight of colorful tapestries mixing with the aroma of authentic native recipes.

The Otovalan Indians are a startlingly attractive tribe — short and squat, with doll-like features — but many seem to be permanently bent forward from carrying heavy loads on their backs. Age and gender are no barriers to that task.

The women's finery always includes choker beads that were originally Czechoslovakian Christmas ornaments. The men wear white pants, bright ponchos and fedora hats covering long black hair twisted into the traditional single braid. Young boys who don't have braids yet cover their heads with American cowboy bandanas. Their hairstyle will be proof that they are an indigenous people. If one cuts his hair, he will be ostracized.

The Otovalans have had land disputes ever since the Spanish conquest. The Spaniards tried to outlaw anything to do with their old religion. They even forbade Inca clothing style. Thus the Indians were virtually forced into wearing these brimmed hats.

Even when we get to play six-person volleyball with a bunch of young men in an Otovalan village, the men keep their fedoras on. At one point, the game, for which each side puts up 60 *sucres*, stops so that an elderly woman may lead a bull through the volleyball court, which is simply a net strung across a dirt road.

Although masculine and feminine roles appear to be clearly defined — men, for example, operate the weaving loom and women do the spinning — there is, nevertheless, an inspiring dignity implicit in a group of well-dressed Otovalan women washing clothes at a dirt road intersection, when they refuse to allow their photos to be taken. In other contexts, they have been eagerly cooperative in posing for our cameras.

Only men can be *brujos* (witch doctors), but some women are permitted to perform abortions by manipulating and crushing the uterus. Two days later there will be a miscarriage. If the pregnant woman has been touched by a rainbow, she will give birth to a monster. However, that can be avoided if a *brujo* cleanses her. Then she will have a normal baby.

Like the Moonies and Scientology and Catholicism — it works. If the universe is infinite, then there is also an infinite variety of paths to connect with the universe.

▪▫◼▫▪

Our bus stops at a marker signifying the exact dividing line between the northern and southern hemispheres. I absolutely cannot resist the territorial urge to urinate on both sides of the equator in one bladder splatter merely by adjusting my aim in midstream.

Later on there will be a billboard proclaiming a NASA tracking station, and as a gesture toward the entire space program, I will be urinating on that too.

Yet another of the Great Moments in Urinating series will occur in an old-fashioned bullfight stadium. It is empty, but as I stride to the center of the arena I can hear a roar, the wild cheering of an invisible crowd of spectators, anticipating my moment of urinary truth.

Between these episodes, there is magnificent scenery, a terrible reminder that there are so many urban Americans who see nature only when it happens to be the setting for a TV commercial. What a pleasure it is now to observe snow-topped mountains that aren't pushing frozen foods, waterfalls that aren't the background for a can of beer, rainbows that aren't advertising a savings and loan association.

The *autocarril* is a bus that travels on railroad tracks. We take it for an eight-hour jaunt to the little Pacific Coast port town of San Lorenzo. They have electricity there, but not until 10 p.m.

We stay at an extremely funky hotel that costs 50 cents a night. The toilets are seatless, but the beds have mosquito netting. We wake up to a chorus of neighborhood dogs accompanying the raucous sounds of a recorded marching band playing "Stars and Stripes Forever" over a loudspeaker. We never find out whether this is a daily morning ritual or just a special welcome for our visit.

Where the Sierra Club leaves off, we begin.

There are no automobiles in the jungle. There are no roads. We travel along remote tributaries of the Cayapa River in giant canoes, each one dug out from a single *sandse* or *wangaripo* tree. The paddles, carved out of the *conalom* tree, are no longer the tools of mobility for our navigators, though.

A few years ago, Yamaha outboard motors came on the scene, offering the combined enticements of status, speed and low down payments. Thus was noise pollution introduced to the natives, along with a significant change in their lifestyle. For they surrendered to the gravitational pull of civilization, forcing themselves into the contemporary version of the Puritan ethic — increasing productivity in order to meet their monthly installments on a five-year payment plan.

It is the ultimate energy crisis — working hard to support your appliances — whether you are delivering a boatful of bananas or working in an office trying to transfer all the stuff from the *In* basket to the *Out* basket in eight little hours.

It's raining heavily, but we get permission to set up camp inside the *Sagra Familia* (Sacred Family) Mission. There is, as an appropriate backdrop to the altar, a mural of the Nativity, apparently drawn by children from this village of blacks who originally migrated from Colombia to escape slavery. The manger has an added local touch. The birth of Jesus is taking place in front of a palm tree with hanging coconuts.

We entertain ourselves with early rock 'n' roll. Instead of the usual religious hymns, the strains of "Silhouettes" and "At the Hop" emanate from the church that evening.

A commune of pigs is stationed just underneath the floor that our sleeping bags are resting on, and we can hear them snorting through the night.

Next morning I find a corroded, naked, pink doll — a tarnished angel, to be precise — in a trash bin behind the church. It seems like a perfect souvenir, so I take it.

A Christian missionary — whose luxurious house and matching yacht on the river edge of the jungle are in shocking contrast to the simplicity of the native shacks — informs us that whereas the Indians are into witchcraft, the blacks are into immorality. These, he asserts, are "the besetting sins" of the area.

He tells us with obvious disdain that the shamans drink *pinde* (another name for *ayahuasca*) and he compares the effects to LSD, which he has never taken. As for blacks, they "can't stand noise or bad news."

The blacks live in small villages. The Indian homes have no walls, but the black homes *do* have walls — the better, presumably, to hide their immorality.

An immoral teenaged marimba player who has just met Holly asks her to marry him, but she declines his proposal, explaining that she wants to finish high school and everything. Besides, we are on our way to spend a week living with the Cayapa Indians, a primitive tribe.

The missionary also warns us to watch out for vampire bats.

The Cayapa Indians live in isolated shacks along the river. Our jungle home belonged to a shaman who died a few months previously. The structure sits on stilts and has a sturdy thatched roof, but no side walls. A raised deck is the kitchen area. The lavatory is downstairs, third cluster of bushes to your left.

The river is for washing and — if you boil the water for 15 minutes — drinking. The muddy bank probably discourages such kinky activities as toe-sucking among the natives.

This is our medialess environment. No television, radio, stereo, movies, telephone, mail, newspapers, magazines. Instead we listen to tree frogs imitating the sound of clinking glasses.

Every day, three generations of the dead shaman's family arrive early in the morning. They sit serenely, as though posing for an official portrait. The women are bare-breasted. One of them is playing with the penis of her small child.

Their social rules are fascinating. Young Cayapas are required to live together for six months before they are permitted to marry. At their wedding ceremony, a couple is given ten lashes each as a sample of the 150 lashes either would receive for marital infidelity.

A bizarre form of role reversal seems to have entered into the process. We are like Martians who have suddenly dropped in on their primitive culture. We are *their* live TV show. They see the therapist doing Tai-Chi. They listen to the harmonica player singing "There's a riot goin' on in cell block number nine." With great curiosity they watch one psychiatrist brushing his teeth and the other one taking notes. So now *they* have become the anthropologists and *we* have become the subjects of their careful observation.

"They are still observing us intently," writes the psychiatrist.

As a Zen Bastard exercise, I once trained myself to laugh when I stub my toe. It has become second nature. I didn't realize that I had been searching for an example of how humor could transcend language and culture, but when I stub my toe and automatically laugh out loud in front of this family of primitive anthropologists, they share in the hilarity.

I become the first to dispense with my bathing suit, and soon all of us are swimming nude except for our native guides. Gossip about these strange naked whites reaches the missionary, who, we learn a couple of weeks later, uses his CB equipment to radio the information back to Quito.

There in the jungle I begin an affair with Dinah, one of the women in our group. On July 23, Holly writes in her journal:

"Today's my half birthday! I'm exactly 15½ years old! Oh, yeah, I haven't written anything about the only romance on the trip. Daddy and Dinah! They are sharing a room & Daddy says that if him & Mommy had treated each other as good as he & Dinah are treating each other they'd still be together. I know that's bullshit but it's a sweet thing to say and it's nice to know things are working so well for them. Daddy seems like a kid again, holding hands in the taxi & when we're eating, little kisses on the cheek, and he's so happy. Dinah is 29, really pretty & intelligent. Daddy says she reminds him of Mommy. She lives with her boyfriend. They really make each other laugh. I'm so happy for Daddy! For my 'birthday' they gave me a rhinoceros beetle's shell that they found."

Dinah and I live 3,000 miles apart and she has a lover at home, so because we both know — and agree in advance — that we will go our separate ways when the expedition ends, our relationship has that much more intensity.

·■■■·

Shamanism goes back 50,000 years. The *curandero* (healer) communicates with those unseen evil spirits responsible for illness. It's also a family business. Built into the overhead costs of our trip was the transfer of enough *sucres* to insure the privilege of observing and participating in their healing ceremonies.

The Christian influence is evident even in the name of one shaman: Jesusito. He is wearing a long silk shirt with short sleeves, resembling a baseball uniform. In front of him is a shrine of hand-carved wooden figures — a soldier, a *mama grande* (female figure) with white beads, a policeman, a bishop, Atahualpa (the last Inca king) — bronze eagle-head staffs, polished stones, a prehistoric clay cast of an ox head, and money.

There is also a pair of perfectly incongruous holy objects: a gray clamshell-like item that opens up and reveals a head of the Virgin Mary that can be lifted out in case you wish to make Jello in the mold; and, the most sacred of all, a sealed-beam headlight from an old Buick, which, deep in the jungle, is transformed into some kind of mysterious crystal ball. There are 40,000 Cayapa Indians, and hardly one has ever *seen* a car, much less driven a stick-shift model.

Jesusito chants over each individual that he is healing. He waves a wand of leaves as he makes this sound: *woosha woosha*. He blows cigarette smoke into the patient's face. Would we not think that a medical doctor who did this was being slightly rude and unprofessional?

He takes a swig of a perfumey beverage, but doesn't swallow. Instead, he spritzes it out through his teeth, in an aerosol mist that helps to cleanse the sickness, without making any holes in the ozone layer.

Jesusito notices my tape recorder, and it becomes the subject of an animated discussion between him and an assistant. I'm fearful that they might resent this technological intrusion, but instead they request a playback of what has already been recorded.

Jesusito listens to himself chanting and going *woosha woosha* with all the attention of Mick Jagger at a recording studio trying to avoid overdubbing on a new album. Then, because Jesusito has been ill and is somewhat fatigued, he *uses* the tape recorder for his next round of healing.

Drifting in and out of sleep, we hear Jesusito continue to chant through the night, as crowing roosters attempt unsuccessfully to harmonize with him.

Earlier, he had asked the physician in our group for a second opinion on a couple of liver and spleen cases. Conversely, there is a hospital that has begun to join forces with local healers.

And in Canada, the Ontario provincial government has actually granted a hospital $26,000 for a medicine man, because doctors had complained that they couldn't help Indians with emotional problems due to language and other cultural barriers. The medicine man substitutes herbs for medication, and rituals for bedside manner.

We visit a shaman of the Colorado tribe. The back half of his head has been shaved. The remaining hair has been dyed orange-red with the *acheoche* berry, mixed with Vaseline and plastered stiff over his forehead. It lasts for eight days.

He does a few sample cleansing ceremonies for us. Cleansing is the first step in the curative process. This shaman has a large magnet — the kind you'd find in a big old 40s Philco living-room console radio — which he hits with a metal cross just above a patient's head, causing a fusion of sound and vibration that will help dispel a disease which was, incidentally, caused by frogs or worms.

There are 50 *brujos* out of a thousand Colorados, and the profession is generally passed on to sons. Our *brujo* has a 22-year-old son who is also a shaman, but his hair is modish and his clothes Western. He has his own peer group.

But who's to say what's really indigenous? There is a theory that the Colorados' hairstyle was originally an imitation of the Spanish conquistadores, whose metal helmets had similarly shaped peaks. More recently, young Indians adopted the custom of hanging a bath towel around the neck, but they were actually copying an idiosyncracy of oil workers.

We visit another shaman who puts on an Indian headdress and displays an outdoor table full of herbs, leaves and roots that are used to heal everything from headaches to rheumatism to severe burns. This is an esoteric counterpoint to the narc squad representative who used to visit junior high schools with his display of dangerous drugs for compulsory hygiene classes. But this display promotes, not fear, but healing:

- The milk of a cactus, *pitajaya*, soaked into a piece of cloth, serves as a cure for gangrene.
- *Chanco piedra* is an herb that reduces and expels kidney stones.
- The leaves of the *juanto* bush cure fractures, while the stems act as an aphrodisiac — so in case you hurt your leg pursuing a potential mate, use both.
- The sap of the *incira* tree will extract — that is, crumble — a decayed tooth, painlessly.
- Take shavings from the bark of a large shrub called *hipocuru*, mix with *aguardiente* (the poor person's rum) and steep for a week, then add honey, and you have an effective medicine that has cured arthritis.

A skeptical Harvard physiologist visiting the area got converted when the profuse bleeding of a machete gash in her arm was halted by drinking the sap of a tree, a euphorbiaceae, the *croton salutaris*.

Magical powers are attributed to various species of the cypress vine, used to cure such diverse ailments as an eye infection and diarrhea, as well as to prevent pregnancy. Two doses, each at the end of consecutive menstrual periods, will render a woman infertile for approximately six years. An herb that causes sterility for only three years is known as *amor seco* (dry love). It boggles the mind to imagine by what means these methods of birth control were originally discovered.

In the late '50s, American pharmaceutical companies combined racism, sexism and imperialism by experimenting with oral contraceptives on Puerto Rican women. Ironically, the properties of contraceptive herbs used by South American Indians were ripped off by North American drug monopolies.

As early as 1920, the Canelos Indians of Ecuador were ingesting a medicine prepared from the *piripiri* plant by crushing the roots and soaking them in water. Many tribes also rub such a liquid on their bows to improve marksmanship. The specific methods of preparing this plant — whether for birth control or better aim — still remain among the secrets of the jungle.

But wait! What kind of mirage is *this*? A beautiful hotel in the middle of the jungle? It was constructed from material brought in via the river. Adorable monkeys roam around and mingle with the guests. A ten-minute walk into the wilderness, and there is an incredibly lush area with a large swimming hole and a place from which to dive.

It is the group's consensus fantasy that this is what Paradise must be like. For one brief moment, I even entertain the notion of staying.

On the way back to a gourmet dinner, while I'm groping my way precariously across a huge log that serves as a bridge, somebody behind me starts jumping up and down on the log, trying to make me fall into the water. It turns out to be the playful hotel owner himself. The absurdity of this situation overwhelms me as I attempt to focus total attention on keeping my balance. *Up and down. Up and down.*

The Zen Bastard rides again!

The time has at last come for us to take *ayahuasca*. It will be that evening. Dr. Andrew Weil had suggested fasting after breakfast, but our group eats lunch anyway, rationalizing that as long as we're all going to vomit anyway, we might as well put something into our stomachs now to throw up later.

In the afternoon, we travel by truck and ferry, then hike for an hour deep into the jungle. There are butterflies with a foot-wide wingspread. A steady stream of bright green leaves is crossing our path with the aid of unseen ants.

When we reach our destination, we are offered plates of boiled *manioc*, a potato-like root, and bowls of *chicha* (fermented *manioc*) ground up and pulverized in water, tasting like sour buttermilk. We have been told that it would be considered impolite to refuse such hospitality.

Ayahuasca means "soul vine." It is innocent-looking enough, an inch or two thick, curving into and beyond a complete circle. There are some 20 varieties of *ayahuasca*. Who can imagine how its psychoactive use was originally discovered? First it is chopped vertically, then horizontally, and then boiled.

In *Wizard of the Upper Amazon*, Bruce Lamb wrote: "Drinking a carelessly prepared extract would only cause violent vomiting, acute intestinal cramps and diarrhea, he (Manuel Córdova, an old Peruvian healer) said, and he went on to tell me that *ayahuasca* must be handled with care and reverence, simmered slowly in a special earthenware pot over a low fire under constant, proper attention."

However, ours is being boiled in an aluminum pot by a young Canelos Indian couple in the midst of a lovers' quarrel. But we can't very well tell *them* that they're preparing it the wrong way.

A leaf, *datura* (similar to belladonna), is added to the potion, which is an unappetizing, rust-colored, muddy liquid that tastes so putrid a bottle of rum must be held in your other hand for an instant chaser. We sit in a circle and pass the bowl around so each individual can drink from it.

After around 20 minutes, the first psychiatrist says, "My thoughts are beginning to become disassociated."

"Oh, really?" the second psychiatrist says. "Mine are *always* that way."

Inevitably, the sounds of violent retching echo through the jungle. One by one the members of our group go outside and vomit as though we were wet towels being wrung out by invisible demons. That old wizard of the Amazon was right — they should've used a clay pot. He had warned that if the *ayahuasca* was boiled in aluminum rather than earthenware, it would make you more sick than visionary.

I pass around the roll of Butter Rum Life Savers I had brought especially for this occasion.

When Holly's insides declare that it's her turn to throw up, I accompany her outside and stand there watching as a volcanic regurgitation takes over her body. *Oh, God,* I think, *I hope I've done the right thing.*

When she finishes, I begin. The power of peristalsis possesses me so thoroughly that I vomit and fart simultaneously. Holly's tears turn to laughter at my involuntary duet, which in turn makes *me* laugh. There I am in the middle of the jungle with my daughter — vomiting, farting and laughing.

"I think this is known as quality time," I finally manage to say.

As we walk back to the shack with our arms around each other and feeling weak, Holly says, "It's nice to be near someone you love when you're in misery."

Under the influence of *ayahuasca,* the local people traditionally have visions of jaguars and anacondas (water snakes), but instead we Americans see elephants and mice, spider webs of memory, a woman wearing an 1890 gown and large brimmed hat, eating a loaf of French bread. The corregated metal ceiling is undulating like the surface of an ocean. Looney Tunes cartoon characters are dancing inside my brain.

"Something's got ahold of my leg," someone shouts. "Oh, it's my boot."

During their healing ceremony, two shamans keep sucking the poisons out of a patient's head, and then, although they don't actually *vomit,* they keep making these awful *sounds* of vomiting in order to get rid of those poisons.

All through the night, we are forced to divert our psychic energy away from exquisite visionary flights simply in order not to throw up again. What was it Tim Leary said about set and setting? How preferable soothing music would be over the continuous sounds of fake retching that punctuate the shamans' chant:

Spirit of the mountain lake
Come, come, come, where are you?
Help cure this sick person
Old spirit man of the forest
Up at the mountain lake.

A flash of paranoia convinces me for a moment that there is some kind of sorcerer's trick being played on us, for these shamans are laughing at us whenever anyone succumbs to vomiting. They almost seem to be displaying a playful pride in their catalytic function.

Each member of our group experiences a certain type of auditory hallucination — perceiving spoken English as the shamans chat in *Quechua* during the healings. This phenomenon is comparable to when you've fallen asleep while watching TV but the voices from the program keep slithering their way into your dream, developing a logic all their own.

In the morning, one of the kids' battery-operated radio wakes us up, not with Bruce Springsteen singing "Jungle Land," but rather a schmaltzy rendition of an old song, "Beware, My Foolish Heart."

We are all thoroughly wasted, but the shamans are up and lively, one playing the harmonica, both looking like Ecuador's primitive version of the Blues Brothers.

Before we leave, one of the shamans asks our medical doctor for Lomotil, to be used for diarrhea, and the cultural exchange is completed.

Our return hike through the rainforest is accompanied by a tremendous rainstorm. While getting thoroughly soaked, Holly and I keep singing "Singin' In the Rain" over and over and over again, as loudly as we can.

Back in Quito, the exact corollary of that corroded, naked, pink tarnished-angel doll appears on the shelf of a fancy boutique.

Holly stage-whispers to a companion, "remember that tarnished angel my dad stole from the church in the jungle?"

I interject, "Why don't you say it out loud for *everyone* to hear?"

But it's a mistake to attempt such light sarcasm on an adolescent who has seen one too many situation comedies.

"Hey," Holly says out loud for everyone to hear — including the clerk, who speaks English—"remember that tarnished angel my dad stole from the church in the jungle?"

Well, of course, we all laugh at that. Holly and I have really grown closer on this expedition. The family that pukes together has visions together.

▪▪▇▪▪

There's a current theory that cannibalism among South American Indians is a myth spread by anthropologists who need to feel superior to those they study. Nonetheless, 32 skeletons of children showing evidence of having been devoured have been discovered in a Colombian jungle. Arms and legs had been almost completely eaten.

Authorities confirm that this was not the first time members of various tribes have eaten their youngsters. It is estimated that about 500 nomadic Indians in that area suffer from extreme malnutrition and occasionally eat the corpses of relatives or neighbors, sometimes killing them specifically for that purpose.

It is with this awareness that I return to civilization. We are of the same species as those cannibals. We merely eat our own children in more sophisticated ways.

A poster at Los Angeles Airport advises, "A Few Extra Minutes Clearing Customs Saves Others From (in threatening red letters) NARCOTICS!"

I have no problem getting through Customs. I certainly haven't brought back any *ayahuasca*. I do have in my suitcase a tarnished angel, but its mate still reclines on a shelf in a boutique on the other side of the equator.

Holly will attend high school in Hollywood and work at a Baskin-Robbins ice cream parlor off Sunset Boulevard. She has come to know her hooker customers by their favorite flavors, and as we walk along the street, she will point them out to me.

"There's Rocky Road... That's Pralines 'n Cream... that's Strawberry Shortcake."

And now I'm home again in San Francisco. TV commercials are trying to program viewers with fear of their own bodies, elevators are getting stuck in skyscrapers without a 13th floor, and MX missiles are enjoying an underground amusement park ride in order to fool the Russians.

How can I explain any of this uncivilized behavior to that primitive Indian family I have smuggled into America, hiding them between the left and right lobes of my brain? They continue to visit me each day. Their image vividly remains as a buffer to my culture shock. They look over my shoulder every moment, never judging, just observing.

And so my own neighborhood has become the site of a new expedition, as I begin to see everything through the innocent eyes of my primitive self-witnesses from the tropical rainforest. In the jungle, canned dog food is unknown. But here, we actually encounter a man walking down the street holding a leash with a four-legged mechanical pet robot. Safari, so good.

Condoms Are Us

There are condoms all over the place. An unofficial slogan for National Condom Week is "Encase your porker before you dork her." On UN World AIDS Day, actress Sharon Stone says that parents should provide condoms for children, that if they truly love them, they need to have a supply of condoms at home. *Getting It On: A Condom Reader*, a collection of stories by several well-known writers, including T. Coraghessan Boyle, Martin Amis and Anne Rice, has been published. The authors note that "Condoms are everywhere. They can be flavored, colored and even patriotic."

The Condom-of-the-Month Club offers "a monthly sampler of sensual and unique condoms packed in a handsome bedside container — an incredible assortment of the world's finest condoms. You'll get colors, textures, natural skins, pre-shaped micro-thins from Japan, Italy, Germany, Korea...."

You can buy Safety Suckers, condoms packaged as lollipops, or you can buy chocolate mint candies in the shape of unrolled condoms, individually wrapped in foil marked, "For internal use only." Someone has found a condom in a McDonald's hamburger. Among David Letterman's Top Ten McDonald's Excuses: "We were test marketing the new McRibbed" and "When you're serving billions and billions, you can't be too careful."

The Supreme Court rejects a parental challenge to a program that makes condoms available free to junior and senior high school students, but attorneys for the American Center for Law and Justice call the ruling "a dangerous precedent that would leave school officials free to provide students with everything from cigarettes to syringes to soft-porn to weapons instruction." According to a study by the Rand Corporation, the free condom program at a Los Angeles high school has increased sexual safety without any corresponding increase in sexual activity.

Former *Baywatch* star Pamela Anderson sends a letter on People for the Ethical Treatment of Animals stationery to Health and Human Services Secretary Donna Shalala, demanding that the government ban non-latex condoms, "not only because they are derived from sheep and lambs, but because they do not effectively block the transmission of HIV." As for the use of animal innards in condoms, she asks a reporter from *TV Guide* these rhetorial questions: "How gross is that? I mean, how unerotic are animal intestines?"

A Massachusetts firm introduces Knight Light, the first condom that glows in the dark. A novelty shop in Budapest sells condoms that play a melody — an old Communist song, "Arise, Ye Worker" — as the condom is unfurled. Japanese researchers develop a condom with a microchip that plays a musical greeting — the Beatles' "Love Me Do" — at the "vital moment." An Italian physics student patents a condom that will play Beethoven if it breaks during use.

A Los Angeles condom importer is sentenced to federal prison for trying to bribe an FDA official to cover up his distribution of hundreds of thousands of defective condoms. The *American Journal of Public Health* tells of a researcher, working on a study of condom usage by Nevada prostitutes, whose job is to examine used condoms for breakage.

Radio Mutiny, a pirate station in Philadelphia, features the Condom Lady Show. Network newscasts capture a Unitarian minister giving out condoms to his congregation. In New York City, Judge Gustav Reichbach distributes condoms to street prostitutes in his courtroom, who are grateful for the attention. The International Whores Convention in Brussels endorses the use of condoms as a safe sex practice. The *Oldest Profession Times* reports on legislation to make it illegal for police to destroy condoms or use them as evidence of intent to commit prostitution. A vice squad officer states, "We definitely do seize condoms. We will seize any physical evidence that enhances the case."

A Vancouver company features greeting cards with condoms and messages such as "Some friendly advice from your mother — Wear your rubbers," or, "You're God's gift to women — Gift-wrap it." In Petaluma, California, condoms are transformed into jewelry, using paint, glitter, feathers and rhinestones to fashion earrings, broaches and bolo-tie ornaments out of square-packaged Trojans and rectangular-packaged Lifestyles.

The president of Lifestyles admits that AIDS is "a condom marketer's dream." Norman Mailer calls sex in the age of AIDS "the condom sub-life," adding: "In my day, you got married so you didn't have to use one." Louisiana sells 100,000 of its own Royal brand condoms. State officials claim it is more economical to make their own condoms than to subsidize higher-priced, brand-name condoms for high-risk-disease clients.

Condoms are used to carry somebody else's urine in order to pass a drug test. The Alabama legislature outlaws strip clubs and adds language that bars the sale of items to enhance sex, including vibrators and certain kinds of condoms.

Twenty-two tons of condoms are sent to France for the World Cup Soccer Tournament. The French government is co-financing five hard-core porn films featuring the correct use of condoms in the hope that they will encourage people to have safe sex. The mayor of the French city, Condom, is promoting a museum of contraception. The Walt Disney Company has stopped an ad in France which features Snow White advocating condoms.

An Italian designer who announces that Monica Lewinsky will make a runway appearance at a fashion show publicizes a condom dress in tight, skin-color latex. Heidi Fleiss markets underwear with a condom pocket. In the novel *Woody* by Peter Lefcourt, there's a character who is a beautiful lobbyist from the National Association of Health Prophylaxis Industries — that is, the condom industry.

Santa Monica High School students sell condoms — with a pacifier at the end of a ball and chain — to raise money for the

Association of Minor Persons. More than 150,000 avant-garde condom covers, in high-fashion packets designed by young Californians, are distributed by the Los Angeles County Sexually Transmitted Disease Program. Winners range from "Condom Power," a green and yellow daisy packet, to an enormous rolled condom floating UFO-like above the planet to "Love Is Blind," a vision of a world of AIDS, genital warts, herpes and chlamydia. Dr. David Reuben updates his 1969 bestseller, *Everything You Always Wanted to Know Abut Sex But Were Afraid to Ask*, stating that, "When my first book came out, abortion was illegal, and you couldn't buy condoms in the supermarket."

A study concludes that 20% of men do not know how to put on a condom. In the theatrical adaptation of John Irving's novel, *The Cider House Rules*, an instruction pamphlet on how to use a condom is read aloud to the audience. Employees at *Spin* manually glue 140,000 condoms onto a page in the magazine, along with explicit instructions for their use, but many distributors and retailers refuse to deliver or sell it. The *Wall Street Journal* reports that, "Even many drugstores that sell condoms won't sell magazines carrying condoms."

Penthouse publishes a full-page ad for Trojans with the headline, "Men Could Use Some Protection From Women." *New York Native* complains of homophobia in the condom industry for not advertising in gay publications, and a spokesperson for Trojans rationalizes that "Gays will see the ads on TV."

The *Village Voice* reports that "Gays have been accused of choking whales to death with condoms in an absurd twist on a disagreement between environmentalists and gay rights activists. The Balloon Alert Project first claimed that prevailing winds could blow the 10,000 balloons (blown-up condoms) originally planned to be released at the Heritage of Pride march, each bearing the name of a person who died of AIDS, out over the East Coast, where turtles may swallow them, thinking them to be jellyfish. Balloons, being made of latex or mylar, which can take months to degrade, could block marine animal intestines, causing the animals to starve to death."

In *Kingpin*, Bill Murray plays a champion bowler whose hand gets crushed and is replaced by a rubber prosthetic. His bowling career is ruined, but he becomes a spokesperson for Trojan condoms. In *Trojan War*, a teenager has his date with a dream girl interrupted when he's dragged through a series of misadventures while trying to buy a condom. In *Killer Condom*, a sex-horror comedy, a gay veteran NYPD detective spends his time searching for a lethal prophylactic.

Julia Roberts, playing a bride in *Steel Magnolias*, is startled to find that friends have decorated the wedding car with inflated condoms. In closing credits for *The Unknown Cyclist*, starring Lea Thompson, Joe Bessara is listed as "Jeweled Condom Box Designer." In *Fools Rush In*, Matthew Perry, in denial about a broken condom, argues, "Its entire reason for being is to work."

Condoms are now free in Iran, with distribution centers set up by the Islamic Republic. Day-long festivities at an annual event in Thailand include a condom-inflating championship. Thirty percent of all condoms in Germany are stolen.

Zimbabwe exports wooden penises for use by family-planning programs in other African countries for demonstrating how to apply condoms. When the government of Saskatchewan tries unsuccessfully to return to the manufacturer almost 1000 five-inch-long "wooden demonstrators" designed for condom-education classes, schools refuse to use them, and opponents of the program call for disposal by "weenie roast."

The world's biggest condom manufacturer, Durex, provides China with 158 million condoms a year. As elsewhere in Asia, the Chinese Durex is one-third of an inch smaller in circumference than the condoms manufactured for Western men. Authorities in Daytona Beach, Florida, are looking for a man who stole a 20-foot condom.

A group of girls go door to door on a Halloween scavenger hunt, asking for condoms. Then they throw the condoms into a pie pan, spray them with whipped cream and proceed to bob for condoms, like apples. A teacher in the U.S. from Ireland doesn't understand why her class of mostly boys burst into laughter at her instruction to "Bring a No. 2 pencil and don't forget your rubbers," since in Ireland rubbers means erasers.

Playboy reveals that British sailors in the Gulf War employed condoms to protect their artillery from sand. Daniel Schorr mentions in his commentary on NPR that Northrop Grumman, manufacturer of the stealth bomber, is suing a small business for producing Stealth Condoms with the slogan, "They'll never see you coming." At the Gennifer Flowers press conference, Stuttering John from the Howard Stern show asks, "Did Governor Clinton use a condom?"

A psychiatrist, the final prosecution witness at the insanity trial of serial killer/necrophiliac/cannibal Jeffrey Dahmer testifies that, by wearing condoms while having sex with his dead victims, Dahmer proved that he *could* control his urge to have intercourse with corpses. And will there be a public service announcement: "If Jeffrey Dahmer is sane enough to have safe sex, what about *you*?"

According to a study by the Women's Sports Foundation, teenage girls who are involved in sports are more likely to use condoms than those who aren't. Organizers of the Commonwealth Games, with athletes from 66 nations competing in Olympic-style events, announce that Ortho McNeil will be the official condoms of the Games in Victoria. The official Woodstock condom proclaims, "I come in peace."

As fallout from the O.J. Simpson trial, a condom named after witness Rosa Lopez is a fast-selling item on the streets of Tijuana. In Los Angeles, billboards warn, "If you can't say no, use condoms." However, the Gannett Outdoor Advertising Company delays displaying them until after the Pope's visit. Miss America is instructed not to say the word *condom* during her safe-sex educational tour.

On *Seinfeld*, George Costanza has sex in his parents' bed, leaving behind a condom. On his Comedy Central TV quiz show, Ben Stein is introduced: "Ladies and gentlemen, meet a man who is so intellectually stimulating he has to wear a condom on his head." Phil Donahue tosses condoms to members of his audience like a rock star throwing flowers to his fans. Michelle Phillips takes condoms out of her purse and hands them to Joan Rivers. Bill Murray removes condoms from his pocket and gives them to David Letterman. A judge rules that Letterman did not defame Martha Raye when he said in his opening monologue that she was a "condom user." She had sued for $10 million, claiming he implied that she "personally uses condoms in some form of deviant, aberrant or socially unacceptable behavior."

A survey by the Kaiser Family Foundation reveals that 77% of those polled say that there should be more references to condoms on TV. On *General Hospital*, a woman tells a man, "You didn't use a condom," and he replies, "Oh, that." On PBS, a woman demonstrates to adults how to put condoms on by using her fingers. On Nickelodeon, Linda Ellerbe shows children how to roll a condom onto a finger. *Felicity* features a demonstration on how to use a condom.

And, finally, one fine afternoon, Oprah Winfrey asks a former prostitute, "How do you get a prophylactic on a person without them knowing it?" The reply: "You put the condom in your mouth and it's under your tongue, and you can do it very easily, without the man knowing it." But now, don't you kids try this at home. Remember, it should be done only by professionals, who know what they're doing.

Speaking of Scumbags

A good laugh is like an internal massage, and the more you get, the better you feel. One of the best laughs of my entire life resulted from my mother saying three simple words. But please allow me to lead up to those words by my own circuitous route.

When I was a kid, condoms were called prophylactics, prophylactics were called rubbers, and rubbers were called scumbags. My friends and I would find used scumbags in a vacant lot or the alley between buildings.

Once I found a large package of unused prophylactics in my father's sock drawer. It must have held a dozen. There were nine left. Each was tightly rolled, bound by a miniature cigar band. I selected one, took the band off, and carefully unrolled it.

There was a legend imprinted on the condom: SOLD IN DRUGSTORES ONLY FOR THE PREVENTION OF DISEASE. What hypocrisy! They were sold for the prevention of *pregnancy*. Which is a condition, not a disease. The irony is that now condoms *don't* carry that message and they *are* used for the prevention of disease.

Anyway, I tried to re-roll my father's prophylactic and stuff it into the band, but it was a losing battle, so I decided not to put it back in the package, figuring that my dad wasn't counting and would never know.

Well, now, you can imagine how shocked I was when Dan Burton publicly called Bill Clinton a *scumbag*. Whatever the word has evolved by usage to mean, a congressman was calling the president a discarded rubber containing a half-million dead sperm. And then, how entertained I was to see Dan Rather, Tom Brokaw and Peter Jennings all trying to say "scumbag" without smirking.

The *Washington Post* and the *Chicago Tribune* used the word "scumbag" in front-page headlines. The *New York Daily News* printed "s — -bag." The *New York Times* avoided using the word altogether, instead referring to Burton's insult as "a vulgarity for a condom." The next day, the *Times* changed it to "a euphemism for a despicable person."

Meanwhile, there was a rumor circulating that openly gay Senator Barney Frank had threatened to reveal a half-dozen members of Congress who were homosexuals, if they voted for Clinton's impeachment. If true, it was an interesting threat, because an outing is not a picnic.

Back in 1991, Assistant Secretary of Defense (now NBC News correspondent) Pete Williams was about to be outed as a closet gay by Michelangelo Signorile in *OutWeek*, but the magazine folded, and Signorile offered his article to the *Village Voice* instead. There was dissent among the staff, and a special meeting was held to discuss the ethics of outing. The dissenters won.

Voice executive editor Richard Goldstein wrote: "I'll abide by the consensus we arrived at by not mentioning the name of the official in Signorile's piece. But I'm glad to report that another publication, *The Advocate*, is considering full disclosure. I believe any gay person who plays a prominent role in the military — especially within the Pentagon — is guilty of political hypocrisy."

The Advocate put the Pete Williams exposé on their cover, and editor Richard Rouliard explained: "We commit ourselves to this singular instance of outing in the name of the 12,966 lesbian and gay soldiers who have been outed by the military since 1982. Since 1989, when Williams was appointed, 2,273 gay and lesbian soldiers have been discharged."

Signorile wrote: "If the military were concerned with blackmail, wouldn't it be more worried about a Department of Defense spokesman with access to all kinds of classified information? Isn't it bizarre that someone as high-echelon as Williams is *not* affected by the policy, while an openly gay drill sergeant, cook or porter who has no access to sensitive information is considered a security risk?"

Syndicated columnist Jack Anderson reported the *Advocate* story, but newspapers including the *Washington Post* and the *San Francisco Chronicle* refused to publish that column. The *New York Times* ran an item on the controversy without naming Williams. Ironically, two weeks after the original *Village Voice* non-outing, their own media critic, James Ledbetter, was allowed to mention Williams by name.

And *Voice* gossip columnist Michael Musto wrote: "In addition to helping censor the (Gulf) war for us, Williams is both a tool and a mechanic of an institution that treats gays as security risks not fit to represent our country. Is he just doing what he has to do? Yes, but so is a light-skinned black who works for the Klan or a Right to Life rep who's secretly had ten abortions."

Back to the present. So far (before it was revealed that Newt Gingrich was simultaneously screwing an employee and orchestrating Clinton's impeachment), these conservative *hetero* sexual politicians have been outed: Henry Hyde was guilty of a "youthful indiscretion" when he was 41; Helen Chenoweth also had an illicit relationship, as foreplay to her love affair with the armed militia; and Dan Burton himself not only committed adultery, but he also fathered a child that he never acknowledged.

Bill Clinton may *be* a scumbag, but Dan Burton should've *used* one.

Okay, so, for my mother's 90th birthday, my brother, my sister and I arranged a big party. The next day, we took her to lunch at a family restaurant, where I finally confessed about what had happened with my father's missing prophylactic. She said that she would've gotten mad then but it was funny now.

Then I asked her if it was true, as my siblings and I had speculated, that when we were kids, our parents would send us out to the movies — every Saturday matinee — so that they could get it on sexually. My mother smiled, shaking her head in denial, and uttered those three simple words that literally knocked me off my chair with laughter:

"No afternoon work."

The Case of the Twinkie Murders

Jim Jones, founder of the 8,000-member People's Temple in San Francisco, once asked Margo St. James, founder of the prostitutes' rights group, COYOTE, how he could obtain political power.

She answered, sardonically, "Arrange for some of your women to have sex with the bigwigs."

Jones in turn offered to supply busloads of his congregation for any protest demonstration that COYOTE organized, but Margo declined his offer.

"I never liked him," she told me. "I never saw his eyes. Even in the dimmest light he never removed his shades. He was hiding something. I figured it was his real feelings. I thought he was a slimy creep."

Margo's instincts were correct. Potential recruits for People's Temple were checked out in advance by Jones' representatives, who would rummage through their garbage and report to him on their findings — discarded letters, food preferences and other clues. Temple members would visit their homes, and while one would initiate conversation, the other would use the bathroom, copying names of doctors and types of medicine. They would also phone relatives of a recruit in the guise of conducting a survey and gather other information, which would all be taped to the inside of Jones' podium, from which he would proceed to demonstrate his magical powers at a lecture by "sensing the presence" of an individual, mentioning specific details.

Sex, Drugs, & The Twinkie Murders

When People's Temple moved to Guyana and became Jonestown, Jones would publicly humiliate his followers. For example, he required them to remove their clothing and participate in boxing matches, pitting an elderly person against a young one. He forced one man to participate in a homosexual act in the presence of his girlfriend. There were paddle beatings and compulsory practice-suicide sessions called "White Nights."

On November 18, 1978, Congressman Leo Ryan, who had been investigating Jonestown, was slain at the Guyana airport, along with three newspeople and several disillusioned members of the cult. Jones then orchestrated the mass suicide-murder of 900 men, women and children, mostly black.

Jones: "What's going to happen here in a matter of a few minutes is that one of a few on that plane is gonna — gonna shoot the pilot. I know that. I didn't plan it but I know it's gonna happen. They're gonna shoot that pilot and down comes the plane into the jungle. And we had better not have any of our children left when it's over 'cause they'll parachute in here on us. So my opinion is that we'd be kind to children and be kind to seniors and take the potion, like they used to take in ancient Greece and step over quietly, because we are not committing suicide. It's a revolutionary act."

Christine Miller: "I feel like that as long as there's life, there's hope. There's hope. That's my feeling."

Jones: "Well, someday everybody dies. Someplace that hope runs out 'cause everybody dies."

Miller: "But, uh, I look at all the babies and I think they deserve to live...."

Jones: "But also they deserve much more. They deserve peace."

Unidentified man: "It's over, sister, it's over. We've made that day. We made a beautiful day. And let's make it a beautiful day."

Unidentified woman: [*Sobbing*] "We're all ready to go. If you tell us we have to give our lives now, we're ready...."

Jones: "The congressman has been murdered — the congressman's dead. Please get us some medication. It's simple. It's simple, there's no convulsions with it, it's just simple. Just please get it before it's too late. The GDF [Guyanese army] will be here. I tell you, get moving, get moving, get moving. How many are dead? Aw, God almighty, God almighty — it's too late, the congressman's dead. The congressman's aide's dead. Many of our traitors are dead. They're all layin' out there dead."

Nurse: "You have to move, and the people that are standing there in the aisle, go stay in the radio room yard. So everybody get behind the table and back this way, okay? There's nothing to worry about. So everybody keep calm, and try to keep your children calm. And the older children are to help lead the little children and reassure them. They aren't crying from pain. It's just a little bitter tasting, but that's — they're not crying out of any pain."

Unidentified woman: "I just wanna say something to everyone that I see that is standing around and, uh, crying. This is nothing to cry about. This is something we could all rejoice about. We could be happy about this."

Jones: *"Please, for God's sake, let's get on with it. We've lived— let's just be done with it, let's be done with the agony of it.* [There is noise, confusion and applause.] *Let's get calm, let's get calm.* [There are screams in the background.] *I don't know who fired the shot, I don't know who killed the congressman, but as far as I'm concerned, I killed him. You understand what I'm saying? I killed him. He had no business coming. I told him not to come. Die with respect. Die with a degree of dignity. Don't lay down with tears and agony. Stop this hysterics. This is not the way for people who are socialistic communists to die. No way for us to die. We must die with some dignity.*

"Children, it's just something to put you to rest. Oh, God! [Crying in background.] *I tell you, I don't care how many screams you hear, I don't care how many anguished cries, death is a million times preferable to ten more days of this life. If you'll quit telling them they're dying, if you adults will stop this nonsense — I call on you to quit exciting your children when all they're doing is going to a quiet rest. All they're doing is taking a drink they take to go to sleep. That's what death is, sleep. Take our life from us. We laid it down. We got tired. We*

didn't commit suicide. We committed an act of revolutionary suicide protesting the conditions of an inhuman world...."

Those who refused to drink the grape-flavored punch laced with potassium cyanide were either shot or killed by injections in their armpits. Jim Jones either shot himself or was murdered.

The *Black Panther* newspaper editorialized: "It is quite possible that the neutron bomb was used at Jonestown."

In San Francisco, former policeman Dan White had resigned from the Board of Supervisors because he couldn't support his wife and baby on a salary of $9600 a year. He obtained a lease for a fast-food franchise at Fisherman's Wharf and now planned to devote himself full time to his restaurant, The Hot Potato. He felt great relief.

However, White had been the swing vote on the Board, representing downtown real estate interests and the conservative Police Officers Association. With a promise of financial backing, White changed his mind and told Mayor George Moscone that he wanted his job back.

At first, Moscone said sure, a man has the right to change his mind.

But there was opposition to White's return, led by Supervisor Harvey Milk, who was openly gay. Milk had cut off his ponytail and put on a suit so he could work within the system, but he refused to hide his sexual preference. Now he warned the pragmatic Moscone that giving the homophobic White his seat back would be seen as an anti-gay move in the homosexual community.

Even a mayor who wants to run for re-election has the right to change his mind.

On Sunday evening, November 26, a reporter telephoned Dan White and said, "I can tell you from a very good source in the mayor's office that you definitely are *not* going to be reappointed. Can you comment on that?"

"I don't want to talk about it," White replied. "I don't know anything about that." And he hung up.

He stayed on the couch that night, not wanting to keep his wife awake. He didn't get any sleep, just lay there brooding. He decided to go to City Hall on Monday morning.

When his aide, Denise Apcar, picked him up at 10:15, he didn't come out the front door as he normally would; he emerged from the garage. He had gone down there to put on his service revolver, a .38 special, which he always kept loaded. He opened a box of extra cartridges, which were packed in rows of five, and put ten of them, wrapped in a handkerchief so they wouldn't rattle, into his pocket.

Because of rumors that People's Temple assassins had been programmed to hit targets back in the States, metal detectors were now set up at the front doors of City Hall. When White went up the stairs to the main entrance, he didn't recognize the security guard monitoring the metal detector, so he went around to the side of the building, entered through a large basement window and proceeded to the mayor's office.

After a brief conversation, Dan White shot George Moscone twice in the body, then two more times in the head, execution-style, as he lay on the floor. The Marlboro cigarette in Moscone's hand would still be burning when the paramedics arrived.

After murdering Moscone, White hurriedly walked across a long corridor to the area where the supervisors' offices were. His name had already been removed from the door of his office, but he still had a key. He went inside and reloaded his gun. Then he walked out, past Supervisor Dianne Feinstein's office. She called to him, but he didn't stop.

"I have to do something first," he told her.

Harvey Milk was in his office, thanking a friend who had just loaned him $3,000. Dan White walked in.

"Can I talk to you for a minute, Harvey?"

White followed Milk into his inner office. Dan White then fired three shots into Harvey Milk's body, and while Milk was prone on the floor, White fired two more shots into Milk's head.

▪▫◼▫▪

Abbie Hoffman had gone underground, and I was scheduled to be a guest on Tom Snyder's late-night TV show, *Tomorrow*, on November 30.

"That's my birthday," said Abbie. "Would you wish me a happy birthday on the show?"

Andy Friendly, producer of the *Tomorrow* show, phoned me to explore areas that the interview might cover. The subject of drug use came up.

"Well, maybe we could talk about my old psychedelic macho. I've taken LSD in all kinds of unusual situations: when I testified at the Chicago Conspiracy Trial; on the Johnny Carson show — Orson Bean was the guest host — I was sort of a guide for Groucho Marx once; while I was researching the Manson case I took acid with a few women in the family, including Squeaky Fromme and Sandra Good. It was a kind of participatory journalism."

I didn't tell him that I planned to ingest magic mushrooms before my appearance on the *Tomorrow* show.

They flew me to Los Angeles, and a chauffeured limousine delivered me to a fancy hotel, where I proceeded to partake of those magic mushrooms. My mood was intensely sensual. What I really wanted was an exquisite, deep-tissue massage. I called an old friend who was a professional masseuse. Since she was also an old lover, it wasn't totally surprising that we began fucking on the bed before she even set up her table. She finally broke the sweet silence of our post-coital afterglow.

"But I'll have to charge you for the massage," she said.

The mushrooms were still coming on strong when Tom Snyder began the interview. He had an FM mind in an AM body.

"You're from San Francisco," he said. "What the hell is going *on* there? First, this guy Jim Jones has 900 people commit suicide by drinking poisoned Kool-Aid. Then the next week this other guy goes to City Hall, kills the mayor and a gay supervisor."

It seemed as if he was asking me to *justify* San Francisco as the scene of such sequential horror.

"Nyah, nyah," I sang, "my city is more violent than your city."

Snyder looked askance at Andy Friendly, as if to say, "What kind of *flake* did you book for me?"

"Actually," I said, "I believe that Jonestown was a CIA mind-control experiment that got out of control."

"Oh, so you're paranoid, huh?"

"Well, conspiracy and paranoia are not synonymous, you know. But I'll tell you a good conspiracy theory. Remember that famous race horse, Ruffian? She broke her leg in a race, and they had to shoot her. Well, do you know why they really shot Ruffian?"

"No, Paul," Snyder said, knitting his impressive eyebrows in mock consternation. "Why?"

"Because she knew too much."

Snyder did a double-take, then started laughing as though he were doing his impression of Dan Aykroyd on *Saturday Night Live* doing *his* impression of Tom Snyder. I could see Snyder's staccato laughter parading before me like musical notes.

Just before the show ended, I remembered to wish Abbie Hoffman a happy birthday.

"Where is he?" Snyder asked. "Can we get him on the show?"

When San Francisco District Attorney Joe Freitas learned of the killings, he was in Washington, conferring with the State Department about the mass suicide-murder in Jonestown. He immediately assumed that Moscone and Milk had been assassinated by a People's Temple hit squad. After all, George Moscone was number one on their hit list.

Freitas had been a close friend of Jim Jones. After the massacre in Guyana, he released a previously "confidential" report, which stated that his office had uncovered evidence to support charges of homicide, child abduction, extortion, arson, battery, drug use, diversion of welfare funds, kidnapping, and sexual abuse against members of the sect. The purported investigation had not begun until after Jones left San Francisco. No charges were ever filed, and the People's Temple case was put on "inactive status."

Busloads of illegally registered People's Temple members had voted in the 1975 San Francisco election, as well as in the runoff that put George Moscone in office. Freitas appointed lawyer Tim

Stoen to look into possible voter fraud. At the time, Stoen was serving as Jim Jones' chief legal adviser. Freitas later piously accused him of short-circuiting the investigation, but after Stoen left the case, the D.A.'s office assured the registrar that there was no need to retain the voting rosters, and they were destroyed.

Several former members of People's Temple had heard about this fraudulent voting, but the eyewitnesses all died at Jonestown. In addition, the *San Francisco Examiner* reported that Mayor Moscone had called off a police investigation of gunrunning by the Temple, which had arranged to ship explosives, weapons and large amounts of cash to South America via Canada.

George Moscone's body was buried. Harvey Milk's body was cremated. His ashes were placed in a box, which was wrapped in *Doonesbury* comic strips, then scattered at sea. The ashes had been mixed with the contents of two packets of grape Kool-Aid, forming a purple patch on the Pacific. Harvey would've liked that touch.

In 1979 I covered the Dan White trial for the *San Francisco Bay Guardian*. There was a certain sense of being back in elementary school. Reporters received written instructions: "Members of the press are asked to line up in the below order to facilitate courtroom entry. You must be in the below order or you will be sent to the rear of the line."

I'm embarrassed to admit that I said "Thank you" to the sheriff's deputy who frisked me before I could enter the courtroom. These official friskers each had their own individual style of frisking, and there was a separate-but-equal female frisker for female reporters. But this was a superfluous ritual, since any journalist who wanted to shoot White was prevented from doing so by wall-to-wall bulletproof glass. It was sort of like sitting in a giant New York City taxicab.

At the pre-trial hearings, White had worn standard jailhouse fashion, an orange jumpsuit, so that the first time he walked into court wearing a regular suit and tie, his mother was pleasantly surprised and said, "Oh, my goodness." There was almost an air of festivity, but when the jury selection began next day, White's mother could be observed uttering a silent prayer to herself.

Defense attorney Douglas Schmidt objected to the dismissal of potential jurors because they were opposed to the death penalty. He cited studies showing that those "who do not have scruples against capital punishment tend to favor the prosecution." Prosecutor Tom Norman claimed that he did not "subscribe to the accuracy of those studies." Judge Walter Calcagno ruled in favor of Norman, and Schmidt was reduced to asking such conscientious objectors if they might at least make an exception in a trial where, say, someone "tortured two or three children to death, for money."

Nor did the defense want any pro-gay sentiment polluting the verdict. Although Doug Schmidt wasn't allowed to ask potential jurors if they were gay, he would ask if they had ever supported controversial causes—"like homosexual rights, for instance." There was one particular prospective juror who came from a family of cops — ordinarily Schmidt might have craved for him to be on this jury — but then he said, perhaps gratuitously, "I live with a roommate and lover."

Schmidt phrased his next question: "Where does he or she work?"

The man answered, "He" — and the ball game was already over — "works at Holiday Inn."

Through it all, Dan White simply *sat* there as though he had been mainlining epoxy glue. His sideburns were shorter than they used to be. He just stared directly ahead, his eyes focused on the crack between two adjacent boxes on the clerk's desk, Olde English type identifying them as *Deft* and *Pltff*.

When White left the courtroom, there seemed to be no real contact with his wife, save for a glance reminiscent of that time she served the wrong brand of coffee. The front row was reserved for his family, being filled on different days by various combinations of his sixteen brothers and sisters. I felt like I was in the middle of a situation comedy that was turning into a tragic soap opera.

Although it was stipulated that Dan White had killed George Moscone and Harvey Milk, his defense would be, in effect, that they *deserved* it.

The day before the trial began, Assistant District Attorney Norman, slated to prosecute the case, was standing in an elevator at the Hall of Justice. He heard a voice behind him speak.

"Tom Norman, you're a motherfucker for prosecuting Dan White."

He turned around and saw a half-dozen police inspectors. He flushed and faced the door again. The cops were his drinking buddies, and now they were all mad at him.

"I didn't know who said it," Norman confided to the courtroom artist for a local TV station, "and I didn't want to know."

One could only speculate about the chilling effect that incident had on Norman, perhaps engendering his sloppy presentation of the prosecution's case. For example, in his opening statement, Norman told the jury that White had reloaded his gun in the mayor's office, but, according to the transcript of White's tape-recorded confession:

Q. And do you know how many shots you fired (at Moscone)?

A. *Uh — no, I don't, I don't, I out of instinct when I, I reloaded the gun, ah — you know, it's just the training I had, you know.*

Q. Where did you reload?

A. *I reloaded in my office when, when I was — I couldn't out in the hall.*

Which made it slightly less instinctive. Norman sought to prove that the murders had been premeditated, yet ignored this evidence of premeditation in Dan White's own confession. If White's reloading of his gun had been, as he said, "out of instinct," then he indeed *would* have reloaded in Moscone's office. And if it were *truly* an instinctive act, then he would have reloaded *again* after killing Harvey Milk.

A psychiatrist testified that White must have been mistaken in his recollection of where he reloaded. The evidence on this key question became so muddled that one juror would later recall, "It was a very important issue, but it was never determined where he reloaded — in Moscone's office or just prior to saying, 'Harvey, I want to talk with you.' "

In his confession, White had stated, "I don't know why I put (my gun) on." At the trial, psychiatrists offered reasons ranging from psychological (it was "a security blanket") to the practical (for "self-defense" against a People's Temple hit squad). But, as a former police officer and member of the police commission told me, "An off-duty cop carrying his gun for protection isn't gonna take extra bullets. If he can't save his life with the bullets already in his gun, then he's done for."

Dan White's tearful confession was made to his old friend and former softball coach, Police Inspector Frank Falzon. When Falzon called White "Sir," it was a painful indication of his struggle to be a professional homicide inspector. Now, while Falzon was on the witness stand, one reporter passed a note to her colleague, suggesting that Falzon was wearing a "Free Dan White" T-shirt under his shirt.

At one point in his confession, White claimed, "I was leaving the house to talk, to see the mayor, and I went downstairs to, to make a phone call, and I had my gun there." But there was a phone upstairs, and White was home alone; his wife had already gone to The Hot Potato. Falzon didn't question him about that. Moreover, he never asked White the simple question that any junior high school kid playing detective would ask: "Dan, who did you call?" — the answer to which could have been easily verified.

Prosecutor Norman simply bungled his case and allowed the defense to use Dan White's confession to its own advantage. The mere transcript of his confession could never capture the sound of White's anguish. He was like a small boy, sobbing uncontrollably because he wouldn't be allowed to play on the Little League team. When the tape was played in court, some reporters cried, including me, along with members of White's family, spectators, jurors, an assistant D.A. — who had a man-sized tissue box on his table — and Dan White himself, crying both live and on tape simultaneously.

If the prosecution hadn't entered this tape as evidence, the defense could have done so, saving it as the final piece of evidence for dramatic effect.

And yet, the heart-wrenching confession was contradicted by the testimony of White's former aide, Denise Apcar. In his confession, White said that after shooting Moscone, "I was going to go down the stairs, and then I saw Harvey Milk's aide across the hall... and then it struck me about what Harvey had tried to do (oppose White's reappointment) and I said, "Well, I'll go talk to him." But Apcar testified that while she was driving White to City Hall, he said he wanted to talk to *both* Moscone and Milk.

On the morning of the murders, although White's aide had let him out of her car at the front entrance to City Hall, he went around the corner to the McAllister Street side and climbed through that basement window because he was carrying a concealed weapon. Now, in court, defense attorney Doug Schmidt was cross-examining a witness as to how many other occasions he had observed such entries being made through this window.

A. *Maybe twenty-five times.*
Q. Then this was not unusual?
A. *It was usually the same person.*

On redirect examination, prosecutor Norman elicited from this witness an admission that he didn't know the name of that individual who entered City Hall through the window, but "always assumed he was an employee, carrying small boxes." Reporters wondered about the contents of those small boxes. Speculation ranged from cocaine to the parts of a nuclear bomb.

I lived on a side street right off the intersection of Castro and Market, referred to as the gay ghetto, where men could comfortably display affection, where a bulletin board announced an "Anal Awareness and Relaxation Workshop," where there was a store named "Does Your Mother Know?" and where gays told jokes about themselves, like, "Why do the Castro clones all have mustaches? To hide the stretch marks."

I had met Harvey Milk when he ran a neighborhood camera shop, and I watched him develop into the gay equivalent of Martin Luther King. Had he lived, he might have been elected the first gay mayor. But he already envisioned the possibility that he would become a martyr. After he was elected supervisor, he taped a message for his constituents, including this prophetic fear and hope: "If bullets should enter my brain, let those bullets blow open every closet door in this country."

The *Los Angeles Times* published a piece by freelancer Mike Weiss which suggested that Dan White's political constituency consisted largely of working-class folks "who are being slowly squeezed out by the advance of a movement whose vanguard is homosexual." *San Francisco Chronicle* columnist Charles McCabe quoted from that article in a discussion of what he called "the homosexual invasion" of San Francisco. He went on to make derogatory remarks about White's supposed dealings with blacks on his high school baseball team. He later backed down from these remarks, telling his readers, "I have since concluded these statements cannot be confirmed and I retract them."

White's lawyer had told the *Chronicle* that McCabe's comments were "actionable." Even though White killed the mayor and a supervisor, the *Chronicle* was evidently worried that he might sue the paper for damaging his reputation.

In his election campaign, White had distributed leaflets referring to the problem of "social deviants." As a supervisor, he was the only member of the board who voted against San Francisco's gay rights ordinance. But his wife, Mary Ann, explained that "Dan is not against homosexuals — he is one of the most tolerant men. When he said 'social deviants' he didn't mean homosexuals, he meant people who deviate from the social norm, criminals, people who hit somebody over the head, people who jail won't help."

Apparently, Dan White's attorney had never said "bullshit" in front of his mother before, but now she was sitting in the courtroom, and he had to use that word in asking Supervisor Carol Ruth Silver if that was how she had characterized the defense in this trial. Thus was she able to provide the jury with presumably their only input from the outside world. However, she did not say on the witness stand what she had said in a KQED interview — that she might have been White's *third* victim had she not stayed downstairs for a second cup of coffee that morning.

Prosecutor Norman asked Silver if she had ever heard White make any anti-gay statements. She told of his "long diatribe" during a debate about the annual Halloween closing-off of Polk Street — "a hostile speech about how gays' lifestyle had to be contained."

On cross-examination, Schmidt asked Silver if she herself was "part of the gay community."

She responded, "Are you asking if I'm gay?"

He said, "Yes."

She said, "No."

In the corridor, Schmidt admitted to me that it had been "a ridiculous question."

Each day of the trial, I would take an hour-long walk from my home to the Hall of Justice. One morning on the news, there was an obituary for the composer of "Happy Days Are Here Again." I found myself singing it ritualistically on my daily walk to court, even as I passed gas line after gas line, every filling station a potential locale for the violence that had already been taking place, every automobile festering with the kind of frustration that could conceivably turn a mild-mannered driver into an instant Dan White. He represented the vanguard of vigilante justice in Stress Wars.

A couple of blocks away from the courthouse there was a "Free Dan White" graffito, only it had been altered to read "Freeze Dan White." That may not have been such a bad idea, for he was a missing link in the evolution of our species. He was the personification of obsolescent machismo. This trial was White's first encounter group, but he never testified in his own defense. He had no close friends to confide in, so he ended up telling his story to various psychiatrists hired by the defense, and *they* repeated those details in court.

Mary Ann White sat behind her husband in the front row of spectators, her Madonna-like image in direct view of the jury. Since she was scheduled to testify for the defense, prosecutor Norman could have had her excluded from the courtroom. For that matter, he could have excluded from the jury George Mintzer, an executive at the Bechtel Company, which had contributed to Dan White's campaign for supervisor. Mintzer was foreman of the jury.

For Mary Ann White, this trial was like a Quaker funeral where mourners share anecdotes about the deceased and you find out things you never knew about someone you'd been living with for years. The day after her own tearful testimony, she was back in the front row again, taking notes on the testimony of a psychiatrist who had previously interviewed *her* and taken notes. So now she was writing down poignant squibs of *her own recycled observations*, such as "Lack of sex drive" and "Danny didn't intend to shoot anyone."

I had wanted to record testimony, but tape equipment wasn't allowed in the courtroom, although the judge did give permission to vice squad officers to place a recording device on two young boys attending the trial. In court that morning, a 63-year-old man had tried to pick them up. According to the police report, he had in his possession two vials with "peach colored pills" plus eight white pills. "The juveniles gave details of how the suspect had began [sic] a conversation and by passing notes in the courtroom, offered them drugs." Now three narcotics officers monitored their conversations and later arrested the dirty old man in the Hall of Justice cafeteria.

There was a moment in the trial when it suddenly seemed to be the courtroom incarnation of a TV program called *Make Me Laugh*. Dan White was the contestant, and all the witnesses were attempting to make him laugh. Laurie Parker, a supervisor's aide, almost succeeded. When she testified that White used to hold the door open for her, his demeanor changed perceptibly. In the corridor, she confirmed that "He was smirking at me." Why was Dan White smirking? Could it have been at the absurdity of his having slain George Moscone and Harvey Milk, yet here was a witness testifying as to his chivalry?

"Smirking" — the exact same verb that White himself had used to describe his perception of what Harvey Milk did to trigger his own death; just as Jack Ruby had referred to Lee Harvey Oswald's "smirky Communist expression" immediately before he shot *him* to death.

J.I. Rodale, health-food and publishing magnate, once claimed in an editorial in his magazine, *Prevention*, that Lee Harvey Oswald had been seen holding a Coca-Cola bottle only minutes after the assassination of President Kennedy. From this he concluded that Oswald was not responsible for the killing because his brain was confused. He was a "sugar drunkard." Rodale, who died of a heart attack during a taping of *The Dick Cavett Show* — in the midst of explaining how good nutrition guarantees a long life — called for a full-scale investigation of crimes caused by sugar consumption.

In a surprise move, Dan White's defense team presented a similar bio-chemical explanation of *his* behavior, blaming it on compulsive gobbling down of sugar-filled junk-food snacks. This was a purely accidental tactic. Dale Metcalf, a former Merry Prankster who had become a lawyer, told me how he happened to be playing chess with Steven Scheer, an associate of White's attorney.

Metcalf had just read *Orthomolecular Nutrition* by Abram Hoffer. He questioned Scherr about Dan White's diet and learned that, while under stress, White would consume candy bars and soft drinks. Metcalf recommended the book to Scherr, suggesting the author as an expert witness. In the book, Hoffer revealed a personal vendetta against doughnuts, and Dan White had once eaten five doughnuts in a row.

During the trial, one psychiatrist stated that, on the night before the murders, while White was "getting depressed about the fact he would not be reappointed, he just sat there in front of the TV set, bingeing on Twinkies."

In court, White just sat there in a state of complete control, bordering on catatonia, as he listened to an assembly line of psychiatrists tell the jury how out of control he had been. One even testified: "If not for the aggravating fact of junk food, the homicides might not have taken place."

At a press conference, Berkeley psychiatrist Lee Coleman denounced the practice of psychiatric testimony, labeling it as "a disguised form of hearsay."

The Twinkie was invented in 1930 by James Dewar, who described it as "the best darn-tootin' idea I ever had." He got the idea of injecting little cakes with sugary cream-like filling and came up with the name while on a business trip, where he saw a billboard for Twinkle Toe Shoes. "I shortened it to make it a little zippier for the kids," he said.

In the wake of the so-called "Twinkie insanity defense," a representative of the ITT-owned Continental Baking Company asserted that the notion that overdosing on the cream-filled goodies could lead to murderous behavior was "poppycock" and "crap" — apparently two of the artificial ingredients in Twinkies, along with sodium pyrophosphate and yellow dye — while another spokesperson for ITT couldn't believe "that a rational jury paid serious attention to that issue." Nevertheless, some jurors did. One remarked later that "It sounded like Dan White had hypoglycemia."

Defense attorney Doug Schmidt's closing argument became almost an apologetic parody of his own defense. He told the jury that Dan White did not have to be "slobbering at the mouth" to be subject to diminished capacity. Nor, he said, was this simply a case of "Eat a Twinkie and go crazy."

Prosecutor Tom Norman's closing argument mixed purple prose — "The defendant had that quality of thought which would embrace the weighing of considerations" — with supercilious sarcasm — "If your friends won't testify for you, who will?"

During the trial, reporter Francis Moriarty had suggested to District Attorney Joe Freitas that prosecutor Norman was blowing the case — echoing similar sentiments by several journalists and attorneys who were monitoring the trial. Freitas passed along the critique to Norman and homicide inspector Frank Falzon.

Falzon challenged Moriarty: "Are you referring to investigative or prosecutorial?"

But the dividing line had become blurred. Falzon sat silently next to Norman at the prosecution table when an ex-cop was allowed on the jury. And neither Falzon nor Norman thought it advisable to subpoena as witnesses those cops with whom Dan White had discussed football shortly after the double assassination.

When Superior Court Judge Walter Calcagno presented the jury with his instructions, he assured them access to the evidence, except that they would not be allowed to have possession of Dan White's .38 special *and* his ammunition at the same time. After all, these deliberations can get pretty heated, you know. The judge was acting like a concerned schoolteacher offering Twinkies to students but withholding the cream-filling to avoid any possible mess.

■ ■ ■ ■ ■

After the jury filed out to decide Dan White's fate, spectators and reporters alike tried to determine for themselves what could possibly be a fair punishment. The prosecutor kept emphasizing that George Moscone and Harvey Milk were "duly elected" — the wording in Proposition 7 which would enable him to push for the death penalty. Ironically, this case indicated that the death penalty did *not* serve as a deterrent, even for someone like Dan White, who as a supervisor had fought for the death penalty because it would serve as a deterrent.

Originally, each potential juror in this trial virtually had to swear eternal devotion to the American criminal justice system. It was that very system which had allowed for a shrewd defense attorney's transmutation of a double political execution into the mere White Sugar Murders. On the walls of the city, graffiti warned: "Eat a Twinkie — Kill a Cop!"

While the jury was out deliberating, reporters passed the time by playing poker or chess, reading books, checking out the porn files in the press room, embroidering sentimental samplers and, mainly, trying to second-guess the jury.

On May 21, 1979, Francis Moriarty brought in a used Ouija Board he had purchased at a flea market. The question we asked it was: "When will the verdict come in?" The answer was between 5 and 6.

At 5:25 the jurors walked in. They appeared somber, except for the former cop, who smiled and triumphantly tapped the defense table twice with two fingers as he passed by, telegraphing the decision of voluntary manslaughter.

"No more Nazi dyke look," the victorious defense attorney announced in the hallway, looking forward to a haircut.

"It was a good fight," the embittered prosecutor pretended, "but we lost."

He should've been grateful the jury had not declared that George Moscone and Harvey Milk were killed in self-defense, or that they had actually committed suicide.

That evening, I was relaxing at home, smoking a joint and remembering how, in 1975, as a state senator, Moscone had been the author of a bill to decriminalize marijuana. I was trying to unwind from the trial, and contemplating the implications of the verdict. Patty Hearst had been kidnapped, held hostage and brainwashed, but she was held responsible for robbing a bank. Dan White had *not* been kidnapped, held hostage and brainwashed, but he was *not* held responsible for executing two government officials.

My reverie was interrupted by a phone call from Mike Weiss. We had become friends during the trial, which he covered for *Time* magazine. He was calling from a phone booth near City Hall. I could hear crowds screaming and sirens wailing behind his voice.

He had to yell: "There's a riot going on! You should get here right away!"

Reluctantly, I took a cab. When I arrived, there were a dozen police cars that had been set on fire, which in turn set off their alarms, underscoring the angry shouts from a mob of 5,000 gays. On the night Harvey Milk was murdered, many of them were among the 30,000 who had marched silently to City Hall for a candlelight vigil. Now they were rioting, utterly furious at the Dan White verdict. But where were the cops? They were all fuming *inside* City Hall — where their commander had instructed them to stay — armed prisoners watching helplessly as angry gays broke the glass trying to ram their way through the locked doors.

I spotted Mike Weiss and a student from his magazine-writing class, Marilee Strong. The three of us circulated through the crowd. Standing in the middle of the intersection, *Chronicle* columnist Warren Hinckle was talking with a police official, and he beckoned me to join them. I gathered from their conversation that the cops were about to be released from City Hall. Some were already out. One kept banging his baton on the phone booth from which Mike was now calling in his story, and he had to wave his press card before the cop would leave.

I found Marilee and suggested that we get away from the area. As we walked north on Polk Street, the police were beginning to march slowly in formation not too far behind us. But the instant they were out of view from City Hall, they broke ranks and started running toward us, hitting the metal pole of a bus stop with their billy clubs, making loud, scary *clangs*.

"We better run," I told Marilee.

"Why? They're not gonna hit us."

"Yes, they are! Run! Hurry!"

The police had been let out of their cage and they were absolutely enraged. Marilee got away, but I was struck with a nightstick on the outside of my right knee. I fell to the ground. The cop ran off to injure as many other cockroaches in his kitchen as he could.

Another cop came charging and he yelled at me, *"Get up! Get up!"*

"I'm trying to!"

He made a threatening gesture with his billy club, and when I tried to protect my head with my arms, he jabbed me viciously on the exposed right side of my ribs.

Oh, God, the pain!

The cops were running amuck now, in an orgy of indiscriminate sadism, swinging their clubs wildly and screaming, *"Get the fuck outa here, you fuckin' faggots, you motherfuckin' cocksuckers!"*

I managed to drag myself along the sidewalk. It felt like an electric cattle prod was stuck between my ribs.

Marilee drove me to a hospital emergency ward. The X-rays indicated that I had a fractured rib plus pneumothorax — a punctured lung. There were several others already there who had been beaten in police sweeps. Another wave of victims would soon arrive after the cops carried out a search-and-destroy mission on the customers in a gay bar, Elephant Walk, at Castro and 18th Street. Although Dan White had acted on his own, he might just as well have been a Manchurian candidate for these cops. When the verdict was first announced, somebody sang "Oh, Danny Boy" over the police radio.

After six weeks of celibacy while the healing process took place, I thought I was ready for sex again, but when my partner embraced me tightly during her climax, I felt a sharp pain and groaned. She got turned on by what she interpreted as a moan of pleasure, and she squeezed me even tighter, which only made me groan louder, turning her on even more. Tighter, louder, tighter, louder. We were riding on a vicious cycle.

The city of San Francisco was sued for $4.3 million by a man who had been a peaceful observer at the riot following the verdict. He was walking away from the Civic Center area when a cop yelled, "We're gonna kill all you faggots!" — and beat him on the head with his nightstick. He was awarded $125,000. I had wanted to sue the police myself, but an attorney requested $75 for a filing fee, and I didn't have it. I was too proud to borrow it, and I decided to forego the lawsuit. This was one of the dumbest mistakes of my life.

The injuries affected my posture and my gait, and I gradually began to develop more and more of a strange limp.

In 1980, on the 50th anniversary of the Twinkie, inventor James Dewar said, "Some people say Twinkies are the quintessential junk food, but I believe in the things. I fed them to my four kids, and they feed them to my fifteen grandchildren. Twinkies never hurt them."

In 1981, the world's largest Twinkie was unveiled in Boston. It was 10 feet long, 3 feet 6 inches high, 3 feet 8 inches wide, and weighed more than a ton.

In 1982, psychiatrist Martin Blinder — who had helped establish Dan White's Twinkie defense — aided Arizona police officer John Clarke in plea-bargaining his way out of sexual assault, kidnapping and armed burglary charges. Dr. Blinder testified that the cop had assaulted, bound and sexually abused a woman while he was suffering from "Fugue State," a disorder which sometimes accompanies hypoglycemia, wild fluctuations in blood sugar. The psychiatrist testified that the policeman blacked out for 90 minutes while driving his car during a hypoglycemic attack. The officer ate doughnuts daily, up until the day he followed a young woman home from a supermarket, confronted her with his service revolver, forced his way into her residence, tied her up and fondled her breasts. He said it was only later that night he realized what he had done. He was allowed to plead guilty to second-degree burglary, for which he would receive probation.

Sex, Drugs, & The Twinkie Murders

In 1983, the *San Francisco Chronicle* published a correction: "In an article about Dan White's prison life, *Chronicle* writer Warren Hinckle reported that a friend of White expressed the former supervisor's displeasure with an article in the *San Francisco Bay Guardian* which made reference to the size of White's sexual organ. The *Chronicle* has since learned that the *Bay Guardian* did not publish any such article and we apologize for the error."

In January 1984, Dan White was released from prison. He had served a little more than five years for killing a mayor and a supervisor. The estimated shelf life of a Twinkie is seven years. That's two years longer than White spent behind bars. When he was released, that Twinkie in his cupboard was still edible. But perhaps, instead of eating it, he would have it bronzed.

In November 1984, prosecutor Tom Norman was convicted of drunk driving. He had been arrested for driving through a stop sign and over the double line twice. Previously convicted for reckless driving, he now received a one-year suspended sentence.

In June 1985, Sirhan Sirhan told the *Los Angeles Times*: "If (Dan White) had a valid diminished capacity defense because he was eating too many Twinkies, I sure had a better one because of too many Tom Collinses, plus the deep feeling about my homeland that affected my conduct."

In October 1985, Dan White committed suicide by carbon monoxide poisoning in his garage. He taped a note to the windshield of his car, reading: "I'm sorry for all the pain and trouble I've caused." White's defense attorney, Doug Schmidt, said, "I expected that he would kill himself. And, in certain respects it vindicates the defense. I don't think a well man takes his own life."

During his trial, an old friend, TV reporter Joyce Shank, who was also covering the trial, came to my house so we could compare notes. While she was visiting, there was an earthquake. She immediately jumped under my desk, just as she had once demonstrated on television what to do in case of an earthquake.

"Paul, get under here with me, hurry up."

I quickly hunched next to her under my desk. Our thighs were touching. Was it possible that my secret lust for Joyce might now become fulfilled?

"Put the radio on," she said.

I got up and put the radio on, then joined her again.

"Not *music*," she said, "the *news...*"

Okay, now that incident is even more embarrassing than saying "Thank you" to the guy who frisked me in the courthouse, but it served as a catalyst to my understanding of the psychological overtones of the Dan White case, because it's such a blatant example of how the process of projection can affect your perception, your empathy, your rationality, your behavior.

And, indeed, it was the lustfulness of George Moscone and Harvey Milk, which may have underlain the more obvious motivation that sexually inadequate Dan White had in destroying them. It was well known around City Hall that Moscone had a predilection for black women. Police almost arrested him once with a black prostitute in a car at a supermarket parking lot. And Harvey Milk had once told White, "Don't knock (gay sex) unless you've tried it." When John Briggs debated Milk, Briggs perpetuated a stereotype of gay promiscuity with the statistic that 25% of gay men had over 500 sexual contacts.

"I wish," said Harvey.

After the Dan White trial, I got a phone call from Lee Cole, an ex-Scientologist I had met in Chicago while researching the Charles Manson case. He wanted to visit me, but I said no.

"Suppose I just come over?" he said.

"You don't know where I live."

"I can find out."

"If you can find out, and you tell me how you did, you can come over."

I wanted to determine how carefully I had covered my tracks, or see which friend would give out my address. A little while later, Lee

Cole called again and told me my address — he said that he had obtained it from the voter registration files — so I told him to come over.

He took me to see Lowell Streiker, author of *The Cults Are Coming!* and a deprogrammer who had counseled one-third of the Jonestown survivors. In the course of our conversation, I mentioned my theory that Jim Jones had served as a pimp at City Hall and maintained power by implied blackmail.

Dr. Streiker told me of his friend — a member of Jones' planning commission — who had told him about the technique that People's Temple had used on the mayor. They sent a young black female member to service him, as a gift, then called the next week about a serious problem — she had lied, said she was 18, when in fact she was underage, but don't worry, we have it under control — just the way J. Edgar Hoover used to manipulate top politicians with his juicy FBI files.

So Jim Jones had taken Margo St. James' sardonic advice after all, on how to achieve political power: "Arrange for some of your women to have sex with the bigwigs." And he had taken it all the way to a mass suicide-murder — which occurred simultaneously with a mass demonstration by the women's movement in San Francisco, called "Take Back the Night!"

They completely shut down traffic on Broadway. But there was not a word about that event in any of the media. It was knocked totally out of the news by the massacre in Jonestown.

Postscript: When Dan White was paroled in 1984, he called his old friend, Frank Falzon — the detective who had originally taken his confession — and they met. A decade later, Falzon, now in the insurance business, told reporter Mike Weiss about that encounter:

"I hit him with the hard questions," Falzon recalled. "I asked him, 'What were those extra bullets for? What did happen?'"

"I really lost it that day," White said.

"You can say that again," Falzon answered.

"No. I really lost it. I was on a mission. I wanted four of them."

"Four?" Falzon said.

"Carol Ruth Silver — she was the biggest snake of the bunch. And Willie Brown. He was masterminding the whole thing."

While White had been waiting to see George Moscone in the anteroom of his office, the mayor was drinking coffee with Willie Brown, chatting and laughing. Finally, Moscone told Brown that he had to see Dan White. Brown slipped out the back door just as Moscone was letting White in the front way. Thirty seconds later, White killed Moscone. Dianne Feinstein, who was president of the Board of Supervisors, succeeded Moscone as mayor and is now a senator. Willie Brown is the current mayor of San Francisco. And Jonestown continues to serve as an occasional joke reference for stand-up comedians.

ABBIE HOFFMAN'S FOREHEAD

I remember the precise moment in 1967 that Abbie Hoffman and I bonded.

"You know," I said, "you're the first one who's really made me laugh since Lenny Bruce died."

"Really? He was my *god.*"

I told Abbie how Lenny had once printed the word FUCK on his forehead with strips of paper towel in a courthouse lavatory to discourage photographers from taking his picture.

A year later, Abbie and I were being interviewed at his apartment by a reporter from the CBS Evening News. The subject was the upcoming protests at the Democratic National Convention.

Paraphrasing Che Guevara, Abbie said, "I'm prepared to win or die." That sound bite never got on the air.

The reporter asked me, "What do the Yippies actually plan to do in Chicago?"

I smiled mischievously. "You think I'm gonna tell *you?*" That portion of my answer was used to end Walter Cronkite's segment on the Yippies, but my follow-up sentence — "The first thing we're gonna do is put truth serum in the reporters' drinks" — was omitted.

They had beaten me at my own game.

In 1996, seven years after Abbie's suicide, the Democrats returned to Chicago, and so did I. A week prior to the convention, Harry Smith, correspondent for the CBS Evening News, interviewed me at my home about the Yippies.

At one point, he asked, "Do you still take drugs?"

"Why, Harry?" I replied. "What do you have?"

He literally fell off his chair, laughing.

Of course, that would never make the cut.

· ■ ■ ■ ·

That scraping sound you heard at the '96 Democratic convention was Herbert Marcuse twisting in his grave as the term he coined — "repressive tolerance" — came to life in the form of a Chicago lottery for those seeking government-sanctioned time slots to voice their causes — from Psychologists for Quality to the Lesbian Avengers — at a location where the delegates couldn't hear them.

It was the ultimate trivialization of protest. No wonder the National Space Society yielded its hour to a marijuana-rights group.

At an officially-approved, fenced-off site opposite the Hilton Hotel facing Grant Park — where in 1968 the whole world was watching as sadistic police turned a peaceful rally into a brutal riot — *nobody* was listening to a man who was standing on a wooden platform, his back to Michigan Avenue traffic, as he spoke into a microphone about the injustice of the legal system.

"I would like to share with you another experience," he announced to himself over the P.A. system.

The schedule called for him to be followed by the American Art Party, which, like several others, didn't even bother to show up.

But then came the most successful demonstration, to honor the work of the late comedian, John Belushi, with a postage stamp. *Chicago Sun-Times* columnist Richard Roeper led 200 spectators in a chant: "Give him a damn stamp! Give him a damn stamp!"

There were two men there, dressed as Belushi characters, and the crowd voted their preference for the Belushi dressed as one of the Blues Brothers over the Belushi in his *Saturday Night Live* bumblebee costume. Democracy in action.

And, just as there are Elvis imitators, the Bruise Brothers troupe entertained at this event. Their performance included what was, in a perverted sense, the defining moment of the Clinton convention — a pair of dancing Chicago cops.

The Bruise Brothers resented the fact that the classic Sam and Dave blues song, "I'm a Soul Man," which had been further popularized by the Blues Brothers, was now being co-opted by the Bob Dole campaign as "I'm a Dole Man."

Probably a more appropriate song for the Dole campaign would have been Beck's 1994 hit, "I'm a loser, baby, so why don't you kill me?"

·■■■·

In my hotel room, I was watching myself on TV being interviewed by Harry Smith.

Me: *"From the feedback we got, it [the Chicago demonstrations in '68] woke a lot of people up, who didn't realize that the government was, in effect, their enemy. They didn't realize what was being done in their name, with their taxpayers' money. So it woke a lot of people up, it radicalized a lot of people. One of the definitions of a Yippie was a hippie who got hit in the head with a police billy club."*

Smith: [*Voice-over, commenting.*] "Krassner and his kind were once viewed by many as radicals, even as evil. His message has changed little over the years, yet now it sounds somehow conservative."

Me: *"I think of the government as the devil, and the devil never sleeps. I don't really think that the government has the interest of the people at heart. I think they have their own re-election at heart. And because of that, they'll take positions that they might not in the depths of their soul really believe, but they kind of think of their reputation as more important than their soul."*

I was stunned — *shocked*, I tell you — that this was considered somehow conservative. When I saw Norman Mailer at the convention, I told him about it.

"Well," he explained, "you have to realize, those media guys think that anybody who's against the government must be a conservative."

．■■■．

I was staying at the same hotel where, 28 years previously, in the restaurant at its base, Abbie Hoffman had been arrested while we were eating breakfast, ostensibly for having the word FUCK written in lipstick on his forehead, but really just to get him off the streets. He might have gotten away with it if only he hadn't tipped his hat to the police who were assigned to follow us.

Now, as a personal pilgrimage, I decided to return to the scene of the crime. It had turned into an upscale restaurant named Topo Gigio, after that dopey mouse from the Ed Sullivan show. Although I didn't eat there, I recalled Abbie's words:

"The duty of a revolutionist is to finish breakfast."

．■■■．

In 1969, a few years after my marriage had broken up, I met Jada Rowland. She was an actress, on TV every afternoon in *Secret Storm*. I fell in love with Jada, but I hated soap operas. They were the ultimate creation of a value system that was the antithesis of my own. Their sole function was to program viewers into becoming greater consumers by manipulating them to identify with the lives of other people who didn't even exist. One woman sent a letter warning Jada that her "husband" was seeing another woman.

Still, within that corrupt context, she maintained a sense of integrity. Once, the script called for her to put down her little daughter by referring sarcastically to her imagination, and Jada refused to say the line.

Photographer Richard Avedon had invited me to be included in a book on people in the counterculture. I accepted on the condition that I could choose the pose with Jada. What we had in mind was a takeoff on the *Two Virgins* album cover, where John Lennon and

Yoko Ono stood nude, holding hands. We would both be naked, smiling, with our arms around each other.

But, she would also be holding a patriotic cup with stars and stripes, and there would be arrows pointing to her breasts and crotch, and I would be holding an American flag. And I would have an erection. If *Two Virgins* was about anatomy, this was about physiology. And Jada was willing to risk losing her $1,000-a-week job to participate just for the fun of it.

I ingested a capsule of THC powder for the photo session. We were standing before the camera, and the only thing missing was my hard-on. I had heard that THC was actually an elephant tranquilizer. I would soon find out if that was true. Avedon asked what music we wanted in the background. I asked for the Beatles' "Hey, Jude," but he didn't have it, so instead we put on Bob Dylan singing "Lay, Lady, Lay."

Jada and I began to kiss.

"This is obscene," she whispered.

"No," I whispered back, "it's very pure. But you're right, it *is* kind of goal-oriented."

We continued kissing. Dylan was now asking the musical question, "Why wait any longer for the world to begin?" My penis rose to the occasion and the crew cheered us on.

I signed a release, assuming the photo would never be seen, because the publishing of an erection was so taboo. However, late last year — three decades later — my bluff was called. Avedon and Doon Arbus published a $75 book of photos, *The Sixties*. A *Los Angeles Times* review said that I looked "sheepish" and "sustained" an erection.

On the back cover of the book, there's a photo of Abbie Hoffman, holding a toy rifle in one hand and giving the finger with the other. He is smiling broadly, sticking his tongue out, and on his forehead the word FUCK is written in lipstick.

The Swinger's Convention

The 24th annual Lifestyles Couples Convention has filled three hotels in Palm Springs, California. The Convention Center is connected to one of them, the Wyndham, which surrounds a large outdoor pool and patio populated by couples busy socializing in 116 degree dry heat. Women and men alike are wearing thongs. From afar they appear like so many eyeless smiley faces among the bathing suits. The law that Sonny Bono signed when he was mayor, banning thongs in public, does not apply to this event, nor, for that matter, to Cher.

The convention is for couples only. Except for me. I've been hired to perform stand-up comedy at their Friday luncheon, and I'm here alone. On the small, propellered plane from Los Angeles to Palm Springs, the right side consists of two-seat rows, occupied entirely by couples on their way to the convention — horny with the expectation of getting laid by the spouse of a stranger, perhaps sitting in front of or behind them — and the left side of the plane consists of one-seat rows, occupied entirely by me. I'm afraid that the plane might tip over upon trying to land.

At the Convention Center, even the plastic-encased lapel name-tags are coupled off: "Ken and Barbie" on his, "Barbie and Ken" on hers. Not all the couples are paired off in real life, though. One person can simply bring along another — known in swinger circles as a "ticket" for gender balance — in order to get into the convention. So everybody has entered two by two, and I feel like a unicorn stowaway on Noah's Ark, surreptitiously balancing on the cusp between love and lust.

There are 3,000 participants at this convention, mostly upper-middle-class, in their 30s, 40s and 50s. They consider people in the outside world to be "straight," even though one would ordinarily consider *them* straight. I mean there are suburban soccer moms here, openly celebrating their secret lifestyle at an oasis of supportiveness. There's a man in a suit with a flesh-colored penis necktie, another wearing a T-shirt declaring, "I'm Not Going Bald, I'm Getting More Head," and another dressed only in a leather jockstrap, who recognizes me and introduces himself.

"I'd give you my card," he says, "but I have no place to keep them."

Inside the 100,000-square-foot Convention Center, the Exhibit Hall has been turned into an "Adult Marketplace," buzzing with commercial activity. I overhear one shopper's complaint: "But we've *already* spent $400." There's a multitude of merchandise on display — pornographic videos, naughty lingerie, fetish paraphernalia, edible lotions — plus booths galore. At the Golden Nipples booth, women are cheerfully having exact duplicates of their nipples created in sterling silver or 14-karat gold, which can be used as pendants, key fobs, money clips or — yes, of course — nipple covers. At the Penimax booth, an Asian vendor is selling disposable cock rings, which, he promises, will maintain your erection even after you ejaculate.

There are several booths dedicated to booking vacations especially designed for swingers, at nude beaches, clothing-optional resorts and ocean cruises. I follow around an elderly woman who is busy picking up brochures at every such booth. It seems incongruous, but I try not to indulge in stereotypes. Finally I engage her in a conversation, and she explains that her boss told her to get as much material as she could, because he owns some property surrounded by government land, and he wants to start a new business.

At the Erotic Massage Wear table, a woman uses my arm to demonstrate a device, which turns her fingertip into a vibrator, not intended for nose-picking. Then she puts Jergen's Lotion on my right hand, dons a pair of Love Mitts — made of vinyl with little nubs all over — and proceeds to massage my hand, while on the VCR there's a tape of a woman wearing Love Mitts and massaging a man's lubricated penis. This is a bizarre mixed-media sensation. Although I don't get a hard-on, the lobes of my brain seem to fuse, and for the next few hours my left hand persists in feeling neglected.

Checking out the functional furniture, I eavesdrop on a (fully clothed) couple testing out the "rocking torso feature" on a Love Table, but I actually climb *into* the Love Swing, assuming a position ordinarily assumed by a woman while the man stands up, crotch to crotch. My body is suspended half upside-down in mid-air with legs spread and feet up in stirrups. I'm feeling mighty vulnerable. As I hang there, the inventor hands me my tape recorder, then proceeds to show me how "the woman can place the man's penis on her G-spot by moving her legs from a position of being out front like this to being in the fetal position" and how "the man, instead of just going in and out like that, he can make his penis a joystick, so every step he takes is a movement inside of her, more like a dance step." He guarantees, "You'll never use a bed again."

Next I inspect the Bungee Sexperience — a harness designed by a company that makes bungee cords — it bounces in the air, so the "rider" can enjoy weightless sex in a variety of positions. I ask the woman demonstrating this how many hours a day she bounces up and down. "At an event like this," she responds, without missing a bounce, "I'd say eight to 12 hours." She tells me that her circulation is excellent, and that her 18-year-old son refers to the contraption as a "bungee humper." In addition to bouncing, it can also create "the illusion of bondage, yet the person can actually be comfortable while restrained."

The Auto Erotic Chair, however, provides *real* bondage. It's equipped with leather restraints and panic snaps for arms and legs, and comes complete with a power box, pneumatically operated anal and vaginal plugs. "Our power source unit is designed to stimulate nerve fibers throughout the genital areas by delivering controllable electro-pulse energy through conductive electrodes on our sex toys. Our precision engineered technology gives you safe and pleasurable electric play." So, for example, in the Electro-Flex Penile Ring/Anal Plug Configuration, "A single conductor butt plug is used in conjunction with a single conductive cock ring to complete the circuit. With a single conductive cock ring, one side of a double conductive butt plug can be used to stimulate either the prostate or the sphincter."

If you'd prefer something, well, less electric, there's always the Crystal Wand, a 10-inch-long, *S*-shaped co-ed tool, hand-carved from pure crystal-clear acrylic, that doubles simultaneously as a G-spot stimulator and prostate massager. I'm reminded of a swing party I heard about, one that took place at the Whispers Club in Michigan. Couples removed from the refrigerator 12-inch summer sausages and cucumbers that the hostess had planned to use for food that evening. When she walked into the "party room," she couldn't help but notice that although the food was being consumed, it was not exactly in the fashion she had originally envisioned. Instead, the sausages and cucumbers were being utilized as organic sex toys.

As I continue to wander around the Adult Marketplace, I realize that the name of the game is penetration. All paths lead to penetration. But I'm not referring to penetration of the sexual kind, although that's an implicit goal — pick an orifice, any orifice, and there's always a corresponding appendage or gadget that can fulfill its desire for penetration — no, I'm talking about penetration of the *market*. There's lots of money to be made here. The persistent question is how can *I* penetrate this market? Maybe I could come up with a combination FM radio and vibrating dildo.

I'm beginning to feel like I'm experiencing an alien encounter, only *I'm* the alien here. Nevertheless, I'm aware that swingers and comedians do have something in common. We both like to have a good opening line. As a performer, I always try to slant my opening line toward a particular audience.

My opening line at the World Hemp Expo was, "Last night, for the first time in my life, I used a hemp condom." My opening line at a Skeptics Conference, attended by the Amazing Randi and the

Amazing Kreskin, was: "This is the first conference I've been to where there were two people with the same first name, Amazing — but the Amazing Randi was born with that name, it's on his birth certificate, whereas the Amazing Kreskin changed his name for show-biz, his real name is the Obnoxious Kreskin." And my opening line at the luncheon during a Los Angeles County Bar Association conference was, "I'd like to begin with a moment of silence, so that you can think about your client's problem, and then you can make this a billable hour."

Now I find myself in a lavish hotel suite, trying to crystallize an opening line while contemplating the bald spot on the back of my head, infinitely cloned in the mirrors of the hotel bathroom, actually the only place I ever get to *see* that bald spot as others do. This will be a serious opening line, since I have been told that, in the introduction to my performance, I will be presented with the Lifestyles Freedom Award. I decided that my opening line will then be, "I just wanna say that freedom of expression existed long before the 1st Amendment." Though it's not my motivation, I realize that this opening line will undoubtedly please Robert McGinley, the bearded co-founder and president of the Lifestyles Organization.

"We hate government intervention in our lives," he has assured me. "We hate censorship. We're against laws that require helmets for cyclists. It's good that a law was just passed allowing women to breast-feed in public, but we shouldn't need permission from the government to do it." He admits to being "libertarian, but not Libertarian Party." He draws his philosophy from Jack London— "The proper function of man is to live, not to exist" — and, more specifically, his credo is, "Adult sexuality is normal." Dr. McGinley (he holds a Ph.D. in counseling psychology) tells me a riddle: "What do you call an Italian swinger?" I give up. The answer: "A swop."

At the luncheon, it turns out that I am *not* presented with the Freedom Award after all, and I have to come up immediately with a replacement opening line: "I'm delighted to be at the Lifestyles Convention — this is the first convention I've ever been to that was named after a condom."

Indeed, condom consciousness (if not condom use) is present at the convention. In one workshop, "The ABCs of Swinging," condom etiquette is described as bringing "the right safety equipment, just as you would for scuba diving or parachuting." Another presentation on "Safer Sex" covers new drug therapies for AIDS, information on other sexually transmitted diseases that are increasing among heterosexuals, and "things you should be doing to protect yourself."

Originally, herpes had caused a certain panic in swinger circles. Some swing clubs closed, though private parties increased. But, paradoxically enough, with the advent of AIDS, *new* clubs opened, as if the disease were anti-climactic. Currently, there's a surge of growth in this subculture — thanks to the Internet — with estimates ranging from 20,000 to three million participants. And, according to Dr. McGinley, "There's been very little increase in condom use. It's the woman's choice."

Nonetheless, at the Adult Marketplace, a woman in a black lace negligee roams around giving out free samples of condoms. There are also Creme Cookie Condoms for sale. They appear to be vanilla and chocolate Oreo-style cookies, individually wrapped in cellophane. I ask the vendor whether these are condoms that look like cookies, or cookies that look like condoms. She tells me that they are edible cookies, but each one has a condom inside.

"They're only a dollar each," she says, adding, as I edge away from her booth, "It's a great joke."

The Art Gallery at the Convention Center, featuring the Lifestyles Convention's 7th annual Sensual & Erotic Art Exhibition, almost didn't happen. The state's Department of Alcoholic Beverage Control had tried to prevent it from opening. When their authority was challenged, an ABC representative became an alchemist, transforming logic into absurdity. Legally, he said, you can't even have sex in a hotel room, which has a mini-bar. Sure, pal, just try to enforce *that* one.

Two days before the convention, the ACLU obtained a restraining order against ABC's interference with the art exhibit. But ABC didn't just give up and assume the fetal position in a Love Swing. Rather, the agency threatened to revoke the Wyndham Hotel's liquor license if they allowed a special two-hour session, the convention's traditional Evening of Caressive Intimacy, to take place in the Wyndham Ballroom on Friday as scheduled. This popular, closed-door, clothing-optional massage clinic, limited to the first 200 couples who sign up, would include the "human car wash," involving, as one veteran swinger portrays it, "a lot of naked bodies and some serious rubbing."

But the ABC regulations on Attire and Conduct — behavior "deemed contrary to public welfare and morals, and therefore no on-sale license shall be held at any premises where such conduct or acts are permitted" — includes this clause as a no-no: "To encourage or permit any person on the licensed premises to touch, caress or fondle the breasts, buttocks, anus or genitals of any other person." The Wyndham chickens out, the massage clinic is cancelled, the money is refunded, Lifestyles will sue the hotel for breach of contract, and the convention will be held in Las Vegas in 1998.

A lawyer, standing on the border of cynicism, suggests, "Just buy a town in Mexico, and all the officials."

In 1996, the convention was held at the Town & Country Hotel in San Diego (for the fourth time), but two ABC officers claimed that they witnessed oral copulation in the convention hall, and the hotel's liquor license was suspended for five days, hence Lifestsyle's move to Palm Springs this year. Lately, ABC has been spreading their particular brand of paranoia in Los Angeles, where they have raided gay, black and Latino bars in Los Angeles, and in Hermosa Beach, where they have imposed restrictions on restaurants, requiring patio patrons to order food with their drinks, and forbidding customers to dance. Proprietors now play less upbeat music so that nobody will be tempted to dance. Those who can't resist are asked to stop.

Incidentally, I find out that, instead of giving the Freedom Award to me, convention officials have decided to present ABC with an

Anti-Freedom Award, but that notion gets lost somewhere in award limbo, along with my unspoken opening line.

On Friday night, the massage clinic that doesn't take place is followed by the Wild West Casino and Dance. One man comes attired in a sheriff's outfit with a rubber penis drooping almost to the floor. A security guard tells him that he'll have to check it. Fake knives, guns and bullets are acceptable, but not a fake sex organ. Another cowboy, with a *real* (unloaded) gun, is stopped by a security guard, but he resists, asserting in his best John Wayne manner, "This is an 1887 pistol, and I'm not about to check it."

Several folks leave the dance at midnight to attend an unofficial 3rd annual spanking party. It ends at 3 a.m. with a bout of fist-fucking. Dear Abby was right. One thing *does* lead to another.

■■■■

I've been sampling many workshops at the Convention Center, and I notice that whenever I sit down on a chair next to a chair with someone else's stuff on it, and the owner of the stuff is sitting on the other side of that chair, they always tap the top of their stuff in a subconscious gesture of territoriality. I also observe that a man with one leg (he walks with crutches) and his wife seem to arrive at every single workshop that I attend. Hmmmmm. I'm beginning to get suspicious. Obviously, I've seen too many spy movies.

A cartoon in the 1991 convention program showed two rooms where lectures were being given. The room featuring "Do It Yourself Porn: Make Your Own XXX Movies" was overflowing into the corridor, and the room featuring "Socio-Political Ramifications of Current Trends in the Erosion of Civil Liberties" was empty, except for the baffled lecturer. It was a nice touch of self-deprecating humor, an exaggeration not too far from reality. At this '97 convention, the audience for porn actress Nina Hartley's "So You Want to Throw a Party: Recipes for a Successful Orgy" attracts ten times the audience of attorney Bob Burke's "Sexual Politics: A Behind the Scenes Look."

Unfortunately, one workshop, "The Undertone of Sexuality in the *Star Trek* Series," has been cancelled — "due," someone added to the notice, "to Federation Regulations and Star Fleet Emergency Order 1007-932." Deborah Warner, in describing her presentation, had written: "Paramount and its parent company, Viacom, have a vested interest in presenting the *Trek* franchise as a family oriented show. To this end, they overtly depict the characters as asexual. Yet there exists erotic subtext.... This has spawned a very large community of fans who create volumes of explicit erotica which are enjoying great popularity in print and an explosion of interest on the Internet." Now, outside the room where her workshop would have been, there is disappointment — "Oh, and she was gonna bring a Klingon" — and nostalgia — "Remember the time Quark and Deanna were french-kissing?"

That theme continues at "American Tantra: How to Worship Each Other in Bed." This workshop — whose motto, "Orgasm long and prosper," paraphrases *Star Trek's* blessing, "Live long and prosper" — is conducted by Paul Ramana Das and Marilena Silbey. "Interspecies intercourse," he muses. "This can't be the only planet where love is made." A writer for *Adult Video News* has reviewed their *Intimate Secrets of Sex & Spirit* and confessed, "I've rarely laughed so hard in my life. No shit, this vid earns a pre-nomination for 'most outrageous sex scene.' Paul actually uses Marilena's pussy as an echo chamber!"

Now, in his regular voice, he is telling our workshop of the need to "approach the body, not for sexual release, but for every single inch of this body, the groundwork, the geography of pleasure. Can anybody name one spot on your body that is not capable of receiving pleasure?" Nobody can. Later, the entire audience, seated around the perimeter of this extra large room, is instructed to come stand in the center area and face their partners. I start to sidle out, but not inconspicuously enough. Ramana Das, who knows me from a previous incarnation calls out, "There goes Paul Krassner. Are you afraid to participate?"

"I'm here as a journalist."

"Ah, he can't participate because he's a journalist. See how everybody has their excuses."

Suddenly I'm saddled with a dose of New Age guilt, as though I have aborted my inner child. Meanwhile, there's a lovely blonde who doesn't have a partner, and I'm tempted to participate, but some guy who's also without a partner links up with her. Unexpectedly, my guilt changes to jealousy. Just a slight pang of jealousy, mind you, but a terrible taboo in this particular world. Jealousy is an outmoded emotion, to be shunned like dandruff. There's even a workshop that advises "How to Handle Jealousy," and another titled "Swing Without Guilt or Jealousy." And so now I not only feel guilty about not participating, I also feel guilty about feeling jealous. I've committed a swinger crime. Any second, I expect to hear security guards shouting "Jealousy alert!" Loud sirens go off. "Jealousy alert!"

Now where will I go? I have been reading about Tantra in *Real Magic* by Isaac Bonewits: "Energy control is a very important part of the exercises; it is essential, for example, that during *Kama-kali* the male be able to refrain from ejaculating under the most harrowing circumstances." I decide to drop in on a workshop, "How to Prevent Premature Ejaculation," but everybody has already been there, and they all left early. Sorry. I blurted that out before I could stop myself.

·■■■·

There are swing clubs all around the country, from "Shenanigans" in Indiana to "Liberated Christians" in Arizona ("for Christians seeking liberation from false sexual repression based on mistranslation of scripture who wish to explore responsible non-monogamy and polyfidelity"). Many clubs designate themselves as an Equal Opportunity Lifestyle Organization, where membership is open to all races, and they belong to NASCA (North American Swing Club Association).

The Spring 1997 issue of *NASCA Inside Report* editorializes:

> "There are political attacks on freedom that citizens should be aware of. It is far too easy to lose, through complacency and ignorance, the freedom that we Americans cherish. These attacks include the proposed censorship of the Internet, now under review by the U.S. Supreme Court, the recently court upheld attempts by states to keep 'harmful' literature from the eyes of children by controlling street news racks, the reintroduction in Pennsylvania of

legislation to outlaw swing clubs, and a similar measure in California. Regarding the latter two, do we smell a conspiracy here?"

In Pennsylvania, Richard Kasunic, a Democratic state senator, failed in his 1996 attempt to outlaw "sex clubs." This year, he has reintroduced legislation to outlaw "swinger clubs." He states, "My bill will outlaw these immoral establishments in every community in Pennsylvania and provide significant penalties for those who choose to continue this offensive practice." The penalty for operating a swing club, even in one's own home: up to two years in jail and $5,000 in fines. For a second conviction: up to seven years and $15,000. For patronizing a swing club: $300 plus court costs.

In California, Tim Leslie, a Republican state senator, has introduced a bill which would provide that "every building or place which, as a primary activity, accommodates or encourages persons to engage in, or to observe other persons engaging in, sexual conduct including, but not limited to, anal intercourse, oral copulation, or vaginal intercourse, is a nuisance and shall be enjoined, abated and prevented, and for which damages may be recovered, whether it is a public or private nuisance."

Swinger periodicals range from *New Friends* to *Fuck Thy Neighbor*. Patti Thomas, author of *Recreational Sex: An Insider's Guide to the Swinging Lifestyle*, is editor at *Connection*, which publishes 13 titles, including *Cocoa 'n Creme*, catering to interracial swingers (not to be confused with *Black'n Blue*, catering to sadomasochist swingers). *Connection* is suing the federal government over a bill that Ronald Reagan sent to Congress in 1987, the Child Protection and Obscenity Act, an outgrowth of the Meese Commission on Pornography.

The specific statute being challenged — known as the record-keeping and labeling law, or the ID law — was supposed to be aimed at child pornography, but has been applied to adults-only swing publications. It requires anyone placing an explicit-photo ad to provide a photo ID, nicknames, maiden names, stage names, professional names, and aliases. These records must be available for inspection by the attorney general's office. *Connection* had attempted to comply with the law by cutting out every explicit photo ad from their magazines and sending them with a letter to those

187

advertisers, explaining the new law and its requirements, asking that they submit the proper ID or send a "soft" photo, which didn't require ID. Out of 500, only 26 advertisers responded with IDs. Patti Thomas spoke about this in her keynote speech at the Conclave '97 Convention in Chicago:

> "It definitely makes it difficult to produce the magazine our readers and subscribers have come to expect when you don't have enough so-called 'legal' ads to fill all those pages. And considering that *swinging itself is not illegal*, why should we have to 'register our sexual choices' with the government just to place a personal ad in a magazine? I've never really thought of myself as an activist, or as one who was 'politically involved,' but over the last few years I think I've finally come to realizing that it's going to be *necessary* to be involved, even if it does mean 'exposing' my lifestyle to those who would repress it. I am *fucking sick and tired of do-gooders trying to tell me how I should live my life!'*

In 1995, *Connection* filed a suit challenging the constitutionality of the law and seeking a permanent injunction. In 1997, the motion was denied. Attorneys filed an appeal and a motion for a temporary injunction relieving *Connection* from complying with the act during that appeal. The motion was granted.

"The justice system in this country just makes no sense to me whatsoever," Patti Thomas tells me. "As far as I know, once we do present our case to the Court of Appeals, if our decision isn't favorable, we will make every attempt to go to the Supreme Court. Our attorneys are the best 1st Amendment attorneys anywhere. Our lawsuit has been very costly, as you can imagine, but our company believes very strongly in fighting for our constitutional rights. Our suit was filed not only for the benefit of our company, but because we felt that this outrageous law was totally infringing on the civil rights and freedoms of people involved in alternative lifestyles. Obviously, the average person involved in swinging would have no way of combating this law on their own."

I ask her whether attempts at repression have resulted in politicizing the swinger community.

"I'm afraid we haven't been very successful," she replies. "We try to inform our readers about political issues threatening our lifestyle, and attempt to get them involved. Unfortunately, many in the lifestyle either don't believe that the government will actually take away their rights, or are too afraid to make a stand. Swingers who have been 'exposed' as active participants in the lifestyle have lost jobs, family, community standing, friends, etc., as a result.

"People I've personally known who have lost their jobs when their swinging activities were discovered just wouldn't fight back because of the fear of further exposure through the publicity that could have been generated. As a matter of fact, my ex-husband was fired from a management position (back in 1980) when someone discovered his photo in one of our magazines and brought it to the attention of his superiors. Luckily, he was able to find a position with one of *Connection's* affiliate companies. So, we pretty much remain an 'underground minority.'"

Her point is underscored by a 29-year-old woman at the convention. "None of us like publicity," she says. "None of us want to be out in the open. The business world is very conservative." She is wearing an American flag bikini, although she has never heard of Abbie Hoffman. She was born the same year that he got arrested for wearing an American flag shirt. Nor did she have any way of knowing that when he wore another American flag shirt on the Merv Griffin show, his half of the TV screen was blocked out all across America. She was, in short, unaware of the roots of her own, limited freedom.

·■**■**■·

It's Saturday night, and the Carnival Masquerade Ball is being held in the huge Convention Center Ballroom. On the wall behind the stage are gigantic masks. Above the tables are gold and purple balloons, fashioned after either somebody's school colors or a Chinese restaurant's hot mustard and soy sauce plate. The taped music is loud, and the dancing is raunchy, enhanced by gaudy yellow, blue and red lights. Pheromones are flying, and the costumes are kinky.

"Costumes," the program states, "may be anything of fertile imagination (genital area must be covered) for an exotic night of adult social fun." Hey, look who's here: Superman. The Phantom of the Opera. The Devil. Mickey Mouse and Minnie Mouse (in a see-through top). An executioner. An Arabian potentate. A gold-plated pharaoh. A chicken lady, covered with big yellow feathers. A guy in a dog collar, being led around on a leash. And the one-legged man, who is wearing a roller skate as his costume.

At one point, an announcement is made that the next dance number will be filmed, so anybody who doesn't wish to be recognized should get off the dance floor. About 80% of the dancers leave. Similarly, taking part in the costume-judging means that permission to be photographed is automatically granted, which results in many contestants not making themselves available to be chosen as possible finalists. The Best Male Costume goes to a 75-year-old man dressed as a biker stud. The Best Female Costume goes to his 75-year-old wife, dressed as a biker slut. The Best Couple's Costume goes to a woman with *papier mache* breasts the size of beach balls and her mate with matching enormous testicles, but covered by pillowcases and a sign that warns "Censored by the hotel and ABC."

A marriage ceremony is performed on stage. The blissful pair have written their own vows; nothing is mentioned about forsaking all others. The newlyweds, their party and a few other couples are invited to a gathering in the suite of a three-time Emmy Award-winning TV producer and his wife. It turns out to be a Tantra-filled wedding night. All the women massage the groom, and all the men massage the bride. One woman, a computer animator who wants to become a sexual surrogate, predicts that, as the millennium comes to an end, Tantric men will be popping up everywhere.

A retired chairman and CEO of a title and escrow company, who attended another Tantra party, tells me, "The difference between the Tantra party and the party next door is the fact that at the beginning of the Tantra party there was a lot of ceremony and shared Tantra ritual, but once we had experienced that, it was every person for themselves. It was like the party next door." These were Closed Parties, by invitation only. But you didn't need an invitation for Open Parties. All you had to do was find them.

The Wyndham Hotel is permeated by a sense of uninhibitedness. In the elevator, a beautiful black woman is looking in the full-length mirror and admiring her new Clit Clip — non-piercing, adjustable, genital jewelry—"not designed to be painful," I learned at the Adult Marketplace, "just very sensual and aesthetically attractive. The Clit Clip is a long, narrow, *U*-shaped piece of metal, designed to fit around the clitoris hood, with some light-catching Austrian crystals, in your choice of clear, red, blue and purple, dangling from the ends." The woman in the elevator turns toward me and says, "Isn't it nice?" Her husband smiles proudly. "It's charming," I reply, "but what are you gonna do if the metal detector goes off at the airport?"

I leave them giggling in the elevator as I get off on a floor where I've heard there would be lots of action. I follow one group, but only the couple in front really knows where they're going. They are on the way to their own room, and when they get there, they go in, close the door, and we are all left out in the corridor, looking like a perplexed ant farm. Everybody turns around. I am now at the front of the line, so I let them all pass by me as they head in the opposite direction, strolling briskly, except for the one-legged man with the roller skate and crutches, who is gliding gracefully along the carpet. Passersby are asked, in vain, "Where's the party?" We finally find a room with a porn photo on the door, which is slightly open.

Inside, there are perhaps 50 people in semi-darkness. Exhibitionists and voyeurs, together again. Here a blow job, there a copulation, everywhere an undulating juiciness. There is an unspoken homophobia — no man is relating sexually to another man — but there is lots of lesbian libido. In order to keep a low profile, I have ripped several pages out of my notebook and folded them in half, so that I can take notes unobtrusively. However, a woman with a feather-duster asks me to hold her panties. She is about to join a threesome on the corner of the king-sized bed near the bureau I'm leaning against. I marvel at the choreography of this foursome. But they are playing, and I'm working. Their moans become my background music.

I wasn't *always* a wallflower at the orgy. I flash back 30 years— it's the Summer of Love in 1967—I'm at a Sexual Freedom League couples-only party at a large theatrical studio in San Francisco. There are 150 people dancing in the nude. Behind the closed curtains on the stage there are 15 small mattresses, in constant use. I remember making love on one of those mattresses with a sweet flower child only 15 minutes after we'd met. It was an exhilarating experience. We were on the front lines of the sexual revolution. We had to hold back from screaming out political slogans at our moment of climax. The seeds of contemporary swinging were planted at that party, but who could have known it would blossom into an industry?

·■■■·

If it's true that, as Bill Maher once stated so poetically, "The real problem with marriage is that it's just very difficult to bump your uglies with the same person every night your whole life," then for some people, swinging is the answer. To them, cheating is not an issue, unfaithfulness is obsolescent, and adultery is merely a concept that deprived former Air Force Lieutenant Kelly Flinn of the opportunity to drop a nuclear bomb. The Lifestyles Convention provides a nurturing environment for these couples the same way a convention of crossword-puzzle enthusiasts or barbed-wire collectors would provide for those folks. Yet, in the case of swingers, one is left with a puzzle. Is impersonal intimacy an oxymoron?

I ask that question of Stella Resnick, author of *The Pleasure Zone*. Her reply: "We can't put a value judgment on this. These are all consenting adults. It doesn't really matter that it's rather impersonal because they are in long-term relationships, so they're getting their intimacy needs met, but not necessarily their needs for excitement in sex, and this is certainly a way to do it. Often they are sexually identified in the sense that they're sexual people, they have strong sexual desires, they're not necessarily into politics or other causes, but this is a good cause — being in the body, being healthy — and it's a way of relaxing and enjoying their bodies. Whatever turns you on, as long as you're not doing any damage to anybody else and you're taking care of yourself, fine, enjoy."

When Tom Arnold was a guest on *Late Show* with David Letterman, he was being pressed by Letterman about his friendship with Kathie Lee and Frank Gifford. This was shortly after the *Globe* had entrapped and videotaped Gifford's extra-marital tryst with a flight attendant in a hotel room. Letterman insisted, "I don't revel in the miseries of others," but Arnold reminded him of his monologues with jokes about Gifford. Letterman defended himself: "It's part of the job." Arnold stammered, searching for just the right words. He finally found them: "Frank Gifford took a bullet for a lot of us." And the audience applauded the accuracy of his assessment.

Certainly, non-celebrities don't have to worry about supermarket tabloids revealing infidelities to *their* spouses. Such exposure could never occur with swinging couples, not only because, as a rule, they are honest with each other, but also because they party *with* each other, so there are no surprises. They are sharing a secret lifestyle, one with an ethic that transcends ordinary romance. Sneaky affairs are for straight people, but swingers can have their wedding cake and eat their fantasies too. Which explains why there have been no hookers hanging around *this* convention.

Allen Ginsberg's Last Laugh

Our countercultural paths had often crossed — at civil rights marches, anti-war rallies, marijuana smoke-ins, environmental demonstrations — and he was always on the front lines. Long before Ellen came out on a sitcom, Allen came out in the streets.

In March 1968, the Yippies held a press conference in New York to announce plans to protest the Vietnam war at the Democratic convention in Chicago. I was one of the speakers. When I mentioned that, in peace candidate Eugene McCarthy's Clean-for-Gene presidential campaign, "Allen Ginsberg wouldn't even be allowed to ring anybody's doorbell unless he agreed to shave off his beard," a reporter asked, "Would you cut your hair if it would end the war?"

Before I could answer, Ginsberg himself popped up like a Zen-master-Jack-in-the-box, his index finger waving in the air, and asked the reporter, "Would you let your hair *grow* if it would end the war?"

Later, Yippie leaders held an impromptu competition to follow up that line of questioning, concerned with exactly how open to self-sacrifice one might become in the pursuit of peace. Ginsberg's fellow poet, Ed Sanders, was unanimously declared the winner, with this criterion: "Would you suck off a terminal leper if it would end the war?"

195

Sex, Drugs, & The Twinkie Murders

Over the decades, Allen and I shared many a stage at benefits for various causes, but in 1988 we were both booked for a paying gig at Lincoln Center, along with New Age musician Philip Glass and performance artist Karen Finley, whose reputation for shoving a sweet potato up her ass preceded her appearance. My opening line was, "Allen Ginsberg is very disappointed. He thought that Karen Finley was gonna shove a sweet potato up *his* ass."

I could hear Allen's laughter reverberating from backstage like a Tibetan gong. When we embraced, he said, "How did you *know?*"

Ginsberg once asked his father if life was worth living. His father answered, "It depends on the liver." This was a touch of inadvertent prophecy, for Allen died of liver cancer on April 5, 1997. But he had indeed lived his life to the hilt and beyond, balancing with dignity and grace on the cusp between rationalism and mysticism, one individual, with curiosity and compassion for all.

On April 7, Michael Krasny hosted a memorial for Ginsberg on his radio program, *Forum*, over KQED-FM in San Francisco. The panel included novelist/Prankster Ken Kesey, poet/publisher Lawrence Ferlinghetti, Digger/actor Peter Coyote and myself. The following is excerpted from that conference call.

Kesey: I was at a party one time when I first knew Ginsberg, and he was standing by himself over by the fireplace, with a wine glass in his hand, and people milling around, and finally some young girl sort of broke off from the rest of the crowd and approached him and said, "I can't talk to you — you're a legend." And he said, "Yes, but I'm a friendly legend."

Ferlinghetti: He lived so many flames. Today the youth, like the 20-year-olds, are really turned on to Ginsberg and the Beat poets, but the thing they're turned on to is the apolitical part. One forgets how political the Beats were in the '50s, which was the Eisenhower and McCarthy era. And that's a flame that seems to be flickering these days.

Kesey: He was a great warrior. I think that's more important than his poetry. In fact, in later times, I haven't read much of his

poetry at all, because the warrior aspect of Ginsberg has
loomed much larger. When we went to the Vietnam Day parade
up in Berkeley (1965), they had been interviewing the Hell's
Angels (motorcycle gang) — all the Hell's Angels were gonna
come out and oppose the opposers — they were gonna come out
and start a riot, is what it was.

So Allen asked me to take him up there, to where the Angels
hung out in this big white house in Oakland, and we went in
there, and here's all these big brutes holding their beer cans,
with their beer bellies and their beards, and Ginsberg goes
right in and starts talking to them. And you look around, here
are these great big mean-looking guys wearing swastikas, pretty
soon Ginsberg has just charmed the hell out of 'em, until there's
not gonna be a riot.

He took himself into that — they marveled at him. It was the
courage, again, the courage of this man to come into this
situation and defuse it.

Krassner: I knew Allen more as a researcher and an activist than as
a poet. In fact, in 1984, at the Naropa Institute in Boulder, at the
25th anniversary of Jack Kerouac's *On the Road*, Abbie
Hoffman was saying how much he and other political activists
like Ed Sanders were influenced by *Howl*, and Ginsberg
dismissed his own poem as "a whole boatload of sentimental
bullshit." But, as a researcher, he had meticulously acquired
files on everything that the CIA ever did, and I'm happy that
these are included in his archives (at Stanford University).

The one image I have of him from Chicago in 1968, when we
were holding our Yippie counter-convention — as opposed to
the Democratic "convention of death," as we called it — the
police were in Lincoln Park tear-gassing and clubbing people,
and Ginsberg sat in the middle of it like some kind of stoned
Buddha, chanting *Om* over and over again, and people gathered
around him, and he led them out of the park, and it created a
kind of mystical force field, so that the cops just ignored them,
and he was like the Pied Piper of Peacemaking.

Allen just articulated the consciousness of people who knew that the mainstream culture was a sado-masochistic bizarre mess.

Krasny: What do you do with the kind of bizarre mess that some people would claim is characteristic of Ginsberg in the wake of his death, all the NAMBLA (North American Man/Boy Love Association) stuff, and his apparently not only supporting that organization, but also expressing favor where little boys are concerned, sexually, and also using drugs somewhat recklessly and excessively as some attribute him to do?

Krassner: Well, that's the risk of free will. Allen has always admitted, you know, he would go to a poetry reading and say he was hoping to meet a young boy there. He was honest about his perversion of pedophilia, if that's what it was, but it may have just been a fantasy. He was for dialogue, and he was nonviolent, so it's just interesting as to what he considered the age of consent. A few months ago he told me it was 18.

Coyote: (chuckling) It's just so funny. I mean, as a father of two kids, I'm repulsed by the idea of pedophilia, but you know, by the same token, it's Allen. It probably wasn't easy being Allen. It's easier to be some of us than others of us, and I think that Allen's great courage was to be unequivocally who he was. And when he went to Cuba and announced that he wanted to have oral sex with Che Guevara, it actually was to Castro's detriment, in my mind, that he threatened to lock him up, or threw him out.

The thing that Allen represented to me was more than the Beats, more than anything else, I harken back to Gary Snyder's great phrase, "the great underground," which he calls the tradition, coming from the Paleolithic shamans on up to the present — the tradition of yogins and healers and midwives and poets and artists and people who stand for archaic, earth-centered values, life-supporting values. It's like a great river that kind of surfaces in various cultures all around the world at different times. It's quenchless, transcendentalist for just one little rivulet of it. And Allen was a great prophet of it.

Kesey: When we (the Merry Pranksters) went to see (Tim) Leary at Millbrook, Ginsberg was on the bus, and we had pulled over somewhere, and he was up immediately, sweeping the stuff out of the bus with a little broom, and (Neal) Cassady at the wheel said, "Looky there, it's our Jewish mother." And he was the Jewish mother, in some way, to a whole literary movement. He did all he could to help all of his friends get into print, all the time. He was a great benefactor to this art, and worked very, very hard to have his friends have as much fame as he did.

We had a poetry festival some years ago up here in Oregon, and the way we were doing it, during the day we had a stage outside of our basketball court, and we had headliners that were gonna be on that night, and during the day people read poetry and we judged it, and they were gonna be the people that read with Ginsberg, and during the day all the people in the field outside gradually trickled into the basketball court, like 3,000 people in there, and we were gonna charge them $5 apiece, but they were already in. Allen said, "Let me see what I can do." And he got up there with his harmonium, and he began, *Om, Om*, pretty soon he had 'em all *Om, Oming*, and he just gave a gesture like that, stood up, walked out, and 3,000 people walked out with him, so we were able to charge 'em money.

Krassner: We've been praising Allen so much, but I'll give you one little revealing story. On one hand, he was a pacifist. I remember when he first started taking LSD, and he thought that world peace would come about if only John F. Kennedy and Nikita Khrushchev would take acid together. And yet, I remember a scene — this was in the early '70s — Ken Kesey and I and my daughter Holly, who was a young girl then, were visiting (William) Burroughs in New York, and he had this huge loft, and a cat, and a lot of cardboard boxes, and he was wearing a suit and tie and high-top red sneakers.

We all decided to visit Ginsberg in the hospital — he'd had a stroke, and part of his face was paralyzed — he was in bed there, and I introduced him to my daughter, and he graciously struggled to sit up and shake hands with her, but he was kind of weak and deep in some kind of medication, and he blurted out

— what they would call in psychiatry a "primary process" — he blurted out, "Henry Kissinger should have his head chopped off!" It was some kind of Ginsbergian Tourette Syndrome.

Krasny: There's been a lot of solemn talk, so I'm glad you added that note of levity. Ginsberg would want, I think, a discussion about his life to be infused with a lot of humor and satire, don't you think?

Krassner: Oh, absolutely. You can't take yourself too seriously if you're walking around with an Uncle Sam hat and Mahatma Gandhi pajamas, chanting "The war is over" when the war was at its height. But that act inspired Phil Ochs to write his song, "The War Is Over," and to organize rallies in Los Angeles and New York on the theme of "The war is over."

Coyote: I think that Ginsberg represented an enlarged notion of sanity — which is not to say it's not without contradictions, which is not to say it's not as stained and tattered as anything else. You may not like the fact that Gandhi tested his celibacy by lying naked with young girls, or that Freud was shooting cocaine while he was working out his psychotherapy theories, or that Martin Luther King had sex with women outside of marriage, but to me what these facts do is reinforce the humanity of the person in question and remind us that we don't have to be perfect to make contributions, that we can struggle against the dark or the undeveloped sides of our nature and still make a contribution, and I think that's kind of the beacon Allen is. The thrust and underpinnings of his life were fundamentally sane in every venue. That's really what I respect him most for.

Ferlinghetti: I think maybe you could say Allen started out mad and became saner all his life, and he then became more quietist, I think, in his last years, and this was an influence of Buddhism, I believe. He died as a Buddhist; he didn't want any life support systems. There were Buddhists around him at all-night vigils the last two nights, and he died the way he wanted to die.

Kesey: Ginsberg had a terrific laugh. I was just trying to think, what am I gonna miss most? Even in the most serious moments, this thing would bubble up and bark forth, his eyes twinkling. It was a great laugh, and I'm gonna miss him.

The Funny Hooker

Dolores French is doing stand-up comedy for the first time. She's wearing a six-foot-wide hoop skirt for her performance at a benefit titled "Ladies of the Evening at the Improv" in Hollywood.

"I am a working prostitute," she tells the audience. "I live in Atlanta where it's very challenging to be a whore. Odd things are illegal in Georgia. Having a dildo in your possession that can be found by a police officer will get you charged with distribution of obscene material. It's perfectly legal to have a dildo in Georgia if the cops can't find it. Actually, you can have a million dildos as long as the cops can't find them. And they will be doing body cavity searches, so don't even think about hiding them there."

Pausing for laughter, she continues: "I love living in Atlanta. But I hate having to always apologize for Georgia being the home of the Hardwick sodomy case. In the state of Georgia you can spend more time in prison for engaging in oral sex with your own spouse in the privacy of your own home than you can for fucking a dead donkey, buck naked on the steps of the state capitol in broad daylight!"

Dolores and I have been friends for 20 years. She had asked me to save all her letters, which eventually became the basis for her autobiography, *Working: My Life As a Prostitute*. She is active on the Internet, where she helps spread information and commentary about her profession, including injustices such as the case of Ma Yulan, who was sentenced to death by a court in China. She was charged with "organizing prostitution" after running a brothel in Beijing.

Dolores has a peculiar sense of curiosity. When it comes to space exploration, for example, she wants "to know more about bodily functions in weightlessness. They talk endlessly about heart function and blood circulation and the attrition of muscle mass, but I haven't heard one word about how the body responds to sexual arousal in zero gravity. Is clitoris and penis engorgement even possible? And how do they catch and contain excrements of all sorts? What do you think those Mir dwellers did to amuse themselves for all those months stranded in space?"

And she is certainly frank about her *own* bodily functions: "Considering how unappealing astronauts' culinary experiences are, I understand that sex in space might have a limited erotic appeal, but I'm curious about how it works. Once I severely sprained my thumb and wrist; wiping, masturbation and a lot of other stuff became adventures of ingenuity. Peeing while wearing a hooped skirt requires assistance akin to air traffic control. I can't imagine what sort of an ordeal it is while wearing a space suit."

According to NASA, "A waste collector has been designed so that both males and females can use it. It has a seat belt and feet restraints to hold the astronaut on the seat. High-speed air currents pull the waste into their respective receptacles. The urine is combined with other water waste and the feces is vacuum dried, chemically treated to get rid of the odor and bacteria, and stored."

Years ago, there was a news item about the Russian cosmonauts requesting that a "privacy curtain" be installed on the Mir space station. Presumably they wanted to jerk off and watch their flesh rockets launch gooey white globlets of semen with millions of unseen passengers floating aimlessly into zero gravity. The closest that the American space program has ever come to official sexual experimentation was the time they sent up some fish embryos, but even those were fertilized *before* the flight.

One correspondent wrote, "As to how sex is done in a weightless environment, from what I understand, the two people having sex would have to be held together with an elastic harness. Otherwise, when they pushed forward, they would then bounce away from each other. They haven't figured out how three or more would do it together. But the harness does sound kinky. Seriously, if this society of ours wasn't so sex-phobic, we would have professional sex workers who would be hired to do sexual experiments in space. Wouldn't we?"

Meanwhile, a porn-movie company has rented an airplane — the same one that "legitimate" filmmakers use when they want to shoot weightlessness scenes while the plane dives from a high altitude to within 1,000 feet of the ground — and recorded the first weightless sex scene for a feature video, *The Uranus Experiment.*

Anyway, a month after Dolores French lost her stand-up-comic virginity, the Georgia Supreme Court declared, in a 6-1 decision, that the state's sodomy law violated the right to privacy guaranteed by the Georgia constitution. That night, couples all over the state were joyously indulging in non-felonious sodomy. And they could thank Dolores for shaming those judges into that ruling with her comedy act at the Improv.

And, of course, Dolores herself celebrated by fucking a dead donkey, buck naked on the steps of the state capitol in broad daylight.

Further Weirdness
with Terence McKenna

The first thing you notice about the naked men and women soaking in the outdoor hot springs overlooking the Pacific Ocean is that they all seem to maintain excellent eye contact while engaging in casual conversation.

They have come to the Esalen Institute — a New Age human-potential resort in Big Sur, California — to participate in various weekend workshops. The group in this particular tub includes Terence McKenna, who will be conducting a workshop titled "Pushing the Envelope." With his curly brown hair and beard, a twinkle in his eye and a lilt to his voice, he could easily pass for a leprechaun.

"I'm convinced," he is saying, "that probably for most people, the most important thing in a workshop situation is nothing that I will say or do, but who you might meet here."

Of course, those who are at Esalen for McKenna's workshop have come mainly to meet *him*. He is a psychedelic adventurer and a visionary author — his books include *True Hallucinations*, *Food of the Gods* and *The Archaic Revival* — who serves as a missing link between botany and technology.

He took his first acid trip in the '60s when he was a student — majoring in shamanism and the conservation of natural resources — at UC-Berkeley, where he became active in the free-speech and anti-war movements. He was influenced by Aldous Huxley,

Timothy Leary and Ram Dass, and now has become a countercultural icon himself.

He handles that role with intelligence, grace and humor. In person, he is spontaneously charming and effortlessly witty. He loves language, and though he is glib without being speedy, he chooses his words carefully. He communicates with the precision of an architect and the passion of a poet, speaking in a friendly, entertaining twang. He is, in short, a Mr. Rogers for grown-ups, and the neighborhood he welcomes you to explore is inner space.

A woman approaches our hot tub from the walkway to tell McKenna that it's time for his massage. When he rises from his sitting position in the water, I can't help but notice that not only is he fairly well hung, but also that he's much too tall to be a leprechaun.

I continue to soak for a while, replaying in my mind the incident that had brought me here.

A few months previously, on the morning of April 1st, I flew to San Francisco, where I had lived for fifteen years. It remains my favorite city — my daughter, Holly, still lives there — and I jump at any excuse to return. My excuse for this visit: I was scheduled to emcee a benefit for Beat Generation novelist Jack Kerouac's daughter, Jan, who had been on dialysis treatment for the last few years.

On that sunny afternoon, I was standing around stoned in Washington Square Park, wearing my *Mad* magazine jacket that Holly had given me the previous Christmas. The smiling face of Alfred E. Neuman — stating his renowned philosophy, "What — me worry?" — graced the back of my jacket. That's exactly what I felt like that day, a harmless innocent.

I was waiting for the arrival of the annual Saint Stupid Day Parade, led this time by Grand Marshal Ken Kesey and his Prankster sidekick, Ken Babbs, in an open-topped convertible. The event was sponsored by the First Church of the Last Laugh. Their sound equipment was surrounded by yellow plastic tape warning,

Police Line — Do Not Cross. Somebody in a clown costume handed me a three-foot section of that tape, and, April Fool that I am, I graciously accepted.

The celebration featured music, comedy and a traditional free brunch, along with such favorite rituals as the Sock Exchange and the Leap of Faith. Kesey — also in town to speak at the benefit — was in fine form. He delivered an optimistic pep talk to the audience sitting contentedly on the grass.

"It ain't over," he concluded, "until the fat lady gets high!"

Then he led a Gong Bong, where everybody stands up, forms a circle, holds hands and, as though a single unit, takes a dozen long, deep breaths, letting out the final exhalation with upraised arms and a group wail of exultation. During this moment of spiritual hyperventilation, a young woman fell to the ground and broke her nose. She was a casualty of peace.

That night, at the benefit for Jan Kerouac — held, let's face it, only because she happened to be the daughter of a groundbreaking literary celebrity, even though he had abandoned her mother when she was pregnant with Jan — I pointed out that "It's not enough any more just to be a sperm donor."

Backstage, someone I knew handed me a baggie of what I assumed to be marijuana. I thanked him and put it in my pocket. Ah, yes, one of the perks of the benefit biz.

Later, as the final members of the audience were straggling out of the theater, I was sitting with my friend Julius in his car, in the parking area at Fort Mason Center. Julius was busy rolling a joint in a cigar box on the dashboard with the map light on. There was a police car circling around in the distance, but we foolishly ignored it. Suddenly, a moment later, there was a fist knocking heavily on the passenger-side window and a flashlight shining in my eyes. *Shit! Fuck! Caught!*

We were ordered outside and, with our arms outstretched against the side of the car, searched. As I was being frisked, I realized that the cop was facing the back of my jacket, with the face of Alfred E. Neuman smiling at him and asking, "What — me worry?" And, indeed, the cop *was* worried. He asked if I had anything sharp in my pockets.

"Because," he explained, "I'm gonna get very mad if I get stuck," obviously referring to a hypodermic needle.

"No," I said. "There's only a pen in this pocket" — pointing toward the left with my head—"and keys in that one."

He found the coiled-up three feet of yellow plastic tape warning, *Police Line — Do Not Cross*, and said, "Where'd you get this?"

"At the Saint Stupid Day Parade."

"What's it for?"

"To keep people away."

But then he found the baggie. And, to my surprise, it contained psilocybin. He examined it. Then, reeking with sarcasm, he said, "So you like mushrooms, huh?" Under the circumstances, it was such a ridiculous question that I almost laughed, but I realized that from his point of view this was a serious offense.

Whereas Julius was given a $50 citation for possession of marijuana, I was arrested on the spot, handcuffed behind my back, and read my Miranda rights. I stood there, heart pounding fast and mouth terminally dry, trying to keep my balance on the cusp between reality and unreality.

That cop's question — *So you like mushrooms, huh?* — was asked with such archetypal hostility that it kept reverberating inside my head over and over again. *So you like mushrooms, huh?* It was not as though I had done anything, which might harm another human being. It was simply an authority figure's need to control. But control what? My pleasure? Or was it deeper than that?

This need to understand the basis of my plight became the impetus for my decision to meet Terence McKenna. He was, after all, the Head Mushroom Guru.

I contacted McKenna in Hawaii, where he lives in happy isolation. "My web site is on a machine in the Bronx," he said, "although I administer it from the big island." However, he was coming to the mainland, and he invited me to his workshop at Esalen.

We met on a Friday evening in the dining room just as a fellow sitting next to him was leaving the table.

"If you see him again," McKenna warned me, "cover your wallet with one hand and your ass with the other."

"Why? What's he selling?"

"A videotape claiming that this guy Hudson has discovered a cure for cancer, the elixir of immortality and the Philosopher's Stone — but needs investors to just dot a few *i*'s and cross a few *t*'s."

After dinner, the workshop convenes with an introductory session. There are 35 participants, sitting on cushions in a circle against the walls of a cabin in the woods. Everybody has arrived with their own personal agendas, and each will hear McKenna through their own individual filters. One by one, they introduce themselves.

Here, a woman who's a professional raver. There, a man who strolled the streets of Paris with a lobster on a leash. Here, a mother and her son, whom she has brought as a gift for his 21st birthday. There, a woman who will spend the entire weekend sucking on a little straw coming out of the top of a plastic water bottle in the shape of a large, pink, erect penis. She introduces herself as "a hooker from L.A.," adding that "I'm here to party with the elves." McKenna turns to the person sitting next to her and says, softly, "Top that."

Someone tells him, "I heard you're one of the greatest minds in the universe." McKenna responds, "More outlandish claims. We'll compare notes at the end." Someone else publicly confides to him, "If my life were a ride through the funhouse at Disneyland, you're like one of the characters who keeps popping up." McKenna confesses, "I'm an epistemological cartoon."

When the formalities are over, he begins his rap, a swirling kaleidoscope of speculation on the influence of another dimension and what's happening at the end of the 20th Century to fracture our understanding of reality. This weekend will turn out to be much more than I bargained for. Mushrooms are only a starting point.

"Why," McKenna asks, "is there so much social tension over this psychedelic issue? Nobody who has informed themselves claims that great criminal fortunes are being made, or that kids are being turned into psilocybin runners in the ghetto. We know that all the stupid reasons given for suppressing psychedelics are in fact some kind of lie.

"And then the more naive on our side therefore assume that, well, shortly, some with reason will climb to its zenith, and all these things will be made legal — *not*. Because this phenomenon is a dagger pointed at the heart of every social system that's ever been in place, from the grain tower at Jericho to modern fascism in China.

"No social system is so confident of its first premise that it can tolerate this. But we don't live for the greater glory of social theories and institutions. We live because we find ourselves, as Heidigger said, *thrown* into being, and we have to sort that out on an individual basis."

And this is where McKenna's concept of novelty comes in. Novelty is the absolute core of his quest. The ultimate battle is between the increase of novelty as opposed to habit or entropy.

"Look at the history of the universe," he says. "Novelty has been increasing since the Big Bang. We need to undergo radical deprogramming before the eschaton — the last thing. We are on the brink of moving into the domain of the imagination. Novelty is maximized and preserved. It changes our position in the cosmic drama, the cosmic accident. We're damn lucky to be here as spectators, we are told by science. Suddenly we matter. We still have freedom to act, to create.

"The bottom line, the final true message of psychedelics — the positive input that comes to you if you accept change — is the message that the culture outside of psychedelics is so keen to deny, with materialism, everything from the calendar to theories of democracy. But nothing lasts, not your friends, enemies, fortune, children, not even you. Nothing lasts.

"Well, if you live your life in denial of that, then it's essentially like being dragged kicking and screaming 60 years to the yawning grave. Strangely enough, the way you cheat the grim reaper is by living as fast as you can, because all time is the seriality of events, and the more events there are, the more time you have, so awareness becomes very important, and even, as the Buddhists say, awareness of awareness."

There is a sculpture of Buddha in the middle of the vegetable garden at Esalen, with a small bench nearby. That night, I take a walk there, and just sit under the stars, listening to the sound of wind chimes tinkling in the breeze as I compose a contemporary haiku. The traditional haiku is three lines — five syllables, then seven, then five again. Ordinarily I'm one for breaking tradition, but I figure that if you don't stick to traditional form in this case, then it's not really a haiku, it's merely free verse. And so I wrote:

> *Aspirins and Prozac*
> *Tums, Nytol, Pepto Bismol*
> *Just say no to drugs*

·■■■·

Saturday morning at Esalen. Fresh fruit and vegetables galore. Hot cereal and stewed prunes. People will be passing gas all over the place, and I remember with fondness my deaf uncle who once struggled to say, when somebody farted, "I can't *hear* it, but I can *smell* it."

At the first session that day, McKenna maintains that "there are not good beliefs, there are just bad beliefs, because they inhibit human freedom. A belief is a closed system. Psilocybin, like all psychedelics, has this quality of dissolving pre-existing mental and behavior patterns. This ability to entertain possibilities is what starts us on the road to free will.

"Our legacy is the legacy of the children of the stoned monkeys. And the chaotic element that a psychedelic introduces into the mental structures of a population is an inevitable precondition for the overcoming of habit and the production of novelty. We are dysfunctional because we have been away from this symbiotic relationship to mushrooms for such a very long time.

"We have got to make a transition to some kind of higher consciousness. If yoga can do it, great. If transcendental meditation can do it, great. The Pope and the Dalai Lama, fine. But in my experience, the only thing that changes consciousness as fast as we're going to have to change it is psychedelics. We have to change it on the dime, because the processes that we have set in motion are going to drag us down.

"If we *don't* make this higher ascent within 50 years, all the easily extracted metal will be gone, petroleum supplies will be dwindled, epidemic diseases, fascism, the erosion of any knowledge by most people with a historical database. We're just turning ourselves into victims of our own processes. That's why I think this is the choke-point. The next 20 years are make or break for the human enterprise. It's a forward escape into a world we can barely conceive of, but the only choice is grim death and extinction.

"We are all very toxified and poisoned by the society we live in, we're critics of it but nevertheless we're products of it. We need to unify heart and head in the presence of super technology. The culture is being left behind by the technology. We have to re-engineer ourselves.

"Fortunately, I have managed to transcend the idea that politics or some social reformation or some messiah is going to bail us out. The reason I'm an optimist is because I think that nature is about some very complex business here, and we are its instruments, and ten thousand years of our discomfort is, from the point of view of the planet, a small price to pay for what is going to be achieved. I don't know about a God, but the laws of Physics favor the production of novelty."

Someone asks, "If psychedelics are such a valuable tool, how do you explain the disappointment of the '60s generation?"

"If psychedelics are so great," McKenna responds, "then what's so great about *us*? Are we better than these poor people who have never taken psychedelics? Are we morally better? Are we wiser? Or are we just some kind of screwball cult like Mormons, who congratulate themselves on having achieved this supreme understanding, and yet to everybody else they just look like geeks? And *we* look like geeks. This really is a problem I carry with me, because I've advocated psychedelics my entire life, yet I often see incredible bad behavior and stupidity and cruelty and insensitivity committed by psychedelic people.

"The bottom line of psychedelics is not how good it makes you feel, but how creative you are, and the acceleration of creativity that is taking place is immense, and most cutting-edge phenomena, if you can get off with the people who are responsible for it, they will admit that it began with psychedelics. I mean all cutting-edge science, art, literature, it's driven from those places.

"I really believe our evolutionary past holds the key to our evolutionary future, and drugs and computers are just two ends of a spectrum. The only difference between them is that one is too large to swallow. And our best people are working on that.

"So I really see recovering ancient values through modern technology and a reconstruction of our lifestyles and our relationships to each other. This is how to make the ride to the singularity of the end of time a more pleasant and palatable experience. If you don't do this, the ride to the end of time will proceed at the same rate, but you may lose it.

"It may go from a white-knuckle ride to truly terrifying, because the change that lies ahead is going to require a great deal of flexibility and openmindedness and a willingness to transform in order to take place without generating a megadose of anxiety.

"Anxiety is already rising. Most governments in the world, their entire function is simply to manage catastrophe at this point, because they have no plan, they have no vision, they're utterly clueless. Basically, they're waiting for flying saucers or the Second Coming to somehow cancel the nightmare that their own institutions and methods have made inevitable."

Jesus, I think, what if McKenna wasn't an optimist? And what if he were *not* so charismatic? Would he be just another guy with a long beard, wearing a toga and sandals, walking along the sidewalk and carrying a big signboard to remind us, *The End of the World is Coming! Are You Prepared*? Only, McKenna has a specific day for it.

"The end of the Mayan calendar," he says, "is the same day that I had calculated. Well, this is not a reason for believing my theory, for you, but for *me* it was a reason. Too weird a coincidence. The only thing that I have in common with the Mayan civilization is that we both used psilocybin, and it's almost as though when you purge the virus off your disc, there is at the bottom line and written in assembly code that cannot be expunged, a discard date that says "Abandon this locality before December 21, 2012 A.D.'"

So, kids, be sure to mark that date on your calendar. Circle it in red.

▪▫◼▫▪

On Saturday, before the afternoon session begins, participants make small talk with Terence.

"How'd you like your massage?" someone asks.

"It was cool," he replies. "I mean like I'm right out of the oven. I should just slip into sleep and meditation, but no hardship is too great."

Someone else asks, "What book are you currently reading?"

"I'm reading a book, it's a hoot, *Time Machines* — time travel in physics, metaphysics and science-fiction — by Paul Mayhem. It's published by the American Institute of Physics, so you need not hang your head in the subway."

Another person asks, "How's your web site going?"

"I'm just so damned proud of having hacked it in the first place. The things we're discussing here, if you go there and download, it's all there in high detail, and you can take your time. I think of it — in terms of my intellectual life — it's more who I am than who I am sitting here, because I might forget a reference or skip over something. On the web site, we got it right."

Except that on the web site you can't appreciate McKenna's speech pattern — which he would pronounce *pat.tern*, as though his inner dictionary were separating his syllables, certainly a *shat.tering* experience.

"The great principle that I've tried to enunciate," he tells the group, "is that nature conserves novelty."

Somebody asks, "Is nature conscious?"

"Seems more reasonable to me than the idea that all of this complexity is just for the purpose of you to run around and have a career for a few years, and then it all is given back to chaos. We're not the chance existential witnesses to a cosmic accident, we *are* Hamlet. The play is about *us*. And so our struggles to attain justice and decency among ourselves are not simply a why-not proposition as Camus thought, but in fact somehow the tone of the universal process is cast by human decisions.

"Nature is not mute, nature affirms the conservation of novelty and is incredibly interested in our efforts to make something more of it. The conservation of novelty lays an obligation upon us to preserve what has been achieved and to go beyond it and to make a contribution to it. So if there is an ethic derivative of the psychedelic experience, I think this is it.

"It's really not entirely for our benefit. I think we are like atoms in some enormous process that is taking place. If there are aliens, they don't talk to people in trailer courts, *species* are addressed. Aliens don't talk to individuals, they talk to species. And they don't say things like, 'Be vegetarian,' they say things like, 'Now do language. Now physics.' Ultimately, everything is a mystery. And it's good, after such an exalted, plodding journey toward explanation, to remember that nowhere is it written that higher apes *should* be able to divine cosmic purpose.

"What wants to save itself is biology, and we're simply a kind of specialized cell that can work at high temperatures or can encode data, and so we've been deputized. I'm sure we're as expendable as any other species and as clueless. The problem is that so much novelty will be lost, and the universe doesn't like that. It wants to conserve novelty at all costs. That seems to be more important to it than conserving biology. It will sacrifice biology if necessary to save novelty. Novelty is the top of the value hierarchy, as I see it, and biology, culture, technology, physics — all are simply means to an end."

I remembered the first time I came to Esalen, in 1970, for a workshop with John Lilly. He played a tape loop of one word being repeated continuously, but after a while you would begin to hear other words.

"When faced with repetition," Lilly explained, "your human bio-computer automatically programs in novelty."

At sundown I keep my eyes focused on the precise instant that the sun disappears over the ocean's horizon, and there is a flash of green. I'm sure there's a logical explanation for it, having to do with refraction of color, but until I saw the green flash with my own eyes, I had always thought it was a myth. And, to quote Terence McKenna, "The truth is more important than anybody's opinion or myth or story or hope or fear about how the universe is put together."

Our evening session will be devoted to demonstrating the results of his work on a computerized timewave of novelty in history, which originally developed out of a mathematical analysis of the deep structure of the *I Ching*.

"At this stage in my life," McKenna admits, "I became a burden to my friends and a joy to my enemies because I knew — [*laughing with self-deprecation*] the way they always *do* know — I knew that this was a map of time, and that the history of universe was here, and a helpful person pointed out a passage in Gurdjieff, who to that point I had always written off, but since it supported my delusion— there's a passage which says, in the future there will be a diagram invented which people will simply unroll and look at, and they will understand everything.

"Finally, after I had alarmed a number of people, and my friends were meeting, speaking of intervention — on an *idea*, for God's sake — Ralph Abraham came to me on his own, he wasn't delegated by the interventionists, and said, 'The problem here is that you have an occult diagram. Only you understand it, and only you can interpret it, and therefore it's not very persuasive.'

"Three years passed, and I basically prayed, and then one day I was sitting in my parlor, and I had twisted a fattie — no, I did not abuse an obese person, it means I had smoked some cannabis — and I was thinking about the great unsolved problem, as I always was in those years, and it was just like, *plunk*, and I saw the solution, I saw how to do it, I saw from end to end, from side to side, in a single moment, and here comes a great piece of good news that you should greet with tears of joy streaming down your face — I'm not going to explain it to you.

"I did it, and the result is the timewave which is totally straightforward and makes extremely precise predictions about where novelty should be found in history. What the computer software is allowing us to do is to move around inside it and see any amount of time at any level of magnification. We could look at something as huge as the condensation of the planet, there it is, or we could look at something as small as the Kennedy assassination, or even smaller. We could concentrate into a single minute and say where the novelty was and where the habit was.

"For me, this is sort of the payoff of doing these weekends. In the other parts of the weekend I basically function as the nutty professor. This is so personal that no one has ever tried to steal it. That's how uniquely and wholly and totally mine it is. So if it's malarkey I get all the blame, and if it's true I get all the credit. On a basic level, the cosmology that I'm proposing is this: that the universe should be thought of as a kind of struggle, or competition, between two enormous forces. We'll name them habit and novelty.

"Habit is repetition of pattern already established, it's conservation of traditional values, it's path of least resistance, it's momentum. Novelty is an equally easy concept to grasp. Novelty is what's never been before. Novelty is emergent. Novelty is new. Novelty makes connections where they were never made before.

"And any span of time, a millisecond, a million years, has within it a struggle between habit and novelty and potentially a signature of how that process proceeded. Like a stock market. The shifts between habit and novelty are like the shifts between high and low prices of commodity.

"The good news in all of this is that novelty is winning and novelty will triumph absolutely at a certain future moment in time. Let me lead us into the future here, and all mysteries will be revealed. Isn't this fun? You see, it's not so much whether you believe it, it's that this causes thinking."

And then, as the group gathers in front of a computer, McKenna takes us on a guided tour of novelty in history.

"We're now at six million years, and this is the story of the evolution of the higher primates, and these are solar energy cycles, glaciations, we're still moving in the realm here of large-scale cosmic input... this is a domain of high novelty, a very long period, longer than the time that separates us from Moses... this may be where that partnership paradise occurs, the early influence of psychoactive plants on consciousness... now we're under a million years. And remember, it wouldn't have any of these correlations if the end date were different... this is the last 62,000 years... 42,000 years... this is the mushroom paradise back here... the crucifixion is here... this is the fall of Rome here...

"This is the birth of Muhammad here, this is the consolidation of Islam — 570 to 630, Muhammad's birth and death — the world had never seen anything like Islam. These guys were desert tribes dealing water to each other for millennia at the edge of organized civilization. They were desert barbarians and suddenly one guy, Muhammad, not only founds a world religion but claims the allegiance of 700 million people, and he founds a political order, too. Buddha didn't pull that off, and neither did Christ. There's a book, *The 100*, that seeks to list the hundred most influential people in human history, and number one, Muhammad, built a political and religious and philosophical order that maintained its coherency."

However, novelty is not necessarily a good thing from the human point of view.

"What happened in 1355?" McKenna asks. "Within 18 months, one-third of the population of Earth died — Bubonic Plague — and no one knows how many died in Europe. It's an interesting signature. It certainly is novel to have one-third of the population drop dead." Because McKenna's predictions of the past are in accurate accordance with history, he is able to extrapolate into the future. "I predicted the fall of the Berlin Wall, Tienamen Square, Chernobyl — I predicted all of these things — I didn't say *what* would happen, but I said the day. 'This day will be the most novel day of this year.'"

The journey through time continues.

"This is 1440, Gutenberg invents printing... 1492, Columbus... the American Revolution begins at a symmetry break at the top of a slide into novelty. It succeeds. The French revolution begins at the bottom of a novelty trough on an upturn into habit, and fails... January 1, 1900, symmetry break occurs, and this is the signature of the 20th Century, an almost continuous descent (ascent, in a sense, but depicted in this computerized graph as descent) into novelty from 1900-1905, the special theory of relativity, 1906, flight, radio, World War I, the Russian revolution, Dada, surrealism — it's the 20th Century, for crying out loud — Hitler, bigtime novelty... World War II, culminates with the atomic bomb, the end of the war and the return to normalcy... 1950, invention of the hydrogen bomb.

"For those of you who are true fans of predictive accuracy, the day of the Human Be-In, January 13, 1967, is the day we go over the hump. Isn't it wonderful that it validates — well, but hell, it *was* the symmetry-breaking moment. And then, just after that, the landing on the moon and the cascade into novelty. Saddam invades Kuwait... Tienamen Square, three million, the largest crowd in human history... we're right about here. This is the pause before the storm. This is the most habituated moment that we will know for maybe the rest of time."

Boy, was I exhausted. Talk about your long, strange trips. Maybe it's all really just self-fulfilling prophecy, but you have to admire McKenna, if for nothing else, for just how far out on a limb he is willing to go.

"Hell," he says, "I *live* on a limb."

■ ■ ■ ■ ■

Sunday morning is our final session. Judging by rearranged seating and body language, a couple of new liaisons — this friendship, that romance — have developed over the weekend. Or what's a workshop for?

"I suppose if I were a different kind of personality," McKenna says, "I would haunt the hallways of major universities and try to drag these guys into my theory. But for some reason, I think the timewave itself empowers a certain kind of fatalism, and I just say if I'm right, I'm right, if I'm wrong, I've probably told enough people already.

"It is a remarkable thing for a non-mathematician to have created, and I know how little I knew when I started. If it's true, I really don't think we'll have to wait 'til 2012. If it's true *[and this has become my mantra, in McKenna's voice],* the world is going to get *nut.tier* and *nut.tier* and *nut.tier.* Eventually it will get so nuts that those at the top, in charge of managing all these interlocking systems, will begin to ask, first themselves and then others, 'What is going *on?*'

"It's a done deal, folks. I feel like I am inside an enormous joke. And that to some degree, each of you is too, to the degree that you understand what's going on here, what's *really* going on here. Then all you can do is act with style and a certain panache, and try to carry things forward, keep everybody happy, keep the levels of anxiety under control. It's a huge, huge joke of some sort, and the real belly laugh is beyond the yawning grave, and then you just look back and say, 'Why didn't I *see* it? It was in front of me all the time, and I lived my whole life in anxiety and doubt and frustration.'

"So the kind of laid-back, chilled-out quality of psychedelic people is simply that they've been there, they've done that, and now they're just living without the illusion of history. It is not the eschaton that is the illusion, it is history that is illusion — three-dimensional space, causality, the structures that we allowed our languages and our science and our mathematics to put in place, to delude us over the last several thousand years.

"As we get closer and closer to the eschaton, there's going to be a lot of panic, uncertainty, unhappiness, because everything in the world is going to change, nothing will survive in recognizable form, into the new modality, and this is good news, but it may be taken for bad news.

"And the task of psychedelic people, I think, is to act as midwives for this collective birthing of a new ontos of being that is going to rend the shell of three-dimensional space and time, and create a new level of novelty and organization in the universe, as has happened so many, many times before. But this is the first time that human beings will be witnesses to and participators in the action, at least since the invention of language. So keep your powder dry and your will protected, and I'll see you, if not before, at the end of the world."

I had a suggestion for McKenna. "You could become like the Unabomber, just send psilocybin in the mail to these professors, and insist that the *Washington Post* publish your thesis on the stoned monkeys."

"Good, well, you can be my advance man. Then they'll believe me."

"Oh, right. I have less credibility than you."

▪■█■▪

For all his pursuit of mysticism, Terence McKenna is essentially a scientist. He may have a cult following, but he is not a cult leader in the sense that he *encourages* challenge rather than forbids it.

"A scientist's job," he says, "is to prove that he's *wrong*. You don't get that at the ashram, or up in a monastery — *[mimicking what such a guru would not say]* 'Well, we crushed *that* hypothesis to smithereens.'"

So, naturally, I had some follow-up questions for him, in person and by e-mail.

Q. "I would feel incomplete if I didn't ask for your comment on the recent news story about the Heaven's Gate cult."

A. *"Like most people, I haven't sorted out the San Diego mass suicide. I imagine that on the mainland, the soul-searching and efforts to determine everyone's collective guilt and complicity are in full cry. But from the slopes of Mauna Loa it looks like simply the latest Southern California Psychodrama with attendant obligatory media jack-off. I encountered Do (then Bo) and Peep in 1972. They were contemptible, power-crazed New Age creepoids then, and apparently things didn't get better."*

Q. "During the workshop at Esalen, you talked about not knowing where the mind is. Do you think that the mind can function without the brain?"

A. *"I have not made up my mind on this but think of the mind as a hyperspacially deployed organ that is ordinarily invisible. As to whether or not it can exist independent of the brain, I am not sure. If the physical world is conceived as a 4-d manifold, it is logically impossible for a physical thing, a 4-d solid, to move or otherwise change. It must be our state of consciousness which changes as we become successively aware of adjacent cross-*

sections of the 4-d manifold. But this makes sense only if we, the observers, are not in space-time. This would imply that our minds exist on a level beyond anything that physics can tell us about."

Q. "You also mentioned how, post-eschaton, we'll look back from the grave and laugh at the futility with which we struggled through life. Were you implying that you believe individual consciousness can survive after physical death?"

A. *"Not really, only that life will show its pattern and plan when we look back on it, and that will redeem some of the weirdness of having to live it essentially without a clue."*

Q. "You mentioned in the workshop, in terms of the coming apocalypse, that people should do things fast. Now, I thought that doing things fast was one of the problems that brought us to this place, and that the antidote would be to slow down and savor the implications of what we do. Maybe you and I are saying the same thing?"

A. *"Well, I didn't really mean do more and more things, I said more and more will happen. I think the thing to do is to eliminate foolishness, having your time vampirized. I agree with you the goal is not to just jam in as much stuff as possible. Basically, one strong motivation for moving to Hawaii was just to escape the silliness, the triviality, of it all, and I've discovered there was apparently no information loss. I can keep up with an O. J. (Simpson) discussion even though I only spent three minutes a week keeping track. The people who watched every day of the testimony, my God, they must be slow learners. And it's amazing how many fields you can participate in as a fully empowered player without investing much time.*

"As pleasant as it is, I can't hold the whole thing in my mind in the states, as we citizens of the sovereign state of Hawaii refer to your country. I just feel like I've been parachuted behind enemy lines, and this is no time for philosophy, let's blow up the damn bridge and get out of here. But in Hawaii I can look at it all and see trends and tendencies and pontificate about it in my rainforest, and it all makes sense. Somebody said,

'Yeah, well, it all makes sense because you never talk to anybody else.' Probably some truth to that."

Q. "At Esalen you stated: 'The technological push that has seemed so relentless and so brutal and so difficult to deflect is, in fact, we are doing the right thing, and the only question is whether we'll make it in time, and it looks like it's going to be a flash photo finish. We basically have until 2012 to figure out how to download all human DNA and other forms of DNA on this planet into some kind of indestructible storage mode. Then there's a chance to ride out this catastrophic wave of extinction.'

"Now, my question is, in view of the recent news which has placed human cloning on the border between science-fiction and reality, might not cloning be an answer to the question posed by your statement? How does cloning fit into your theory of the need to prepare ourselves for the apocalypse?"

A. *"In spite of the cloning of Dolly, we still have a great deal to learn about DNA. What was remarkable about the Dolly episode was how far the research team got without really understanding why they were succeeding. There is still a great deal to understand about the cloning process and how it works. Which does not mean that it will not be applied before it is fully understood. But at this point, it is a kind of stunt. Clones are simply people with a strange family history, and who among us does not fit that description?*

"The interesting thing about the recent cloning news, both regarding Dolly the ewe and the two cloned monkeys, is that both fated births occurred right around the same time, July/August 1996. That was a time that my timewave had long predicted would be a period when there would be some enormous scientific breakthrough.

"I was very excited, therefore, by the announcement, at the time, of the discovery of microfossils in a Martian meteorite. Now with the news of the clones I am more convinced than ever that my prediction of a period of novelty and scientific breakthrough was correct. As for the clones themselves, I am reminded of Brave New World, *Aldous Huxley's dystopia of*

clueless clones. More scary than 1984, that is for sure. And more likely, long run. So corporate, so elegant."

Q. "What are your visions of alternative scenarios that are upcoming, either in December of 2012 or before?"

A. *"Well, I've spent a lot of time thinking about this, although I realized about a year ago that, in a sense, it's not really my issue. The funny thing is, here I have this wave, it predicts every second between here and December 21, 2012, I show it to people and their first question is, 'So what happens afterwards?' It doesn't address that. It addresses all moments* before *that. Nevertheless, I feel the force of the question, and I've created a series of scenarios in ascending weirdness which answer the question.*

"A low weirdness answer would be, suddenly everyone begins to behave appropriately. This is kind of a Buddhist, Taoist approach. Now, the interesting thing about that scenario is, the first 30 seconds of that we can predict — appropriate behavior would probably be to take your foot off your neighbor's neck. Step back from what you're doing.

"And then I always imagine — for some reason, I don't know why — that everybody would take off their clothes and go outside. But after that I can't figure *— that's only the first 30 seconds of appropriate behavior. If you change the context of reality so radically that predicting what would be appropriate in the next 30 seconds is impossible, and so we would just dissolve into appropriate behavior. Since we've never had that, we can' t imagine what it would be like.*

"Then there's the transformation of physics scenario, which basically says, 'All boundaries dissolve.' What that would probably be like, the first hour of it would be like a thousand micrograms of LSD. After that we can't imagine or predict, because again it would have so totally changed the context that you could no longer predict it.

"Then there are the catastrophic scenarios that revolve around the question, 'Death, where is thy sting?' And probably the most efficient of those is the planetesimal impact scenario. A

very large object strikes the earth and kills everybody, and that's that."

Q. "A blunt object?"

A. *"It's a blunt solution. Sort of in that same category is the blue star in Sagittarius. And then a kind of intermediate between those two — the sun will explode. That would certainly clear the disc and fulfill the whole thing. The planet vaporizes, and collectively we and all life on earth move into the shimmering capsules of the post-mortem realm, whatever that is. Novel, novel.*

"When I worked with the timewave, I argued strenuously that it reflects all ebb and flow of novelty, but somebody will come up with something like the release of the 'Sergeant Pepper' album or the O.J. Simpson trial, and then we see that it's lost in the noise. What the wave seems most pristinely to predict, or what parallels the wave most closely, is the evolution of technology, and I think technology is something that we haven't really understood. In a sense, technology is the alchemical journey for the condensation of the soul and the union of spirit and matter in some kind of hyper object.

"The rise of the World Wide Web has been a great boost to my fantasies along these lines because now I can see with the web from here to the eschaton. Apparently it's a technology for dissolving space, time, personality, and just releasing everybody into a data stream, something like the imagination. Then that's why the ultimate technological fantasy along this line of thought is what is conventionally called a time machine.

"There's an interesting aspect to the time machine. The wave describes the ebb and flow of novelty in time, but then you reach a point where it's so novel that it fails beyond that point. Well, a time-traveling technology would cause such a system to fail, because it's a description of the unfolding seriality of linear events, which a time machine would disrupt.

"So it may be that it isn't the explosion of the sun, or the coming of the aliens, or the descent of the second person of the Trinity, it's simply that a technology is put into place that destroys linear time and, from thence forward, when you give

your address you have to say not only where but when. There are some problems with this.

"And then here is a slightly more interesting and woo-woo scenario. The thing that's always held out against time travel, especially time travel into the past, is what's called the grandfather paradox — somebody pointed out it's not called the father paradox because apparently you want to avoid an Oedipal situation — and it's simply the following objection: If you could travel into the past you could kill your grandfather. If you killed your grandfather you wouldn't exist. Therefore you couldn't travel into the past. Therefore time travel is impossible.

"One idea I have for an end-of-history scenario: Time travel becomes more and more discussable, finally there are laboratories working on it, finally there is a prototype machine, finally it's possible to conceive of a test, and so on the morning of December 21, 2012, at the World Temporal Institute headquarters in the Amazon Basin, by a worldwide, high-definition, three-dimensional hook-up, the entire world tunes in to see the first flight into time. And the lady temponaut comes to the microphone and makes a few brief statements, hands are shaken, the champagne (bottle) is smashed, she climbs into her time machine, pushes the button and disappears into the far-flung reaches of the future.

"Now, the interesting question is, what happens next? And I already established for myself that you can travel backward into the past, but you can't travel further into the past than the invention of the first time machine, for the simple reason that there are no time machines before that, and if you were to take one where there are none you get another paradox.

"So what happens when the lady temponaut slips into the future? Well, I think what would happen a millisecond later is tens of thousands of time machines would arrive from all points in the future, having come back through time, of course, to witness the first flight into time. Exactly as if you could fly your Beechcraft back to Kitty Hawk, North Carolina to that windy morning when the Wright brothers rolled their flier out and

fueled 'er up. And that's as far as the road goes. That's the end of the time road.

"But the grandfather paradox persists. One of those time travelers from 5,000 years in the future, on their way back to the first time travel incident, could stop and kill their grandfather, and then we have this whole problem all over again. So I thought about this for a long time, and I think I've found my way around it. But as usual, at the cost of further weirdness.

"Here's what would really happen if we invented a time machine of that sort. The lady temponaut pushes the button, and instead of all time machines appearing instantly in the next moment, in order to preserve the system from that paradox, what will happen is the rest of the history of the universe will occur instantly. And so that's it. I call it the God whistle.

"This is because you thought you were building a time machine, and in a sense you were, but the time machine isn't what you thought it was. It caused the rest of time to happen instantaneously, and so the furthest out developments of life, matter and technology in the universe come right up against you a millisecond after you break that barrier, and in fact you discover that traveling time is not traveling time, it's a doorway into eternity, which is all of time, and that's why it becomes more like a hyperspatial deal than a simple linear time travel thing.

"There's been a parallel development which has caused me to feel even more confident. We're now beginning to build this parallel world called the World Wide Web. And you can bet that long before we reach 2012, the major religions of the world will build virtual realities of their eschatological scenarios. There will be the Islamic paradise, the Christian millennium, the Buddhist chunyata — these will be channels that you tune into to see if you like it and want to join, so in a sense guaranteeing we will have a virtual singularity.

"It's all very well to try and understand the end point, but recall that where we are relative to the end point is in resonance with the year 950 A.D. We're like the people in 950

A.D. trying to understand the World Wide Web, the hydrogen bomb and the cat scanner. How can we? My God, we don't even have calculus yet. Newton hasn't been born yet, let alone Einstein. I mean we're running around — essentially we're primitives *is what I'm saying. We don't have tools yet to conceive of the object of 2012. We must build those tools between now and then. And good places to start are with the World Wide Web, psychedelic drugs, whatever is most cutting edge, and most far out."*

Q. "So that saying, 'May you live in interesting times,' is supposed to have been a Chinese curse, but if the ruling class had control of the language, it was a curse to *them*, but it was a blessing to the people who *made* it interesting times."

A. *"I think it's saying the same thing as the Irish toast* (heavy brogue): *'May you be alive at the end of the world.'"*

Q. "Meanwhile, my Chinese fortune cookie predicted that you and I will cross paths again, and also that I will enjoy another Chinese repast soon."

A. *"We must meet in a Chinese restaurant and save the oracle unnecessary embarrassment."*

Epilogue:

Jan Kerouac had met her father only twice. The first time she was nine. The second time, six years later, he sat drinking a fifth of whiskey and watching *The Beverly Hillbillies*. Jan died of kidney failure at the age of 44, never having fulfilled her fantasy of becoming *"drinking buddies"* with her father, who died when she was a teenager.

As for my psilocybin bust, I was lucky. With the aid of a terrific attorney, Doron Weinberg, I got off with a $100 fine and nothing on my permanent record. But I finally understood what that cop had meant when he snarled, "So you like mushrooms, huh?" What was his *actual* message? Back through eons of ancestors — all the way back to those *un*stoned apes — this cop was continuing a never-ending attempt to maintain the status quo. He had unintentionally revealed the true nature of the threat he perceived. What he had really said to me was, "So you like the evolution of human consciousness, huh?"

Well, yeah, now that you mention it, I do. I mean, when you put it like that — *So you like the evolution of human consciousness, huh?* — sure, I do. I like it a whole lot.

The Neo-Pagan Festival

As an investigative satirist, I rarely work the comedy club circuit, but rather, I tend to appear at more offbeat venues.

In the summer of 1997, I performed at the 17th annual Starwood Neo-Pagan Festival in Sherman, New York, Amish country on the border near Ohio and Pennsylvania. This event — a female-oriented subcultural celebration of the sensual and the spiritual — took place on private campgrounds, where clothing was optional. Many women were bare-breasted, and several men and women walked around fully naked, a practice known as the "sky clad" experience.

Instead of camping out, I stayed at a nearby bed-and-breakfast place. It was run by a Christian family, and there were crucifixes and angels on the walls of my room. I would sneak up to the attic whenever I wanted to smoke a joint. Downstairs in the living room, I asked a woman — assuming that she was the proprietor — where the key would be left if I came back late at night.

"I don't know," she replied. "I'm here for the festival."

"Oh. In what capacity?"

"I'm in the craft."

"Witchcraft?"

"That's right," she said.

And, indeed, a positive perspective on witchcraft was one of the themes at the Neo-Pagan Festival, along with such workshops as "Privacy Rights and Drug Policy," "Cultivating Consciousness in

Your Child," "Live Meditations in Drumming and Dance," "The Supreme Court and the Free Exercise of Religion," "A Procession to Honor the Earth Goddess," "Safer Sex," and "Dark Ecstasy: The Ritual Use of Pleasure, Pain and Sensory Deprivation as Psychedelic Experience."

When I walked on the outdoor stage, my opening line was: "I'm gonna start with two words that have been *thought* year after year at these festivals, but which have never actually been uttered out loud, and those two words are, 'Nice tits.'"

The audience hesitated a nano-second, because in that context this could be a politically incorrect observation — I had deliberately taken that chance — but then they laughed and applauded, because they knew it was true.

I was invited back to perform at Starwood again in the summer of 1998. The previous month, two Amish men here had been arrested for distributing cocaine they bought from a biker gang, the Pagans, one of whose members was a police informer.

The two men were from a particularly conservative Amish sect, where not only electricity and tractors were forbidden, but even zippers. Did those tempting zippers on the Pagans' leather motorcycle jackets serve as a gateway drug to cocaine?

Speaking of illegal drugs, at the festival, I came across the only individual I've ever known who has actually hallucinated on toad slime. I pictured him as a young lad with a tadpole in his pocket — right out of a Norman Rockwell painting — and now as a grown man with a frog in his pocket.

I also met Reverend Ivan Stang, leader of the infamous Church of the SubGenius. He talked about "how to milk the Internet for all it's worth, and get away with murder, before the Conspiracy figures out how to spoil it for us."

But Stang was deep in embarrassment mode, since this was only a couple of weeks after the failure of his widely circulated prediction that, on July 5th at 7 a.m., Pleasure Saucers would descend to Earth as part of the great "Rupture," and take away all those SubGeniuses who had paid $30 for the privilege.

The highlight of the festival was a 25-foot-high bonfire, around which neo-pagans danced and pranced and cavorted late into the night. My own personal highlight was when a beautiful woman approached me. She was in the process of transforming her breasts from fetish to functional by nursing a baby that had been conceived there the year before.

During that festival, she had walked in on my performance at the precise moment that I uttered the words, "Nice tits." She assumed that I was referring specifically to her, and was flattered, so now I didn't have the heart to disillusion her.

I hope she doesn't read this.

A Survey of Drug Comedy in the '90s

Okay, let's start with television. Except for the old Cheech and Chong movies, or maybe a sitcom rerun like the hash-brownie episode of *Barney Miller*, there's hardly any humor about drugs for couch-potato-heads. But it's usually a matter of self-censorship. Certainly, when I was a guest on *Late Night* with Conan O'Brien, my pro-pot reference was greeted with applause by the audience.

If dope is in the news and jokeworthy, Jay Leno is likely to go there, as he did in a *Tonight Show* monologue: "The Santa Clara County Cannabis Club announced that it is looking for an experienced marijuana grower who meets government requirements. They want to grow marijuana for the government. How do you prove you're qualified for the job? Show up late covered in Cheetos dust? How does that work? Fall asleep? Say 'Willie Nelson and Keith Richards are my references?'"

Similarly, on *Late Show* with David Letterman, a drug reference can occasionally find itself included in the Top Ten list. When the subject happened to be, "If a college student could be elected president of the United States," one possible consequence was "Federal disaster aid for severe attack of the munchies."

On the ever-popular *Seinfeld*, the subject of psychedelics is as rare as the presence of an African-American, although LSD was mentioned once in a throwaway line when Kramer — suddenly noticing an elderly man who had passed out on the couch —

muttered to Jerry and Elaine, "He must've dropped acid when you weren't looking."

Dennis Miller often peppers his opening rants with drug metaphors. Example: "Your mother pushes buttons like a peyote dealer working straight commission."

On *Politically Incorrect*, host Bill Maher *and* his guests (such as Timothy Leary, Michelle Phillips and Robert Anton Wilson) have been able to play with the funny side of dope. With a veteran stand-up comic's timing, Maher can spout a cute one-liner — "I just quit smoking... crack" — but he has also taken the following principled, electronically public position, with a keen sense of wit, in praise of certain illegal drugs.

"Why is Halcyon — which is banned in most countries and which caused one of our presidents to throw up on a Japanese prime minister — why is *that* drug and Valium and liquor legal, but not marijuana or mushrooms? Why did God make so many different kinds of mushrooms, and then one kind that's *really* different? I mean, when one species of mushroom is perfect for a cream sauce, and another for an omelette, and then there's one that makes you laugh for eight straight hours — that doesn't seem random to me. I believe God wanted us to laugh for eight straight hours sometimes, because God knows life sucks.

"In the Bible, Job says to God, 'God, why is there suffering? Can't you take away misery?' And God says, 'No. Of course not, don't be silly. If I took away misery, no one would talk to me. But here's what I'll do. I'll give you drugs.' This, of course, is a paraphrasing of God's sentiments — which I read in the *New Yorker*. Nevertheless, God did make a rather perfect world, and it seems positively sacrilegious to question His hand in the creation of any form of life, including herbs that induce giddiness as well as insight and creativity.... It's true that the most interesting place you can ever travel is inside your own head, then some people just never leave home."

But, let's face it, such honesty was an exceedingly rare moment on TV. Another such moment occurred, however, when prolific craftsman George Carlin, during an epilog to his HBO special, told fellow comedian Jon Stewart that smoking pot really helps him to fine-tune his material. Carlin's vintage monologue on how to roll a joint was an extremely funny bit, and he obviously continues to follow his own creative instructions.

"One hit is all I need now," he said. "One hit and it's punch-up time."

Richard Pryor is a living legend — his description of setting himself on fire while free-basing remains a classic of confessional comedy — whereas Bill Hicks, Sam Kinison and Lotus Weinstock, all outspoken performers who died too young, have joined Lenny Bruce on stage at that great comedy club in the sky, The Last Laugh.

Lenny was, of course, the World Heavyweight Champion of drug humor, partly because he got arrested so often. Since he would always share the embellishment of his personal experiences with audiences, it was only natural that he would satirize the inhumanity of drug law enforcement.

Probably the most drug-positive comic working today is Rick Overton, who deals with politics, conspiracy and the environment. His own agent told him that he's "too intelligent for colleges."

He tells a long involved story about the time he and fellow comic Rich Hall were both turning 40 and decided to go where they could have their midlife freakout in style, so they went to Amsterdam—"a Euro-Disney for adults" — and enjoyed a Cannabis Cup for two. He describes cops walking around like pro-wrestling referees, because they have nothing to do. "Hey, what are you doing there? Oh, smoking dope. Very good. Welcome to Amsterdam. Enjoy your dope." The cop sees something with his peripheral vision: "What is this on the other side of me? Oh, a blow job in the window. Welcome to Amsterdam, young lovers, good luck with your scheme."

They go to the Bulldog Cafe, which "not only serves coffee, liquor, sweets, but you can flick the menu over and there's the special menu on the other side. You can see this is a rosy, piquant, but unpretentious hashish. 'Well, I'll have a brick of that, my good man.' And of course they actually produced a brick of it. This moment transcended my vocabulary. I didn't know what to say. I held it, I smelled it, and then I just started crying like Miss America, holding it like a bouquet."

He gets philosophical: "Amsterdam has it figured out. There's no drug problem there because they don't call it a drug *problem*. It's not a crime problem because they don't call it a *crime*. Being human shouldn't be a crime. Certain drugs, yeah, they make them illegal, but the ones that shouldn't be called drugs they *don't* call drugs, and everyone just levels off, and there's no violent crime over there because everyone's just too busy having fun." But then he winds up — with hysterical physical humor — trying to smuggle through Customs a brick of hash hidden up his rectum.

But Overton is an exception. Stand-up comics these days hardly ever perform extended doper routines, but they do manage to get in an occasional zinger. Some samples:

Frazer Smith: "Clinton still has his bad leg. I bet he's in favor of medical marijuana now. "Doc, it's my trick knee. How about a bong load?'"

Nora Dunn: "Did you see Janet Reno? It's just ludicrous. She's on TV about how they're gonna fight this use of pot for relieving pain, and I'm not sure she doesn't use pot, but whoever cuts her hair does."

Jack Coen: "Jerry Garcia died of a heart attack in a drug rehab center. I guess the message is, when you do drugs for 35 years, don't stop. Apparently, it's bad for your heart."

Bill Bronner: "I remember when my daughter was around 12, she was head of her 'Just Say No' group. We drove to Lake Tahoe and she cried on the way up there begging me not to smoke pot."

Kathy Ladman: "My very first acid trip in college, I took blotter acid, and as soon as I dropped it, felt guilty, and I *literally* had a guilt trip. Every person I ran into that night, I said, 'Do you hate me? Have I done anything wrong?' — the entire night — and I think that would've been a better trip if it was legal."

Argus Hamilton: "Paul McCartney says that it's wrong to make criminals out of people who smoke pot. The problem is, pot is a gateway drug. One day you're not inhaling, the next day you're violating campaign finance laws."

Jonathan Pekar: "Pot's gonna be legal pretty soon. I mean it's just gotta be. It'll be legal soon and then there'll be a two-joint minimum here [the Comedy Store]. I guarantee it. It won't take management long to put two and two together, but it's pretty scary, though. You think, if they're charging ten bucks for a drink, what are they gonna charge for a joint?"

▪▫█▫▪

Drug humor is most likely to be heard on the alternative comedy scene, which has been erupting at offbeat venues — book stores, coffee houses, art galleries, and even (as with Jeannine Frank's Parlor Performances) people's living rooms.

Comedians talk about what's been going on in their own lives, occasionally referring to notes sitting on the stool that a stand-up comic would ordinarily sit on, sometimes resorting to their usual programmed schtick or trying out new material, often hoping to get those six magic minutes on a TV talk show that could lead to a sitcom deal and movie career, but always surrendering to that existential moment of trying to make *this* audience laugh *now*.

Beth Lapides is the mother of alternative comedy. Conception took place in 1990 at the Women's Building in downtown Los Angeles, where she was performing her one-person show, *Global Mania*. The audience (all women except for three men) responded with unusual enthusiasm, starved for what they couldn't get at comedy clubs — material which didn't reek of mysogyny and homophobia. Lapides promised she would come back with a different kind of entertainment—"the UnCabaret" — thus naming her offspring-to-be. But the Women's Building lost its funding, and in 1991 her concept was born instead at Highways, a performance art space in Santa Monica. Lapides had been doing a joke in her act about running for First Lady: "It's such an important job. And how does she get it? Sleeping with the president." Then it occurred to her that "it would be a lot better to actually run than to just keep saying this joke. To do a sort of joke in action." She started researching First Ladies, and in 1992 the UnCabaret went on hold so that she could conduct her campaign. "It's a full-disclosure campaign. I've smoked pot, not just to try it, but because I *liked* it. I inhaled, I exhaled, I used my entire respiratory system." Everyone wanted to know if she had a good recipe for chocolate chip cookies, but it was a moot point, because Hillary got the job.

In 1993, the UnCabaret opened for a three-week run at Luna Park, a Hollywood night spot, and has been there every week since — becoming, as Lapides says, "The *Gilligan's Island* of comedy shows." Julia Sweeney, who played the androgynous "Pat" as well as other characters on *Saturday Night Live*, had never before performed as herself, but the true, tragicomic family stories she told at the UnCabaret evolved into her highly praised theater piece, *God Said Ha!*

On the other hand, Bob Goldthwait has *maintained* his blustery character; at the UnCabaret one night, he strained and stammered, "My PTA was looking for fundraising ideas, so I said, 'Hey, let's sell crack! Not to *our* kids, but there's a public school down the street.'"

Lapides serves as host at the UnCabaret, and does her own rap before the introductions. Her advice about having marijuana in a car: "Our current dealer says if you put the pot in an envelope as if it's being sent somewhere, the cops can't open it." [Her husband-producer, Gregory Miller, from an offstage microphone: "I don't think it's the sending, I think it's a sealed envelope."] "Oh, really? A *sealed* envelope. But I thought it was a pre-addressed envelope, like responding to *The Nation* subscription service." [Miller: "*The Nation* envelopes, they'd open."] "Yeah, they do open *The Nation*, but maybe like — definitely not *High Times*, don't put it in a *High Times* subscription, put it in *The Republican National Party Convention* envelope, then you're safe.

"I love the pot. I don't love *buying* the pot, though. I'm not a pot buyer. I send other people to do that. Every now and then a little diva behavior comes in. 'I can't be buying it, uh-uh, I don't know anything about the buying.' Which is so funny because when I lived in New York, I had no problem going to 14th Street and handing my money over to a hole in the wall. There was no problem with that for me, but now that I live in L.A., 'Ooh, how did *this* get here? I don't even know.'"

"We have very special joint rolling albums. And they're all old. For some reason, no new albums. I guess there *are* no new albums.

There's no joint rolling CDs. Gotta buy the old albums. Hot Rocks is one of our big ones, even though he totally did no drugs, so it's ironic, which adds a special little twist. Electric Lady Land is another one of our big ones. Every now and then I roll one on Court and Spark, just for a crazy thrill."

While others are performing, Lapides remains at an offstage microphone, so that she can ask questions or make comments. And now, ladies and gentlemen, here for your stoned pleasure is a montage of dope humor brought to you directly from some very special Sunday nights — three of their annual Drug Show presentations — at the UnCabaret.

Andy Kindler: Lapides introduces him by mentioning, "We were on the road, and Andy made a pipe out of an apple," so Kindler, a truly fearless performer, begins by parodying the way comedians' drug stories, if told at all, are almost always in past-tense nostalgic form: "That was before the projects I have going on *now*, which I wouldn't wanna jeopardize. I wanna keep my mind *straight* now, those are the *old* days, so if there's any industry people in the room..." Then he proceeds to be himself. "In my first year of college I worked in a day camp, and I thought, 'It's 3 o'clock in the morning. If I do the organic mescaline *now*, I should be down in time to go to day camp and be in charge of the kids. Should be no problem.' And it was the day that we were taking the kids to the top of the Empire State Building. How's everybody handling that?

"All I remember is, at 9 in the morning I'm with the kids, just laughing hysterically, and the kids are like tied into my energy— they're laughing, I remember that, and then I black out — the next thing I remember I'm on the top of the Empire State Building and four hours have gone by. 'How many kids do I have, six, seven, eight, who's missing?' I took the organic mescaline, I don't know where Jimmy went, but I'm sorry about that."

Greg Behrendt: "My first friend who was a homosexual came out when we were in college. I went to my first gay club with him on ecstasy — I think that's the way you should go if you're gonna go and you're straight — you figure, I'm a little uptight and then you take some ecstasy and you're not that uptight any more. In fact, you don't even mind getting a few phone numbers from fellas. 'Well, what the hell, yeah, it's fine, thank you very much. Well, you have nice hair too. I probably won't *call* you, though, but thank you. Want mine?'"

Henriette Mantel: "The first time I ever smoked pot, with my friend, Katie, who's a shrink now, we hooked up this electric water pipe, and we did it every day for two weeks, and we took notes while we were smoking pot, because we were gonna write this paper on it for school. So we would take notes, how I was feeling, what I was going through, the spacey thing I was feeling, the stoplights — I was stopping like 20 feet on the wrong side of 'em — we totally wrote it out. And then when she got busted for coke a couple of years later, the cops took the notes as evidence."

Mark Ebner: "In New Orleans, Louisiana, I got a job as a barker on Bourbon Street in a place called the Hotsy Totsy. 'Live nude girls! Live nude girls! 100% female entertainment live on stage, gentlemen! Take a looky-looky at all that nookie! Have a drink and see some pink! Oh, we got the pretty little ladies here, guys! Put a rise in your Levi's! One whiff it'll make it stiff!' And I'd bark all night long, ten hours a night, ten bucks a shift, and all the tips I could muster from some of those dancing girls. Drugs kind of crept back into my life at this point to take the edge off all those mint juleps and hurricanes.

"I needed another job to support my habit. The only marketable skill I really had was ranting, so I got the same job on Royal Street, to bark in front of a restaurant. 'Dinner time, dinner time, dinner time, it's seafood time, courtyard dining here! We got the oysters, we got the jambalaya, we got the shrimp creole, we got it all here! Get an ice cold beer here!' One night, during the Mardi Gras festival, I did a shitload of acid, and motherfucker, I forgot where I was. And I'm standing out there, and I'm going, 'Yeah, we got the *pussy* here!' And I'm barking there for pussy in front of a fine gourmet restaurant."

Julia Sweeney: "A year ago I had a hysterectomy, and then I had to go through nine weeks of radiation. There was this one phase of the radiation that was really horrible — they had to show you the room the week before so that you could emotionally prepare yourself for it — and I actually burst into tears when I saw it, which is amazing to me because I have no emotional reaction in the moment for anything. It always takes me like a year and then I go '*What?*'

"Anyway, there was a table and this dildo of radiation, this thing that you had to scoot onto and up to, and then they had to leave the room and radiate you, and then they came in, in big outfits with like a Geiger counter to see if you had enough radiation to go into the real world. So I went into the doctor's the next day, and they said, 'We understand this might be very upsetting, and we have ways to help you with this. You have a choice. You can either have an IV of valium, or we can send a wonderful woman in and she can give you visualization exercises.'"

David Cross: "I always write notes to myself before I trip. I plot it out, and I leave little surprises for myself, shit like that. I remember one time, I was kinda in the process of breaking up with this girlfriend, and I had gone around the apartment in all these places, writing, *Don't call Faith. Don't call Faith. Don't call Faith.* On my money: *Whatever you do, don't call Faith.* And then it's like, 'Oh, I should call (*snapping his fingers as he remembers his own warning*) — right!' And then you become two different people, where you're tripping and you respect your non-tripping self, where you're saying, 'Don't call Faith, it's set, I wrote that.' Then I wrote, *I really gotta respect what I thought before.*"

Merrill Markoe: "I sent my friend out to get some marijuana — I think I was 15 — and he got some and he got us an empty house in which to smoke it, but he forgot to get rolling papers. But that didn't stop us. He went ahead and he rolled us a nice joint the size of a stuffed cabbage, in toilet paper. So we lit it up, and it went right on fire — cascading embers were burning right down into the carpet — and it set a nice little chunk of this shag carpet on fire. We stomped it out and then we spent the next hour cutting pieces of the carpet off with a manicure scissors."

Dana Gould: "Cocaine in the '80s in comedy clubs was what blow jobs were to Caligula's court. It was what you did when you punched-in in the morning. I remember working at the Punchline in Atlanta, 1987, and afterwards you'd go back and they'd go, 'How do you wanna get paid, white or green?' People would get *paid* in cocaine, that's how fucked up it was. And now all those people are straight and in the (12-step) program, and they're more fuckin' annoying than they were when they were dopers.

"Every person I know in the program — and that's basically every person I know — they all assume that you have the same lack of restraint that they do. Like, 'What are you doing today?' 'Oh, I think I'm going to the movies.' 'Okay, just fuckin' be careful with that shit. You go to the movies today, man, and in three months your family won't talk to you and you're selling your stereo trying to get matinee tickets.'"

Taylor Negron: "When I started out in show business, I got involved with these comedy people, and a lot of them did cocaine, which I never did. Robin Williams was a good friend of mine at the Comedy Store, and Robin was completely out of control on coke. He was a coke *fiend*, and he used to hang out with all these Euro-Indo-Hippie-Pakistani jet set people, and they were all called like Uva and Hercules and Oleo and Klemglah and Corinthea and Tibo, and they were always around giving him cocaine.

"So we had a party at my apartment in Hollywood, and Robin lost his vial of cocaine somewhere in my furniture, and he totally went maniacal and took all my furniture outside of the apartment and put it in the hallway, found the vial of cocaine, and left with Hercules, Uva, Corinthea, Libo, Kibo and Dada. And there it was, 4:30 in the morning, and there wasn't anything in my house, it was all in the hallway."

Ellen Cleghorne: "Thank you for inviting me to your drug show. I just knew there was gonna be some free drugs. Right? Is it after the show or what? Well, of course, I'm black, I don't get the free drugs. See, I was so high all my life that I never knew I was black, I always thought I was like a 5' 5" blond girl. I came out to L.A., I got sober, I was like, 'Oh, my God, this is me, and who the fuck is *that* in the mirror? Not *me*. I don't know who the fuck it *is*. So it's very sobering, this blackness. Well, when I get high, I'm gonna be looking just like you.

"I have a daughter, she's 12." (Lapides asks, "What do you tell her about drugs? Do you tell her not to take them?") "Well, after she *finds* my drugs, I tell her not to take them, and to buy her own. 'Bitch, you got money!' The school has indoctrinated them so much. They teach the kids, you know, the war on drugs. And my daughter walks around making posters about no drugs, with the X in the (circle) thing. 'Mommy, what do you think I should do for ecology and the war on drugs?' I go in my room, get some of my pot, just smoke and think about it.

"My daughter is on drugs. They give her Ritalin. I wish somebody would've given *me* some Ritalin or something when I was a kid. I was a terror! All that fuckin' and carrying on, but with a little Ritalin I would've sat my ass down, I'd be president right now."

Patton Oswalt: "Drugs don't give you revelations, they lower your revelation threshold so that *everything* becomes a revelation. If you're walking around straight, you gotta wait your whole life for the epiphany to hit you, and when it does, you get a fleeting glimpse, that's it. But if you're taking acid, you can glance at a bowl of Lucky Charms and, 'Oh, that's *it* — it's so fucking clear! Get the camera! Don't touch the bowl!'

"A friend of mine, a comedian, he was out of his mind on some kind of window pane, and he goes, 'This is the whole subtext behind Lucky Charms. If you look into a bowl of Lucky Charms you will notice that the little crunchy marshmallow things that are sugary and they're bad for you, those are shaped like little diamonds and horseshoes and clovers, traditional pagan symbols Now if you look at the little crunchy wheat things with all the vitamins and minerals and they don't taste too good, those are shaped like little crosses and little fishes, that's the Ichto symbol that the Greeks drew over their doors to signify they were Christians so the Romans wouldn't slaughter 'em. So what Lucky Charms is saying is that the path to paganism may be sweet in the moment, but it'll eventually give you tooth decay. And the road to Christianity might not be too much fun right now, but it'll keep you regular, man.'"

Jackie Beat (a drag queen who performs as himself only at the UnCabaret): "Am I the only person here who will endure the most amazing dental pain to save the drugs for later? 'Oh, my God, it so fucking hurts!' And my friend says, 'Take one of the pills.' And I'm like, 'Are you crazy? I'm gonna wash those down two months from now with some vodka.'"

Judy Toll: "Ludes are the greatest thing for me because I'm so hyper, and they make me like a little less hyper but still really very active. What's better for an overweight girl who's never had sex to take a drug that makes you really, really horny? So I did, and I thought they were God's gift to the world. There was this quack doctor downtown, and that's how you could get your prescription for ludes. 'Hi, doctor, I'm just so anxious. I can't seem to relax. I mean, well, *I* can relax but my muscles can't relax.'

"Well, one day I came home, and my mother was crying. 'I was cleaning your room, and I picked up your pillow, and it rattled.' *'Give them back*!' 'We need you to see a psychologist.' 'I will if you give me them back!' And the psychologist made me promise, she said, 'No quaaludes at your prom, okay?' I don't really think I stuck to the promise, because when I came to, I was on my knees, unzipping a guy's pants, with a crowd standing around me, chanting, *'Go! Go! Go!'* And that is unseemly behavior for the chairman of the decorations committee.

"I should tell you about the Scientology drug rundown that they do. I had to make a list of all the drugs I'd done." (Lapides warns her, "Tell them you're out now, people might be afraid you're still in.") "Oh, please, not only am I out, I got all my *money* back!" (*Applause and cheers*) "Thank you. Oh, I am such an enemy of the church. I'm like one of the top Suppressive People. Anyway, this is what the drug rundown consists of. L. Ron Hubbard must've spent *hours* coming up with the technology to be able to get the harmful effects of drugs out of our system forever. You sit with the E-meter — those orange juice cans with the wire — Beth calls it 'the 1950s hair dryer machine.'

Meanwhile, I'm spending like $6700, some *enormous* amount of money, because I want my memory back, I wanna get all the drugs *out.*

"So they have this list of drugs — they had to cut down a few rainforests for the paper to fill the list up for me — and they start at the top. And she [the Scientology auditor] goes, 'Okay, Judy?' And they give you a command, and then you answer, and they say, 'Good, thank you.' And if you say the right answer, and your needle [on the E-meter] is floating, they'll say, 'Thank you, your needle's floating.' And if it's not, then they keep asking until you get the right answer. 'Judy, how many times have you smoked marijuana?' 'Uh, four thousand!' 'Thank you very much, your needle's floating.' And that's it. Gone. All the marijuana out of my system. That's what it means. 'Judy, how many times have you done Quaaludes?' 'Uh, a hundred and seventeen.' *[The needle is not floating.]* 'Good, thank you. Judy, how many times have you done Quaaludes?' 'Okay, two hundred and twelve.' 'Thank you, your needle's floating.' And it went on and on. And I'm going, 'You've got to be kidding. I'm spending all this money to give you the right *number*?'"

Bob Odenkirk: "On mushrooms one time I got to meet God. I walked into a very crowded bar, and I stood there, and then I collapsed on the floor, and while I was down, unconscious or whatever, I went out into space and I saw God, and God said, 'You must go back.' I went back, and I woke up in the bar, and my friend picked me up, and everyone was a constellation, and I walked through them to go outside, and then I ran into the back and sat down in the grass behind the bar where everybody pees, and I sat there and thought how wonderful the grass was. It occurred to me today that God must be really thankful that the '60s are over, because He mustn't have gotten any work done in the late '60s with all the hippies showing up."

Laura Kightlinger: "I think anybody who says that sex is better on drugs is used to really shitty sex and really shitty drugs. I remember kind of like being at the end of my cock in this relationship with this guy, and we were both on mushrooms, and I thought, 'All right, if we can't get anything going on now,' but I was really like, my body was rejecting him. There wasn't a drop of moisture outside on a leaf when we were together anyway. So mushrooms, yeah, that would have to help. I remember lying in bed, and he's just looking at the ceiling, and I'm just as clear as I've ever been about how boring he is, how I don't like him, except on the mushrooms it's in Sensurround — *Oh, no, I should be with somebody funny right now, we should be flying!* — and then he thinks he's being really funny, like he's going, 'God, look at the ceiling, doesn't it look like a black shag rug, but like it's moving towards us?' And I said, 'Do you wanna fuck me?' And he goes, 'Yeah, yeah, I *do*, I *do*,' and he starts giggling. And then he was kissing my shoulder and my back, and I was like, okay, doggie style, that's fine with me, and he starts giggling some more, a high-pitched giggle, like all of a sudden I'm in bed with a 13-year-old girl, which actually, that thought kind of got me through it. So he's touching my back and then he starts giggling some more and he goes, 'You know those beetles that are like green and silver, that's what your back looks like.' I was going, *fuck me*, so that was that, nothin' went on, the mushrooms didn't make anything better."

Andy Dick: "Glass, what a funny name for a drug. Glass, what a silly name for a drug. Glass, what a lovely name for a drug. Yes, glass, I've tried it. I don't do a *lot* of drugs, but I tried this drug called glass. So glass to me is this sharded-up window pane, dudes. It's like somebody said, 'Let's get high,' well, fuckin' break the *glass*. It *is* like little shards of — I think what happens is these tiny shards go into your blood vessels and start cuttin' up your brain, choppin' up and slicin' your *thoughts*."

Blaine Capatch: "I was in a Navy boot camp, and I'm standing in my barracks with all the other fucking assholes, and I'm being inspected by our chief petty officer. He's like frisking me and making sure everything's buttoned. 'Where ya from, recruit?' 'Dallastown, Pennsylvania, sir.' 'Pennsylvania, huh? Lotta guys hanging out in the cornfields smokin' dope, getting' high?' 'No, sir, that was the other guys, not me.' 'Well, y'know what, lemme tell you something, a lotta guys from Pennsylvania' — he pulls out my Chapstick, because we're all issued a Chapstick — 'a lotta guys get their girlfriends to send acid out to 'em, and what they do is, they hide it up in the cap of their Chapstick. You don't have any *acid* in your Chapstick cap, *do* you?' 'No, sir, no acid in the Chapstick cap.' He screams at me and I just blank it out. I learned something very important that afternoon. You can hide your acid in a Chapstick cap."

Scott Silverman: "I could tell my parents were smoking pot when I was a kid, because my hamster would be in its habitrail, and our house had a really strange ventilation system. My parents would go into their bedroom—'G'night, kids' — at like 8, and then all of a sudden we'd like have smoke *billowing* from the ventilation system, because we couldn't tell what *that* was. 'Oh, they're burning rope.' The pot would go into the habitrail where my hamster was running on its wheel, furiously, and then it would get a contact high and would slow down, and then it would get off its wheel and it would lay down, and then it would get up and eat everything in its cage."

Beth Lapides: "Pot is my drug. I enjoy very much sitting in my big green chair, with my huge notebook opened, listening to Hole or Liz Phair, the candles lit, and I have four tokes. That's how I smoke pot now, okay? This is not the way I was brought up. I was brought up to smoke a lot a long time. The problem with drugs in our country is parents are not teaching their children how to take them. Children are having to learn on their own how to take the drugs. Sometimes a nice brother or sister, older sibling, might show you a thing or two, give you a pipe, a few hits, but children can't learn on their own.

"If you're not gonna let children learn on their own how to *read*, how are you gonna leave such an important thing like taking drugs to their own devices? You know, I believe you can never have too much meaning. For my taste, the more meaning, the better, and drugs can get you there. Drugs can make a simple thing like a glass of water become a symbol of the infinite. Drugs can make this fluid become the condensation of all that is invisible. Drugs can make this funny."

▪■▪

It would be a sign of false humility not to include myself in this survey. Drug references are an integral part of my shows, as is drug use. I almost always perform while stoned on pot. I talk about the president being against medical marijuana — in Clinton's voice, 'I feel your pain, I just don't want to help you relieve it' — and about the drug war itself — "We have a secret weapon, the neutron bong. The neutron bong wipes out the user but leaves your stash intact."

At a recent performance, I told the story of ingesting acid just before testifying at the Chicago Conspiracy Trial in 1970. An audience member at the show, who was visiting from Canada, told his 17-year-old son about this and wrote to me: "Since the 'new' acid is approximately 60-75 micrograms — and kids drop before going to school! — my son wasn't particularly impressed until I mentioned that in our days, to drop meant a 300-microgram Owsley barrel or some such. As he mentally calculated the possible effects of 5-6 tabs, he smiled and said, 'You guys were fuckin' *nuts*.'" And (*toke, toke*) we still are.

Oral Sex Is On the Rise

The following story, which I published in *The Realist* several years ago, was widely circulated on the Internet:

When astronaut Neil Armstrong first walked on the moon, he not only said, "That's one small step for man, one giant leap for mankind," but also, just before re-entering the craft, he uttered, enigmatically, "Good luck, Mr. Gorsky."

At headquarters back on Earth, they assumed that this referred to a rival Soviet cosmonaut, but there was no Gorsky in either the Russian or American space program.

Until recently, Armstrong always refused to answer reporters' questions about that remark, but he finally gave in. Gorsky had died, and so Armstrong felt it would no longer be inappropriate to respond.

When he was a boy, playing baseball in the back yard, his brother hit a fly ball that landed in front of a neighbor's bedroom window — the Gorskys. As young Armstrong was retrieving the ball, he heard Mrs. Gorsky shouting: "Oral sex? You want oral sex? You'll get oral sex when the kid next door walks on the moon!"

And now, thanks to Monica Lewinsky's big mouth, oral sex is all over the place. Forget about Jay Leno, David Letterman and Conan

O'Brien — people who have never even *tried* oral sex have been openly discussing it. Biblical scholars are busy checking to see where God said that oral sex is not adultery. And now, *every* kid, not just Neil Armstrong, can embarrass his parents by asking, "What's oral sex?"

Oral sex is so much in the air these days, it's hard to remember what a tremendous taboo it once was. Yet there is a certain twisted sense of continuity. We used to practice oral sex as a way of preventing pregnancy. Young people today mistakenly practice oral sex as a means of preventing AIDS.

Oral sex was the running theme of an entire episode of *Seinfeld*. In one high school, where free condoms are available for students, there was a sign proclaiming that "The Peppermint Condoms Are For Oral Sex Only."

Gennifer Flowers, whose claim to infamy is that she had an affair with Bill Clinton, wrote a tell-all in which she praised the then-governor's skill at cunnilingus, though the book wasn't exactly a bestseller. But, ever since Paula Jones accused Clinton of dropping his pants, exposing his gubernatorial gonads and requesting oral sex — a story which *Village Voice* columnist Ellen Willis assumed I made up — this country has not been the same.

Surprisingly enough, oral sex was missing from a proposed amendment on sexual misconduct in the Student Council Code at the University of Oregon.

In an effort to prevent date rape, a motion was presented to the University Senate, defining rape as "an offense committed by a student who engages in penetration of another person, and who does not obtain explicit consent."

Penetration means "any degree of insertion, however slight, of the penis or any material object into the vagina or anus."

Hey, what about the *mouth*? Forcible fellatio is rape!

Explicit consent is defined as "voluntary, non-coerced and clear communication indicating a willingness to engage in a particular act

[and] includes an affirmative verbal response or voluntary acts unmistakable in their meaning."

So, how specific does one need to become? Is a kiss just a kiss, or is it a step-by-step process? "Now that our lips have touched — with your stated approval, of course — may I insert my tongue an inch or so and gently rub it along the outer ridge of your upper gum?"

This could make it difficult to be spontaneous, but presumably, if one is given permission to fondle a female breast, that would cover *both* breasts, or else it gives new meaning to the legal concept of double jeopardy.

Of course, the ironic implication of this policy is that sexual activity which thrives on trust will be allowed to proceed only on the basis of a *lack* of trust.

Indeed, why should such an agreement be merely verbal? Why leave it to one person's word against another's? Why not have a *written* contract?

Moreover, there could be individualized clauses promising *to do* certain things. Like, "There must be at least 23 minutes of foreplay." Or, "Men have to share the wet spot."

Don't you think that when Neil Armstrong became the first human to walk on the moon, Mrs. Gorsky would like to have chosen *in advance* whether or not she would swallow the results of her now-immortalized husband's spasm of pleasure?

The Great
Kurt Vonnegut
Cyberhoax

I confess. Although I didn't handle the technological end of the Kurt Vonnegut hoax, the *idea* was mine. A friend I'll call Hacker took care of the cyberspace aspects.

I've always loved pranks. In my high school yearbook, under Hobbies, I put "Eating new recipes and playing practical jokes" — not realizing that I had unintentionally described the best way for somebody to play a nasty trick on *me*.

When I started publishing *The Realist* in 1958, I printed a rumor that IBM, whose employees sometimes seemed as standardized as the machines they sold, required all personnel to have their teeth capped by a company dentist. IBM's Medical Director wrote in response: "We do not maintain dental services nor do we provide remedial dental care." Of all the hoaxes since then, my most infamous one was "The Parts Left Out of the Kennedy Book" in 1967.

Of course, I have had pranks pulled on me in return, from an announcement of my demise in the short-lived *Cheetah* magazine — they rationalized that I had published a fake obituary of Lenny Bruce two years before his death (in order to call attention to his plight while he was alive) — to an interview that I had supposedly done with Bob Dylan, which was actually made up by Marvin Garson and published in the *San Francisco Express Times*. It was circulated throughout the underground press and critiqued in *Rolling Stone.*

When I stopped publishing in 1974, many readers thought *that* was a hoax. Others didn't realize publication had been suspended until it was resumed in 1985. The *Los Angeles Times* published a series on plagiarism by their media critic, David Shaw, and I reprinted an excerpt from it, using Pete Hamill's byline. *The Realist* was back in business.

Then along came the World Wide Web. A prank could now be communicated with greater speed and reach more people than ever before. For example, the following "Virus Alert" has been spread with altruistic intent and Malthusian multiplicity:

"Warning — If anyone receives mail entitled Pen Pal Greetings, please delete it without reading it. This is a warning for all Internet users. There is a dangerous virus propagating across the Internet through an e-mail message entitled Pen Pal Greetings. Do not download any message entitled Pen Pal Greetings.

"This message appears to be a friendly letter asking if you are interested in a pen pal, but by the time you read this letter, it is too late. The Trojan horse virus will have already infected the boot sector of your hard drive, destroying all of the data present. It is a self-replicating virus, and once the message is read, it will *automatically* forward itself to anyone whose e-mail address is present in your mailbox.

"This virus will *destroy* your hard drive, and holds the potential to destroy the hard drive of anyone whose mail is in your In box, and whose mail is in *their* In box and so on. If this virus keeps getting passed, it has the potential to do a great deal of damage to computer networks worldwide...."

However, the Virus Alert was *itself* a hoax. As Hacker explains, "E-mail can't contain a virus. E-mail is pure data. A virus has to be an *executable* code. No e-mail can contain a virus except for e-mail with executable attachments. This includes Microsoft Word, which has a macro language that can execute immediately when you open a document. So it's possible to do great harm by opening an *attachment* to your e-mail, but *not* by reading it."

■■■■■

In June 1997, a subscriber sent me several clippings, including the following column by Mary Schmich in the *Chicago Tribune*:

Inside every adult lurks a graduation speaker dying to get out, some world-weary pundit eager to pontificate on life to young people who'd rather be rollerblading. Most of us, alas, will never be invited to sow our words of wisdom among an audience of caps and gowns, but there's no reason we can't entertain ourselves by composing a Guide to Life for Graduates. I encourage anyone over 26 to try this and thank you for indulging my attempt.

Ladies and gentlemen of the Class of '97:

Wear sunscreen.

If I could offer you only one tip for the future, sunscreen would be it. The long-term benefits of sunscreen have been proved by scientists, whereas the rest of my advice has no basis more reliable than my own meandering experience. I will dispense this advice now.

Enjoy the power and beauty of your youth. Oh, never mind. You will not understand the power and beauty of your youth until they've faded. But trust me, in 20 years, you'll look back at photos of yourself and recall in a way you can't grasp now how much possibility lay before you and how fabulous you really looked. You are not as fat as you imagine.

Don't worry about the future. Or worry, but know that worrying is as effective as trying to solve an algebra equation by chewing bubble gum. The real troubles in your life are apt to be things that never crossed your worried mind, the kind that blindside you at 4 p.m. on some idle Tuesday.

Do one thing every day that scares you.

Sing.

Don't be reckless with other people's hearts. Don't put up with people who are reckless with yours.

Floss.

Don't waste time on jealousy. Sometimes you're ahead, sometimes you're behind. The race is long and, in the end, it's only with yourself.

Remember compliments you receive. Forget the insults. If you succeed in doing this, tell me how.

Keep your old love letters. Throw away your old bank statements.

Stretch.

Don't feel guilty if you don't know what you want to do with your life. The most interesting people I know didn't know at 22 what they wanted to do with their lives. Some of the most interesting 40-year-olds I know still don't.

Get plenty of calcium. Be kind to your knees. You'll miss them when they're gone.

Maybe you'll marry, maybe you won't. Maybe you'll have children, maybe you won't. Maybe you'll divorce at 40, maybe you'll dance the funky chicken on your 75th wedding anniversary. Whatever you do, don't congratulate yourself too much, or berate yourself either. Your choices are half chance. So are everybody else's.

Enjoy your body. Use it every way you can. Don't be afraid of it or of what other people think of it. It's the greatest instrument you'll ever own.

Dance, even if you have nowhere to do it but your living room.

Read the directions, even if you don't follow them.

Do not read beauty magazines. They will only make you feel ugly.

Get to know your parents. You never know when they'll be gone for good. Be nice to your siblings. They're your best link to your past and the people most likely to stick with you in the future.

Understand that friends come and go, but with a precious few you should hold on. Work hard to bridge the gaps in geography and lifestyle, because the older you get, the more you need the people who knew you when you were young.

Live in New York City once, but leave before it makes you hard. Live in Northern California once, but leave before it makes you soft.

Travel.

Accept certain inalienable truths: Prices will rise. Politicians will philander. You, too, will get old. And when you do, you'll fantasize that when you were young, prices were reasonable, politicians were noble, and children respected their elders.

Respect your elders.

Don't expect anyone else to support you. Maybe you have a trust fund. Maybe you'll have a wealthy spouse. But you never know when either one might run out.

Don't mess too much with your hair or by the time you're 40 it will look 85. Be careful whose advice you buy, but be patient with those who supply it. Advice is a form of nostalgia. Dispensing it is a way of fishing the past from the disposal, wiping it off, painting over the ugly parts and recycling it for more than it's worth.

But trust me on the sunscreen.

▪▪▪▪▪

At a recent memorial for Allen Ginsberg in Los Angeles, Robert Weide (who wrote and produced the film version of Kurt Vonnegut's novel, *Mother Night*) read a statement from Vonnegut which began, "Please, stop dying." Somehow, "Wear sunscreen" reminded me of that. When I chatted with Vonnegut in New York a few years ago, I got the impression that he was saddened that young people might not be familiar with his work. The perverse motivation of my prank was to help remedy that situation.

Replacing Mary Schmich's byline and opening paragraph with "This speech was given by Kurt Vonnegut at MIT's commencement this year," Hacker proceeded to transmit the text of her column over the Internet in such a way that it could not be traced to him.

The non-commencement speech traveled fast and furiously. It was even posted to the Vonnegut Newsgroup. Many of his fans thought it was valid, including Vonnegut's wife, photographer Jill Krementz, who e-mailed it to several friends (her husband was out of town at the time). *Mademoiselle* magazine asked Vonnegut for permission to reprint his speech. Peter Lasally, who used to be a producer for Johnny Carson, tried to book Vonnegut on the Tom Snyder show.

Actually, the commencement speaker at MIT — five days *after* Mary Schmich's column had been published — was Kofi Annan, secretary general of the UN, who didn't mention sunscreen *or* flossing. Schmich, who had written the piece "while high on coffee and M&Ms," called Vonnegut to let him know that *she* wasn't behind the hoax. He responded that it revealed the gullibility of people on the Internet.

Schmich traced one e-mail backward from its last recipient, a professor at Malcolm X College in Chicago. He had received it from a relative in New York, who received it from a film producer in New York, who received it from a TV producer in Denver, who received it from his sister, who received it from... At this point, Schmich gave up her quest for the culprit.

I apologize to Vonnegut and Schmich, but I'm happy to say that the revelation that the commencement speech was a hoax reached more people than the hoax itself did, not only on the Internet, but also in print and electronic media. The truth had triumphed in a truly free marketplace of ideas.

Fuck Sunscreen

On April 3, 1999 — ten days after NATO began dropping bombs on Yugoslavia, I spoke at MIT. My role was to provide comic relief as the culmination of their week-long Democracy Teach-In. A CD of my performance, titled Sex, Drugs and the Antichrist, *has been released by Danny Goldberg's Artemis Records. The following is an excerpt from that evening.*

Inside every adult, there lurks a little child who once said, with great pride, "When I grow up, I want to be a pundit." Now, for me, that dream has at last become a reality. And so I would like to take this opportunity to pass along whatever wisdom I've gained during my lifetime.

Ladies and gentlemen of the class of '99: Fuck sunscreen. Global warming is actually a cruel hoax, a conspiracy. There is no such thing as global warming. It's all propaganda from the monopolistic sunscreen industry.

Take a sacred vow never to floss again. Explain that you're trying to avoid wax build-up between your teeth. Or, if you must, try using floss imbedded with tiny pieces of food in case you have to skip a meal between flossings.

Do one thing every day that scares you. Eat bikini wax. Admit publicly that you were extremely bored by *Shakespeare in Love*. Try masturbating with sandpaper.

Practice safe sex. Practice, practice, practice. And when you've practiced enough to reach perfection, then throw away those annoying condoms. Or at least put some pinhole pricks in the reservior tip. Give those spermatozoa a fighting chance.

Remember, the personal is political. If you find yourself in an unsatisfactory relationship, develop an exit strategy.

What this civilization really needs is an answering machine for your online communication so that people will stop calling you on the telephone to find out if you got their e-mail.

In this age of low sodium and high tech, you can still make a difference. You can still make your individual voice heard. Don't hang up on pollsters. Infiltrate a focus group. Steal ideas from a think tank. Transcend your own demographic.

When election time comes, do not familiarize yourself with the issues. More importantly, *do not vote*. Even if you prefer one candidate over another, don't even *think* about casting your ballot. I mean, look what happened in Minneapolis. Young people, who said they would not have voted otherwise, elected as governor a wrestler who favors decriminalization of marijuana. Let us stick to the lesser of two evils.

Always strive to have empathy. Understand that from a policeman's point of view, a police state is a *good* thing. Dedicate yourself to the security of working for a multinational corporation. Show your support of the war on drugs by voluntarily bringing a cup of urine to your first interview.

Be discriminating in your life. And be especially discriminating in the field of education. Discriminate against women even if you *are* one.

Remember, the economic system affects everybody. Build more prisons. Assure inmates that they will never have to suffer from overcrowded conditions again.

Learn the fine art of snitching. Snitch on your friends and your enemies with equal venom. Snitch on your classmates and professors, even if you have to make stuff up.

Of course, there are times when it becomes inappropriate to snitch. If you ever see a crime taking place, don't be a tattle-tale. Do not call 911 unless your cat has climbed up a tree.

On an international scale, if you are witness to a horrible injustice taking place, an utterly evil crime against humanity, simply bomb the perpetrator's city back to the stone age — I mean the peace table. If they resort to anti-aircraft missiles, accuse them of escalating the war. Above all, be sure to ignore every tenet of conflict resolution in order not to appear wimpy.

And finally, allow me to reiterate: Fuck sunscreen. Sunscreen will not serve to ease your transition into the 21st century. For that you need Y2KY Jelly. Trust me on this. Thank you.

Anita and the Blow-Up Doll

Exactly five weeks before Sunday, December 27, 1998 — the day that Anita Hoffman had chosen to die — she was talking on the phone about a blow-up doll that she and her husband, Abbie, had once bought as a present for me. That was almost three decades ago. The blow-up doll never arrived, and Anita now found it necessary to reassure me that they really had ordered it. Their gift may have been a gag, but it wasn't a hoax.

"We were probably the only ones that happened to," she said.

"Oh, no," I replied, "I think they probably screwed everybody. No one *ever* received their blow-up doll, but they were all too embarrassed to report it to the Better Business Bureau."

My missing blow-up doll was just another loose end from Anita's past. She was in the process of tidying up her life before taking it. Three of my closest friends had ended their lives too early — satirist Lenny Bruce in the '60s, folksinger Phil Ochs in the '70s and revolutionist Abbie Hoffman in the '80s — and I was deeply saddened each time, but it was different with Anita.

"There's no despair here," she said. "I'm happier than I've ever been. I'm really looking forward to my death ."

She had been suffering from breast cancer, which metastasized to her hips. In September she e-mailed:

"I've been very ill. Too sick to sit at my computer, thus offline for several weeks. Today felt like sitting here and catching up. I'm undergoing radiation treatment. The cancer in my spinal column is affecting my spinal cord, and thus weakening my right leg. I can't walk so good. Use cane. Bedridden. Anyway the radiation is in hope of stopping that encroachment."

She spent her time on the Internet, watching television and reading the *New York Times*, which didn't carry program listings for California, so I got her a subscription to *TV Guide*.

"I must admit," she said, "that I'm hypnotized anew by the visual medium."

But now she was paralyzed from the waist down and had been informed that she had two months to live. "Maybe four," she said, "but, you know, I've always been a pessimist." So here she was, at the age of 56, in an altered state bordering on ecstasy from painkilling drugs — morphine, Marinol, marijuana — combined with the self-empowerment of orchestrating her own departure.

When we lived in New York City in the '60s, Anita and Abbie's TV set had the word *Bullshit!* taped on the lower right-hand corner of the screen. Our friendship was permeated with media manipulation and punctuated by LSD sessions. So, when CBS News wanted to film a hippie acid trip at the Hoffmans' apartment on the Lower East Side, being countercultural propagandists, we agreed to do it.

As a joke, I suggested to CBS that they ought to pay for the LSD because I was curious to see whether they would charge the expense to Entertainment or Travel. Blaming my suggestion, they changed their corporate mind, expressing fear that the trip would now be "staged." We took the acid anyway — Abbie, Anita, my friend, Phyllis, and me — and we watched CBS. Every commercial seemed to be trying to sell us the high we were already on.

At one point, Abbie and Anita left the living room, and when they walked back in, they were both totally naked, smiling broadly. I suspected they might have an impromptu foursome in mind, but Phyllis whispered to me, "I think we ought to leave now." Just then a phone call came about some trouble at the 9th Precinct. Abbie and

Anita quickly got dressed, and we all strolled down to the police station.

Some African-American kids had been busted for smoking marijuana in Tompkins Square Park. Abbie wanted to indicate that there could be solidarity between hippies and blacks, so he insisted on getting arrested too. The cops refused to oblige his request, but Abbie just stood there in the lobby of the stationhouse. Captain Joseph Fink beckoned to me.

"Paul, do you think you can persuade Abbie to leave?"

"Abbie's his own man," I replied.

Abbie was standing in front of a display case filled with trophies. Suddenly he kicked backwards with his boot, breaking the glass as though there were an emergency. Since Abbie was most meditative when he was most actively engaged, this was for him a transcendental moment.

"Now you're under arrest," yelled Captain Fink.

Abbie enjoyed the rest of that particular acid trip behind bars. Phyllis went home, and I accompanied Anita back to the apartment on St. Marks Place, where she immediately got on the phone to contact lawyers — and journalists.

"Hi," she would begin each call, "this is Anita Hoffman — Abbie's wife...."

That was her role, and she played it with diligence. She would have preferred a simpler lifestyle, but Abbie functioned as a community organizer, and Anita was his willing helpmate. Whether bailing him out of jail or bringing him to a hospital after he was beaten by cops at a demonstration, she was always there for him, planning and participating in guerrilla theater events, from showering $1 bills on the Stock Exchange to levitating the Pentagon.

Abbie provided an adventurous vehicle for the radical consciousness that Anita had already been exercising before they met. She had become politicized simply by reading between the lines of the *New York Times*. With a master's degree in psychology, she had intended to get a Ph.D., but dropped out because she was so upset about the Vietnam war. She began working for the New York Civil Liberties Union, but quit her job, afraid, ironically, that she wouldn't get promoted because of sexism. This was in 1967.

She met Abbie — who also had a master's in psychology — when she went to volunteer at Liberty House, a store he founded as an outlet for items crafted by poor people in the South. That same evening, Anita and Abbie had their first date. She put on the Beatles' "Revolver" album, and while they were dancing she told him that she wasn't a good dancer but that she *was* a good kisser. Abbie stayed the night.

Soon after, they got married in Central Park in an alternative ceremony. Without telling her, Abbie had leaked an invitation to the press, and a photo of their wedding appeared in *Time* magazine, where they were identified only as "a hippie couple." Anita wore dark glasses because she didn't want to be recognized by her parents.

She had taken her vows with Abbie, and now she was also married to the media.

There was, for example, the fake orgy that took place in their apartment. In order to build up interest in the exorcism of the Pentagon, Abbie had invented an imaginary drug, LACE — supposedly a combination of LSD and DMSO — which, when applied to the skin, would be absorbed into the bloodstream to act as an instant aphrodisiac. It was to be sprayed on military police and the National Guard in Washington.

Actually, LACE was "Shapiro's Disappero," a novelty item from Taiwan that leaves a purple stain, then disappears. A press conference was called to demonstrate the effect of LACE on three hippie couples. Mattresses were spread across the living-room floor for them to have sex on after being sprayed with LACE from squirt guns, while the reporters took notes. For some reason, Abbie wasn't even there, leaving the shy Anita to host this bizarre prank.

Originally, I was supposed to be there as a reporter who got accidentally sprayed with LACE. To my surprise, I would put down my notebook, take off my clothes and start making love with a beautiful redhead who had also been accidentally sprayed. I was looking forward to this combination media event and blind date. Even though the sexual revolution was at its height, there was something exciting about knowing in advance that I was guaranteed to get laid, although I felt guilty about attempting to trick fellow reporters.

But there was a scheduling conflict. I was already committed to speak at a literary conference at the University of Iowa on that same day. So Abbie assigned me to go to a farm in Iowa and purchase some cornmeal, which would be used to encircle the Pentagon as a pre-levitation rite. I was a rationalist, but it was hard to say no to Abbie.

In Iowa, novelist Robert Stone drove me to a farm.

" I'd like to buy some cornmeal to go."

"Coarse or fine?" the farmer asked.

I looked at Stone. He shrugged. "Since it's for a magic ritual," he said, "I would definitely recommend coarse."

"Coarse, please," I said to the farmer.

"How many pounds?"

"Thirteen, please."

"The farmer smiled and said there would be no charge. And I flew back to New York with a 13-pound sack of coarse cornmeal properly stored in the overhead compartment.

Meanwhile, there were stories about LACE in the *New York Post*, the *New York Daily News* and *Time* magazine, as well as the wire services, perpetuating the promise that three gallons of LACE would be brought to Washington, along with a supply of plastic water pistols, so that LACE could be sprayed at police and the National Guard at the Pentagon demonstration, who would then make love, not war.

The hippie who substituted for me in that ostensibly accidental sexual encounter with the beautiful redhead at the LACE press conference ended up living with her. Even though I had never met her, I was jealous. Somehow I felt cheated out of a romance.

"You really should have a steady girlfriend," Anita teased.

Abbie and Anita had an open marriage, but only Abbie acted on it. He was insatiable. He occasionally stopped by my loft on Avenue A with his latest lust object for a matinee performance. I would be at my desk, writing something for *The Realist* or on the phone, and they would be screwing away in my bed.

Abbie obviously wanted his trysts to be kept secret. Yet, since he and Anita were my friends individually as well as a pair, I felt conflicted — strangely disloyal — as though I were part of a conspiracy to keep the truth from her.

In December 1967, the three of us decided to take a vacation in the Florida Keys. We rented a small house-on-stilts in Ramrod Key. We heard on the news about black leader Stokely Carmichael's return from Africa to the United States, and Anita remarked that we should have been at the airport to greet him. Instead, we ingested acid at the Seaquarium in Miami and watched the dolphins frolicking.

"I think hippies have been using dolphins for their role models as pioneers in a leisure economy," Anita observed.

We had planned to see *The Professionals* with Burt Lancaster and Lee Marvin — "That's my favorite movie," Abbie said — but it was playing too far away, so instead we saw the Dino Di Laurentis version of *The Bible*.

On the way back, Anita mediated our debate about the implications of Abraham being prepared to slay his son because God told him to do it. I dismissed this as blind obedience. Abbie praised it as revolutionary trust. This was the week before Christmas, and we stopped to buy a small tree and spray-painted it with canned snow.

Still tripping, we watched Lyndon Johnson being interviewed. The TV set was black and white, but LBJ on LSD was purple and orange. His huge head was sculpted into Mount Rushmore. "I am not going to be so pudding-headed as to stop our half of the war," he was saying. Now the huge heads of the other presidents — George Washington, Thomas Jefferson, Abraham Lincoln, Theodore Roosevelt — were all snickering to themselves and covering their mouths with their hands so they wouldn't laugh out loud.

Abbie, Anita and I talked about the different styles of protest that would be taking place at the Democratic National Convention in Chicago the next summer. While the Democrats would present politicians giving speeches at the convention center, we would present rock bands playing in the park. There was no separation between our culture and our politics. We would have booths with information about drugs and alternatives to the draft.

I went outside and, under the glow of moonlight, I followed a neighborhood crow named Alice down the road to a gas station, where there was a phone booth. First I called Dick Gregory in Chicago, since it was his city we were planning to invade. He told me that he had decided to run for president, and wanted to know if I thought Bob Dylan would make a good vice president.

"Oh, sure," I replied, "but to tell you the truth, I don't think Dylan would ever get involved in electoral politics."

Instead, Gregory would end up with attorney/assassination-researcher Mark Lane as his running mate.

Next I called Jerry Rubin in New York to arrange for a meeting when we returned. The conspiracy was beginning. And, concomitantly, egos were expanding. Jerry would later insist that *he* had called *us*. However, there was no telephone at our house-on-stilts.

When I got back there, I could hear the rambunctious sounds of Anita and Abbie in bed, alternately moaning and giggling. This, then, was the original conception of the Yippies — the Youth International Party — an organic cross-fertilization of psychedelic drop-outs and political activists. We had come to share an awareness of the connection between putting people in prison for smoking marijuana in this country and burning them to death with napalm on the other side of the globe. It was the ultimate extension of dehumanization. And we were planning to play our part in helping to turn the tide.

This was the most exciting acid trip we'd ever had.

Two days before Thanksgiving 1998, Anita moved from Petaluma to San Francisco, carefully chauffeured by photographer Robert Altman.

"Goodbye, room," she said to her little cottage. "Thanks for giving me cancer."

Her immobility had prevented her from seeing the sky, but her friend Cindy Palmer was living at a house in San Francisco owned by her daughter, actress Wynona Ryder, and offered the master bedroom to Anita. The plan was to have a steady stream of visitors there. Poet Diane Di Prima, for instance, might be coming over to read some Buddhist death prayers.

Timothy Leary had been Anita's role model during the final months of his life, except that, unlike him, she would not be seeing groupies or reporters. Leary had said, "You couldn't choose how and when and with whom you were *born*, but you can take charge of your own death," and now that's precisely what Anita was doing.

"I'm in total hostess mode," she said, joyfully. "I'm on automatic party time."

My wife, Nancy, and I flew to San Francisco in early December to visit her. Steve Wasserman, a friend and editor of the *Los Angeles Times Sunday Book Review*, arranged to be on the same flight. He had once edited the *Times'* Sunday Opinion section, but moved to New York to escape the pain of an unrequited crush on Anita. Now he was going to see her for the last time.

My friend Julius picked us up at the airport. We brought him a red Buddha candle and a 1999 calendar. For Anita we brought a multi-colored mushroom candle, a CD — Krishna Das' "Pilgrim Heart" — and a bag of cookies. At her bedside, I panicked at the possibility that I had given Julius the candle intended for Anita, which would mean that the one she was now unwrapping would have the calendar for a year in which she would be dead. What could have been an unintentional sick joke didn't occur, though, and the relief was worth the tension.

Anita was living her fantasy. She could not only see the sky, but also the San Francisco Bay and the Golden Gate Bridge. Alcatraz Island was included in the view, though not from the angle of her bed, and she preferred it that way.

Her appetite was ravenous, and her humor was dark. After devouring a pastrami sandwich, she remarked, "I better brush my teeth, I don't want to get gum pockets." Someone was bringing over "pineapple-coconut ice cream to die for," and Anita responded, "I guess I'm ready for that." And when we were talking about an upcoming movie, she said, "I'm sure we'll all be going to see that — oops."

In this frame of mind, she would act on an impulse immediately because, as she explained, "I'll never have a chance to do it again." And so she asked for a photo that was on a bookshelf. The rest of us in the room assumed that perhaps she was going to share a memory, but instead she simply ripped the photo in four pieces and tossed them in the trash. Who was in that photo and why she tore it up remains a mystery.

The question rose, since Anita was so euphoric, why not continue living? But her euphoria came from knowing exactly when there would be closure. Of course, Anita's family — her mother, her sister and her son — were not quite so elated. Nevertheless, she wanted them to be at her bedside "to comfort each other."

■■■■■

Before the debacle outside the Chicago convention in the summer of 1968 was officially labeled as "a police riot," Mayor Richard Daley's office produced a documentary, *What Trees Do They Plant?* — asserting that reporters were accidentally beaten by police because their credentials were hidden in their jacket pockets. Even if that were true, it only indicated that the cops did in fact attack at random, but the truth was that clubbings took place as a *result* of being shown press cards. Notebooks were seized, cameras were smashed, film was thrown into the lake.

When this anti-protesters documentary appeared on network TV, the Yippies managed to get rebuttal time. Abbie asked me to write a script. At one point, I included this line: "It is not that we hate America, it is that we feel the American dream has been betrayed."

"But we *do* hate America," Anita scolded me.

"No, we hate what America has *become*."

We argued, but they finally agreed with me, and the line stayed. Indeed, at the Chicago conspiracy trial, Abbie repeated that line in his final statement. Moreover, when Anita gave birth to a baby in 1971, he was named america — with a lower case *a* "because we didn't want to be pretentious," she explained. "We chose that name because he was our vision of what the country could be." While america went to school, he was called Alan, though he would later reclaim his name and his heritage.

In 1974, Abbie went into hiding for several years after he was arrested for selling cocaine. He and Anita had already separated, but she continued to be supportive, even after he met Johanna Lawrenson while he was on the lam and she became his "running mate." In a letter included in a collection of correspondence between Abbie and Anita, *To America With Love: Letters From the Underground*, she had written, "I needed to live desperately, separately from you in order to become a separate person. Do you understand?"

Now on her own, Anita founded a self-help center for mothers and children who were receiving public assistance. She gave me an inscribed copy of *To America With Love*. And she made sure that Abbie, still a fugitive, mailed me *his* inscription on a yellow Post-It.

·■███■·

In the final weeks of Anita's life, members of her extended family visited her in San Francisco.

Yippie organizers Stew and Judy Albert flew in from Portland, Oregon. They had a reunion with Anita and Rosemary Leary, whom they had last seen twenty years ago, when they were all tripping on the beach in Algeria. Anita had been there trying to renew an alliance between the Yippies and the Black Panthers, but she found Eldridge Cleaver so authoritarian and misogynistic that, afraid for her safety, she climbed out a window to escape. Now they were laughing about it over an afternoon snack of matzahs and jam.

Sam and Walli Leff, Yippie archivists and the cornerstone of Abbie's overground support system, flew in from New York. At Anita's request, they brought from Zabar's delicatessen a carton (packed with dry ice and properly stored in the overhead compartment) containing kippered salmon, sliced sturgeon, smoked sable, herring in cream sauce, herring in wine sauce, whitefish, Jewish rye bread with caraway seeds, cole slaw, potato salad, Russian coffee cake — and they all had a lovely picnic in her bedroom.

Ron Turner, publisher of Last Gasp Comics, brought a whole case of grape soda, and promised to deliver a video of *A Bug's Life*.

Janeane Garofalo — who had successfully sought to portray Anita in Robert Greenwald's unreleased film biography of Abbie, *Steal This Movie*, for which Anita was a consultant — came to visit her fading prototype. They had met during the filming. She called Anita "a very, very bright woman who definitely marched to the beat of her own drummer. She was very dynamic. When she walked into the room, you knew she was there." Garofalo said the whole experience reinforced her desire "to live a very Berkeley life wherever I am."

Anita felt she had to warn certain visiting friends — Martin and Susan Carey from Woodstock; Nancy Kurshan from Chicago (who ran the Yippies' New York office and was Jerry Rubin's girlfriend) — that they would not be portrayed in the movie.

"The film makes it seem as though Stew and Judy were the only other Yippies and our best friends," she told me. "Everything other people did, such as donate their kid's bar mitzvah money (the Careys) or forward underground mail, is credited to Stew and Judy. When I mentioned the paucity of other characters, Robert replied that on a low budget film we just can't afford a lot of major players. This is Hollywood."

Robin Williams learned about Anita's situation from his co-star in *Good Will Hunting*, Matt Damon, who had been told about it by his girlfriend, Winona Rider. Williams had never met Anita, but he called and offered to pay a visit, in keeping with his benign case of Patch Adams syndrome. After all, if Patch could travel to Trinidad to entertain murderers who would be hanged three days later, why shouldn't it be appropriate for Robin to make Anita laugh on Christmas day? Anita hesitated — "I've never really been a fan of his work" — then invited him to come.

Jay Levin — who had been a reporter for the *New York Post* assigned to cover the Yippies, then became a Yippie himself, and years later launched the *L.A. Weekly* — was also there, and described Williams as "an incredibly funny human being." He did conversational schtick for a solid hour, and Anita became an instant fan.

Wavy Gravy, the socially conscious clown who became a Ben & Jerry's ice cream flavor, originally met Anita at Liberty House in 1967, when she and Abbie were busy stringing love beads. Now Wavy came to her bedside holding a stiff knotted, leather dog leash, leading a large rubber fish named Saul Bass. Anita wanted to touch it, but Wavy wouldn't let her.

"No," he said, "you don't know where this fish has been. People try to kiss him all the time, but he's been out sniffing a lot of dogs' asses."

Wavy sang a plaintive song, "She Carries Me to the Other Side," while Anita sat in bed wearing his red plastic clown's nose.

·■■■·

On February 14, 1969, I was a guest on the *Tonight Show* — host Orson Bean, substituting for Johnny Carson, had invited me — and naturally I ingested a tab of LSD for the occasion. I was wearing a black Mexican hat Abbie gave me and a bright orange shirt Anita embroidered with an Aztec Indian design of an owl.

They and many other Yippies had spent the previous day rolling some 30,000 joints, wrapping each one in a flyer wishing the recipient a Happy Valentine's Day and containing facts about marijuana. Over 200,000 arrests for pot-smoking were made the previous year, and Mayor John Lindsay had just petitioned Governor Nelson Rockefeller to raise the penalty from one to four years for possession.

The Valentine joints were sent anonymously to various mailing lists — teachers, journalists — and to a guy listed in the phone book as Peter Pot. The project was financed by Jimi Hendrix. One newscaster who displayed a joint was visited by a pair of narcotics agents on camera while he was still delivering the news — a TV first.

Without revealing the culprits, I discussed this political prank on the *Tonight Show*, and Anita would later recount it in *Trashing*, a fictionalized account of the Yippies, under the pseudonym Ann Fettamen. "There was no way of knowing how many people got high on Halloween [sic]," she wrote, "but we knew it was the busiest night in the history of the Narcotics Division."

The next day I was visited by a pair of narcotics agents who had seen me on TV. I told them that the Mafia must have sent out all those marijuana joints in order to discredit the Yippies.

And, although I was the one who had been tripping on acid, it was a viewer who wrote to NBC complaining that I had worn a shirt with the internal diagram of a uterus.

∙■■■∙

Anita was efficient in death as in life, taking care of business right to the end. And so it was that I received a refund from *TV Guide* for the unused portion of her subscription. Details, details...

At 10 p.m. on Saturday, December 26, she ingested a cocktail that had previously been provided by a compassionate doctor. That she would administer her own deliverance in such a way had been kept secret from almost everyone. Not even the hospice volunteers knew. On Sunday, at 4:15 p.m., Anita accomplished her goal. She died in peace and serenity, believing in the continuation of her consciousness.

"I know I'm not enlightened," she had said, "so I'll probably have to come back."

In her latter years, Anita had become intrigued by the twin towers of mysticism and conspiracy. She read books and magazine articles about those subjects, and loved to listen to Art Bell's late-night radio show. She believed that there is life on other planets, and accepted the notion of certain UFO aficionados that extraterrestrials have been making a movie of the earth's progress.

Her last words to me were, "I hope I remember to ask to see that movie."

∙■■■∙

"Somehow, Abbie will see the movie," Anita had said — referring to *Steal This Movie*, in which she appears briefly in a courtroom scene. "He was the love of my life," she added. "One of the best things about dying is that I'll be able to say hello to him again."

Meanwhile, she continued to serve as the keeper of Abbie's image. She wrote a letter to the editor of the *Los Angeles Times Sunday Book Review*, which had stopped printing such correspondence several weeks earlier. Finally, she called Steve Wasserman and told him that she was dying — yes, she played the death card — and he published her letter:

"Abbie's legend has a life of its own by now and is surely beyond correction, but I can't help sending in a small correction to J.

Hoberman's otherwise fine review of *Steal This Dream* and four other books about the '60s counterculture. Contrary to the quotation from one observer, Abbie Hoffman did not ingest LSD 'like corn flakes' every morning. I would estimate he took LSD about four times a year for three years during the late '60s.

"Also, Abbie never took acid or any other psychedelic during the Chicago conspiracy trial. It was Paul Krassner who was on acid during his testimony in that trial. Abbie and I were furious and didn't speak to Krassner for several years thereafter. I think it's important to be accurate about this for the sake of young people who may be influenced. I continue to believe that psychedelics are a useful tool or sacrament for special occasions."

Actually, it was not several years, but ten months, that Anita and Abbie didn't speak to me, although it *seemed* like several years. Ten months after the break-up of our friendship, I had noticed a tiny ad in the movie section — *The Professional* was playing at the Charles Theater on Avenue D — so I mailed the clipping to them, and forgot about it. But that gesture broke the ice, and we proceeded to have an emotional reconciliation. It was then — when I still didn't have a steady girlfriend — that they had ordered a blow-up doll for me, the one that never came. But it really was the thought that counted.

THE MISSING EPISODE OF *SEINFELD*

[Jerry is on stage at the comedy club.]

Jerry: Did God look down at Adam and Eve one day and say, "Oops, I forgot something. Let there be erections." So Adam got the first hard-on in history. But God forgot to say *when*. And that's why men don't always get an erection when they *want* one. Women don't know it, but sometimes men have to actually *pray* for an erection. "Please, God, I'll be sensitive to her needs, I promise, oh God, please, just make it hard...."

[George is having dinner with his parents. There is no conversation, but George's father is smiling, then chortles out loud.]

George: What! What! What's so funny? Is it because I'm becoming more like *you* every day?

George's father: Should I tell 'im? I'm gonna tell 'im.

George's mother: No, don't tell 'im. It's private between you and me. It's none of his beeswax.

George: C'mon, stop teasing me, I wanna know, whatever it is, I wanna know, so c'mon, tell me.

Sex, Drugs, & The Twinkie Murders

George's father: Okay, I'm gonna tell 'im. I've been taking Viagra. George, it really works. Your mother and I have been making whoopie like it was going out of style.

George's mother: Yeah, but it's not me *he gets excited over. It's only because of the Viagra.*

George's father: What difference *does it make? George, listen to this, they cost $10 each. But a friend of mine goes to Mexico and he gets me a bottle of fifty for $42.*

George: Gee, that's less than a buck a fuck, isn't it?

George's mother: George! You must never say the F-word in this kitchen! See, I told you, we never should've told 'im.

■■■■■

[In Jerry's apartment, Kramer bursts through the door.]

Kramer: Jerry! Jerry! I'm gonna be rich! I bought a bunch of shares in Pfizer when it was real low and now they put Viagra on the market and all the doctors are getting writer's cramp from writing prescriptions and the stock is going up and up like it took Viagra! Jerry, I'm gonna be able to retire!

Jerry: Retire from *what*? Kramer, you don't do anything *now*.

Kramer: Yes, I do. I scheme. I spend a lot of time scheming, Jerry. But now I'll be able to finance *my schemes. I'm gonna be able to call my own bluff, every day! If that's not retirement, I don't know what is.*

Jerry: Anyway, I might get this stand-up comedy award tonight, and I'm trying to think of what to say that will sound completely spontaneous. So, what's your *current* scheme?

Kramer: Okay, I got this idea because of the insurance companies. Blue Cross will pay for six Viagra pills a month. Well, that's very arbitrary, isn't it? I mean I get six hard-ons in one day.

Jerry: That's the national average, you know, six hard-ons a day.

Kramer: Jerry, believe me, Kramer doesn't have *"average" hard-ons. But here's my merchandising idea. It's for one-night stands — a combination package of Viagra and RU486, the morning-after pill. It's a natural for the unisex market.*

280

[At the restaurant, Elaine and George are sitting at the table.]

Elaine: But, George, that's stealing.

George: Yup. And from my own parents.

Elaine: You have no scruples. How do you know your father isn't counting the number of times he "makes whoopee" with your mother? He'll know that you took some of his Viagra pills when he thinks he has seven more times to go and the bottle is empty?

George: You think he keeps a tally sheet? He'll never suspect.

Elaine: You're in denial again — but you have to give me a couple. I would just love *to put a Viagra into Jerry's and Kramer's coffee.*

George: Oh, really? I thought you had *scruples*, Elaine. Dosing somebody is unethical, especially friends.

Elaine: Oh, didn't I tell you? I had my *scruples removed with laser surgery.*

George: But what about the side effects of Viagra?

Elaine: Stop worrying, George. Hurry, let me just have two. Jerry and Kramer will be here any minute.

[At the stand-up comedy award ceremonies, Jerry, Elaine, George and Kramer are sitting at the table. Suddenly the table rises slightly.]

Jerry: Kramer, stop that, what are you *doing*?

George: Maybe he's holding a one-man seance.

Kramer: I can't get it *down*! Jerry, I can't get it *down*!

Elaine: Gosh, Kramer, you must have been thinking about sex, huh?

Kramer: No, I was thinking about my business plan. That's the only thing that really arouses me. When I'm with a babe, I just think about my latest scheme and I get aroused. But I always let the babe take the credit.

▪■▉■▪

[Courtney Cox is emceeing the event. Now she's announcing the winner.]

Courtney: And the best stand-up comic award goes to... Jerry Seinfeld!

[Jerry walks up to the stage. Courtney and Jerry embrace warmly. She gives him the statuette. As the audience applause subsides, the blood flow increases to the spongy tissue in Jerry's penis. He tries unsuccessfully to hide his erection with the statuette.]

Jerry: Thank you very much. Well, as you can *see*, I'm very excited about receiving this reward. I feel all tingly. And I have a headache. I'm a little dizzy too. An erection is like a cop. When you *want* one, it's never there. But when the *last* thing in the world you want is a hard-on — a *public* hard-on — then *boing*! I'm busted, right here on stage, with a spotlight, in front of 500 strangers. I may have to vomit. I'll try to avoid the first few rows. And everything looks blue. Especially my balls. Is there a groupie in the house? Well, I'm not actually a group. Is there a *singly* in the house? Who would like to get laid tonight? I'll point the way. So I've become a human dowsing rod. Now I think I'm gonna faint. But even while I'm lying unconscious here on the stage *[Jerry is fainting]*, my penis will still be a stand-up....

Worship at the Celebrity of Your Choice

"Circus freaks, celebrities," says Roseanne, "it's all the same thing."

As a kid violinist, I understood that connection; I was the object of an audience before I was a member of one. At the age of six, wearing a Little Lord Fauntleroy suit and playing my violin, I became the youngest concert artist ever to perform at Carnegie Hall. It didn't seem like such a big deal to me — I almost fell asleep in the middle of the Vivaldi Concerto in A Minor — but strangers kept complimenting me and rubbing my hair. I understood viscerally that they were doing it for their needs, not mine. One woman even asked me to sign her program.

"What for?" I asked.

"This makes it more personal," she explained, "and I can show my friends that I met you."

I wrote my name right above my photo, unaware that the word to describe my feeling was *absurd*. But, besides being a child prodigy, I was also a professional brat, and I said, "Well, if they're really your friends, why won't they believe you?" She laughed, and I discovered my true calling.

Twenty years later, instead of becoming a violin virtuoso, I launched a satirical magazine, *The Realist*. I was still intrigued by the implications of fame, and would occasionally ask an interviewee how celebrityhood had changed his life.

"Sometimes it helps," replied professional curmudgeon Henry Morgan. "It gets you tables in full-up restaurants, and sometimes people give you stuff for nothing because you can afford to buy it and they just charge it to the people who can't afford to buy it. All you have to pay for it is a loss of privacy for the rest of your damned life, giving autographs to mindless little girls, listening to jokes forced up your leg by imbecile truckers, answering questions in small papers of dubious repute and miniscule circulation — and which use jerky words such as 'celebrityhood' — overpaying tradespeople because they know you're a big star and make a million dollars a year and don't need the money, being stared at in the street whether you're blowing your nose or not. On the other hand, I used to be shy when I went to a party. Now I'm not."

And Woody Allen said, "None of the *internals* get changed, and that's what really kills you. You get in trouble with a better class of women, that's all that happens. Years ago, I lived in a tiny one-room apartment and went out with fairly drab women. Now I come in contact with more exciting women, but the problems are still the same. I may get a suit custom-made, but I still can't relate to the tailor. I can afford a car but I don't buy one because I have too many emotional problems driving. You know, all the things just recur on a higher economic scale."

Recently, a friend told me how she was once at an event where she was standing near the young, handsome Marlon Brando while she was eating a *samoza*, and she was so flabbergasted by his presence that she ate right through the napkin, with pieces of it hanging from her mouth. I also heard about a woman who saw Robert Redford in an ice cream parlor and ended up putting her ice cream cone in her purse, but in another city I heard the same story, except it was Paul Newman and frozen yogurt, so it's probably an urban myth.

Orson Bean admits, "I deliberately chose to walk that thin line between fame and oblivion because being a celebrity is part ego trip and part inconvenience. They say that savage tribes get upset if white hunters or anthropologists take their photograph; part of their soul will disappear. Conversely, autograph hounds think they're stealing part of the soul of a celebrity when they get his autograph, and they run away with it, thinking that some of that fame is gonna rub off on them."

Joan Baez used to sign autographs only for children. To others, she'd smile and say, "Let's shake hands instead. That way I'll get something out of it too."

And, at a peace demonstration during the Vietnam War, Muhammad Ali would only sign his autograph on draft cards.

Alley Mills told me about the conclusion of a research project. "It's an actual phenomenon," she said. "When you've seen someone on celluloid, and then you see them in person, your heart starts to pound and you start getting all excited, even if you hate them. I remember seeing Jamie Farr, that guy from *MASH*, in a restaurant, and I got all excited. I don't like Jamie Farr. I didn't even like *MASH* that much. It's a physical thing."

Stanley Young, who interviews celebrities for *People*, agrees. "There's an inevitability behind it, because when somebody whose face is on the screen for an extended period of time, or on the tube and they're in your house, eventually you begin to emotionally identify with them. That's why faces sell on magazines, because people have an emotional identification with them."

Joe Levy, an editor at *Rolling Stone,* says, "I don't think it's the end of the world that celebrities are on the cover of all these magazines. I *do* think it's the end of the world if they're on the cover of *every* magazine. If it gets to the point where you can't put a large-mouth bass on the cover of *Field and Stream* unless you've got Jenna Elfman holding that large-mouth bass, then you've gone too far."

Celebrities and the media have developed a totally symbiotic relationship. They need each other so desperately it's giving co-dependency a bad name. Although *In Style* publishes a feature titled "Truth or Tabloid," fundamentally the only difference between the *National Enquirer* and *In Style* is in the slickness of their packaging and the elegance of their language. Whereas the *Star* calls Calista Flockhart "scrawny" and "waif-thin," *In Style* refers to her "swanlike beauty" and "a frame as slender as a tulip stem." In a *George* magazine interview (where she is described as "wafer-thin"), Flockhart is asked about a story in an Australian magazine that reveals her "secret lover." She laughs and replies, "He was a reporter from *In Style* who was interviewing me. He was one of their own."

Each fan projects upon a star, their own individual perceptions. When the Beatles came to America, there was a concert at Shea Stadium. You could hardly hear them sing above the screaming of the crowd. One young girl held up a poignant poster: "It's all right, John — I Wear Glasses Too!"

The perverted extension of that sense of identification occurred when Mark David Chapman asked John Lennon for an autograph, then a few hours later killed him. Ken Kesey observed, "You have to remember, whenever there's a spotlight, there's always a crosshairs in the middle." A couple of months later, John Hinckley tried to execute Ronald Reagan in the hope that Jodie Foster would be so impressed that she'd go bowling with him. And don't forget, Rebecca Schaeffer was killed by a deranged fan, while Selena was murdered by the president of her own fan club.

With the aid of technology, however, things happen so fast that even the rate of acceleration has been increasing, and irreverence has been accelerating along with everything else. Although it took more than a decade after the assassinations of John and Robert Kennedy for there to be a band called the Dead Kennedys, it took only a few months after the attempted assassination of Ronald Reagan for there to be a group called Jodie Foster's Army. Other bands have been named Sharon Tate's Baby, Jim Jones and the Suicides, and Lennonburger.

I asked Lew Harris, editor-in-chief of *E! Online*, how the Internet has changed the nature of fan clubs. His response: "Anybody who has anything they want to say about a celebrity has a voice now. The anarchy of the net is the most exciting thing, but celebrities don't like it very much, because we're in a period now where celebrity control is higher than it's ever been in the history of show business. The contract system in the studios is over, all these celebrities now have their personal publicists and most of the time their job is to keep their clients *out* of the press.

"The fascination with celebrityhood is unparalleled at any time in the history of the world, and now there's a medium for it. Along comes the Internet, you've got thousands of people out there, millions, who can say anything they want about a celebrity, they can put their pictures up, they can put somebody else's nude body — *TV Guide* got in trouble for running a picture of Oprah with Ann Margaret's body — this happens on the web all the time, except they're nude. You've got Alyssa Milano nude, and her mother is now out trying to get all these nude pictures off the web. Meanwhile, there are pictures of everybody else — Courtney Cox, Drew Barrymore, Brad Pitt — superimposed, done by Photoshop. And the fans don't care. To them a fake picture of Brad Pitt nude is just as good as a real picture of Brad Pitt nude."

Just like it doesn't make any difference to those matrons who seek autographs from Elvis Presley look-alikes.

Larry Flynt has offered a million dollars to many celebrities to pose nude in *Hustler* — Cher, Farrah Fawcett, Olivia Newton-John — who have refused, but no matter. There is now a CD-ROM being sold on the Internet with this pitch: "Are you tired of spending countless hours searching for pictures of nude celebrities? Well, the search is over! Celebrity Nudes CD-ROM with over 8500 different images... contains some of the hottest actresses, *Playboy* centerfolds, singers, models and every other celebrity out there."

As Colin Quinn said on *Saturday Night Live*, "Charlize Theron is upset about appearing nude in *Playboy*, saying she intended the photos for her private use. I guess that makes two of us."

On KPFK, Amanda Parsons was talking about researching her new book, *High Exposure, Hollywood Lives: Found Photos From the Archives of the Los Angeles Times*:

"I discovered what may be, and I came to think of as, the most powerful cultural phenomenon of our century. These [celebrities] are people that are under our skins in ways that we can't possibly imagine until we let it happen, and it's a phenomenon felt all the way around the world. There's also something about it that's tawdry and unpleasant. What I learned from working on this subject of fame — I learned that I don't want it — as I sit here on the radio. I think it's toughest for the person that *is* the celebrity, but for those of us who are out there, the fans, I think that we use these celebrity lives in ways that transform our own. I sometimes think of it as these are our gods and goddesses, these are our icons, and their stories become kind of parables for how to lead our lives."

Indeed, fan clubs on the Internet are known as altars. One site is actually named "Worship Janeane Garofalo." Another, more specialized, Web site declares, "No one in his right mind would call Janeane Garofalo fat. No one, that is, except the agents, casting directors and other assorted weight Nazis who've sworn to protect America from the sight of a woman without visible hip bones. Sure, Hollywood thinks we're ready to see a leading lady come out of the closet, but not out of a bakery." The site — surprise! — is sponsored by a weight reduction plan: "Click here and we'll send you all the secrets of automatic fat control."

There is a sense of continuity in fan fetishism, though, from a sale of the Beatles' bedsheets cut up into thousands of one-inch squares — fully authenticated by hotel managers and suitable for framing — to the Fox network siphoning water from the swimming pool in *Melrose Place* and filling hundreds of tiny plastic vials that can be distributed to fans as souvenirs.

If the Beatles were, as John Lennon said, more popular than Jesus, then Madonna is more popular than his mother. Salman Rushdie sent her an autographed copy of his latest novel, *The Ground Beneath Her Feet*, coincidentally about a troubled rock star who is constantly reinventing herself. The bedeviled author was told that she shredded the book. Rushdie announced, "I suppose 'Shredded by Madonna' is a higher recommendation than 'Burned by fundamentalists.'"

Fame, as both Rushdie and Madonna know only too well, is a two-sided coin. Where there is love, there is always the potential of hatred. Last month, in *E! Online's* mean-spirited, reality-twisting, weekly series, "Diary of Madonna's Baby," the precocious child wrote: "Well, Mommy's been in a good mood lately, 'cause she just started shooting that dumb ol' movie *The Next Best Thing*. You remember that, doncha, Diary? It's where Mommy plays a woman who uses a man to help her have a baby. No, it's not an autobiography, silly! It's a romantic comedy.... Mommy's so into this movie that as soon as she wakes up, she starts right off shouting and cursing at the nearest bodyguard. Then, by the time she reaches the set, she's all warmed up and ready to yell at the makeup girl, the hair-dresser, the masseur, the pedicurist, the yoga teacher, the Tarot card reader and anyone else she hoodwinked the producers into hiring who has the misfortune of being within 20 feet of her luxury trailer."

The anonymous writer of this feature told me, "I see it personally as the antithesis of celebrity. It's the true meaning of iconoclasm — a shattering of the icon. It's satirical iconoclasm, an attempt to de-flate — I think of it as celebrity deconstruction — and some of the support that I've heard from people who read it around the world is that they feel that more of that needs to be done, there's not enough vinegar out there being poured on these celebrities, there's only adu-lation and adoration. I think it's something in the human psyche."

At the various award ceremonies, so many celebrities thank God that you realize God is the Ultimate Celebrity. And a forgiving de-ity, at that. The MTV Awards telecasts have served as a redemption center for fallen celebrities. One year it was Pee Wee Herman ask-ing the audience, "Heard any good jokes lately?" The next year it was Michael Jackson kissing his wife on stage as a public relations gesture to dispel the notion that they had gotten married as a public relations gesture.

A letter to Walter Scott in *Parade* magazine — "I fell in love with Latin hunk Ricky Martin at the Grammy Awards. Is he mar-ried?" — reeks with a vague delusion that the letter-writer has a chance with him. That same delusion was catered to by Tom Jones' manager, who kept it a secret that Jones was married, and it is still catered to by the publicist for Reese Witherspoon and Ryan Phillipe who didn't want it known that they were girlfriend and boyfriend.

Here's a case history of a literary fan. Robert Weide first met Kurt Vonnegut in 1982. Over the past ten years, Weide has been filming a documentary on the author's life. He wrote and produced *Mother Night*, based on Vonnegut's novel. "In high school and col-lege," he told me, "I worshipped Vonnegut out of all reasonable proportion. I guess I still do, but it's hard to remain that fanatical over someone who's become one of your best friends. Despite the age difference, we've become something akin to brothers. This is a guy who, twenty years ago, I would have walked a mile, naked, in a blizzard, to shake his hand or get an autograph.

"Now we speak on the phone almost daily, and see each other whenever we're visiting the other's coast. I've spent weekends at his country home, we've had countless meals together, downed numerous glasses of scotch together. He even mentioned me in his book, *Timequake*. So I'm basically carrying on the friendship with him that every fan dreams of having with their idol. You know, 'If only he met me, I know we'd hit it off and become best friends.' I guess you could say I'm the world's most successful stalker. I've told Kurt that I'm glad he accepted me as a friend because it's much easier than having to camp out across the street with binoculars."

There's a journalistic tradition that whenever a celebrity dies, you're supposed to interview other celebrities and ask how they feel about their friend's death. On the evening that Lucille Ball was about to undergo serious surgery, I was having dinner with Steve Allen at a Hollywood restaurant. CNN's entertainment reporter had made an appointment to meet Allen at the restaurant, and interviewed him there — *twice* — once for if Lucy survived the operation, and once for if she didn't. Although I could understand the practicality of such foresight, somehow I was offended by it.

Sure enough, the next day, there was Allen on CNN, standing outside the restaurant, saying, "We all hope Lucy will pull through. There have been many success stories in the history of television, and yet the affection that millions of Americans hold for Lucille Ball is unique." A week later, she died, and sure enough, there was Allen on CNN again, standing outside the same restaurant, saying, "Lucy will be greatly missed." Then George Burns came on and said, "I had a lot of fun with Lucy," but I couldn't tell whether he had taped that before or after she was dead.

In *Notting Hill*, Julia Roberts, who got $20-million for her marquee value as well as her acting ability, tells Hugh Grant, "The fame thing isn't really real, you know."

Nevertheless... Ben Stiller has stopped counting the number of times people come up to him and say, "You've got something in your ear." A man who would never go to a peep show brings his binoculars to the theater, the better to see Nicole Kidman's bare buttocks. Michael Jordan becomes the top celebrity endorser, while Dennis Rodman is dumped as a TV pitchman. The removal of Pamela Lee's breast implants generates worldwide interest. A crazed fan asks Ron Howard, "Can I have your chicken bones?" And Monica Lewinsky — the *New York Post* calls her "the portly pepperpot" and the *Globe* refers to her as "the tubby temptress" — has come to represent the ultimate triumph of notoriety over talent. Yes, some day everybody's name will be in boldface type.

A few years ago, when my autobiography was published, I was a guest on *Late Night* with Conan O'Brien. Since I was scheduled to do a reading immediately after the show was taped that afternoon, NBC arranged for a limousine to take me downtown. That morning, there had been an article about me in the *New York Daily News*, and now a group of strangers was waiting along with the uniformed driver for me to exit the stage entrance.

A few people asked for my autograph. Then an attractive woman requested to have her photo taken with me. The presence of her friend's camera automatically gave us permission to put our arms around each other. A man walking down the street observed this whole scene and realized that there was a celebrity in sight. So, when this photo-op was over, he approached the woman who was posing with me and asked for *her* autograph. As the limo drove away, I looked out the window. She was signing her name.

And, simultaneously, restoring my perspective.

The Memoirs of Monica Lewinsky

The following is an exclusive sneak preview of an autobiography by Monica S. Lewinsky, titled Going Down in History. *The manuscript in progress was leaked to* The Realist *by, of course, a reliable source.*

I am not an airhead. I'm a victim, partly of my own making. And, mostly, I'm a political pawn of the spin doctors. There are several books being written about the White House scandal, but only a few individuals know what really happened, and only I know who I really am, which is why I have decided to write this book. I would write it even if I didn't need the money for legal expenses. My life may be ruined — at least my reputation will be forever tainted — but the truth must be told.

I don't like being a one-dimensional symbol. If anybody were to take a free-association test, the psychiatrist would say "Monica Lewinsky" and the patient would immediately respond, "Oral sex." Maybe soon my name will be in a crossword puzzle — eight letters across — and the answer will be "Fellatio."

This country was originally founded by puritans and pioneers, and I feel trapped between those two forces.

Back home in Brentwood, I've been listening to talk radio a lot. Ronn Owens on KABC had listeners phone in with nothing but jokes about me for a solid hour. First he warned the audience that if they were easily offended, they should tune out. I have never felt so objectified in my life, and yet, at the same time, I found the program quite riveting.

The best call came from a nine-year-old who said "Bill Clinton violated the Eleventh Commandment: Thou shalt not put thy rod in thy staff." The worst call came from a man who asked, "What do The Titanic and Monica Lewinsky have in common?" The answer was, "They both have dead seamen (semen) floating in the hull."

And remember that ridiculous rumor — the one Lucianne Goldberg *admitted* she made up in order to get attention from the press — that I kept a dress stained with Clinton's dried ejaculation as a souvenir? Well, Jonathan Brandmeier on KLSX invited listeners to call in and suggest euphemisms for presidential semen. My favorite was "Bubba butter." Apparently, my role is to serve as a vehicle for the destruction of taboos.

I have also become an automatic comedy reference. So, to Jay Leno, David Letterman and Conan O'Brien, I'm very useful in punchlines. To *Saturday Night Live*, I'm just a character in their sketches, and never without that beret from my famous hugging Bill TV footage. But I did think it was hilarious to cast John Goodman in drag as Linda Tripp. That cheered me up. I've been simultaneously depressed, scared and, strangely enough, exhilarated.

As an instant celebrity, I've learned that everybody always sees everybody else through their own particular filters. Democrats, Republicans, men, women, the other interns — all perceive me subjectively. For a manufacturer of novelty items, I was simply a disembodied inspiration for the marketing of "Presidential Kneepads." And for *Penthouse* magazine, I would only be their next notorious masturbation enhancer.

In the eyes of the media — from NBC News to *Dateline*, from CBS News to *60 Minutes*, from ABC News to *Nightline*, from *Time* magazine to *People*, from the *New York Times* to the *National Enquirer*, from the *Washington Post* to the *Globe* — I am purely a commodity. Naturally, I believe in the First Amendment, so I'm against censorship. All I'm saying is that while America is achieving adolescence publicly, the tabloids have won the war.

The battleground is like an ongoing contemporary Shakesperean tragicomedy, but there is no script, there is no producer, there is no director. There is only the process of everyone's karma interacting. I recall the words of Terence McKenna when he was a guest lecturer at Lewis & Clark. He said, "Chaos is the tail that wags the dog."

Damage control is the name of the game. It was Dick Morris who advised Clinton to get a dog. Buddy, huh? They should've named him Photo-Op. It was also Dick Morris who suggested taping that ostensibly candid scene of the First Couple dancing on the beach. And I would bet my entire book advance that both Hillary and Bill *knew ahead of time* that Dick Morris was going to release a trial balloon that *if* the rumor about Hillary being a lesbian were true, *then* it would be perfectly reasonable that her husband would need to seek sexual gratification elsewhere.

In fact, the reason I think that Clinton's approval ratings have been so high is because people can *identify* with him fooling around. I mean, when Jimmy Carter admitted that he had lust in his heart, it was the adultery vote that helped get him elected. And that was only lust in his *heart*. Bill Clinton is an *activist*.

I've been reading a book, *Spin Cycle* by Howard Kurtz, and there's a story in there about that time in 1996 when the president said he "might like to date" a shapely, 500-year-old mummy whose remains were on display at the National Geographic Society. Later, chatting after a few cocktails, Press Secretary Mike McCurry told a dozen journalists on the press plane that he could understand Clinton's remark. "Compared to that mummy he's been fucking," McCurry chuckled, "why not?"

Without bothering to mention that it was off the record, McCurry assumed his joke wouldn't be reported, and it wasn't until that book. Washington is a very cynical place. Everything is stated carefully and deliberately, with the *intention* that it will be repeated. When McCurry told the *Chicago Tribune* in an interview that Clinton's relationship with me could turn out to have been "complicated," it was no slip of the tongue. He was fully aware that his observation would appear in print.

Unlike Richard Nixon, who never dreamed that *his* words would be published in a book, *Abuse of Power, The New Nixon Oval Office Tapes:* "Bob (Haldeman), please get me the names of the Jews, you know, the big Jewish contributors to the Democrats. Could we please investigate some of the cocksuckers?"

My mom is a member of the Book of the Month Club, and in their brochure they printed it "c*cks*ck*rs." Anyway, that's how everybody thinks of *me* now. I'm the nation's official c*cks*ck*r laureate.

The image of me on my knees giving head to the president has become a cultural icon. The irony is that *it never happened.* When Wolf Blitzer from CNN asked Clinton at a press conference what he would like to say to me, Clinton smiled and said, "That's good, that's good." It was extremely ironic, because that's *exactly* what I *imagined* he *did* say to me: "That's good, that's good." And I replied, "I gave you a blow job, but I didn't swallow." He started laughing hysterically, just like that time he did with Boris Yeltsin. Bill liked my sense of humor. That's why we went from flirtation to friendship.

However, the reason I visited the White House 37 times was not for Bill — it was to be with Hillary — *she* was the one who desired me physically. The rumor about her being a lesbian was *true.* And so my relationship with Bill *was* complicated. He just acted as a middleman for Hillary, and now he's telling the truth *and* taking the fall for her. In that sense, he's an incredibly loyal husband. Despite what the public may think, Bill is absolutely devoted to Hillary.

Everyone is watching so closely for him to commit the next indiscretion, but it would have to be somebody he can *totally* trust, who could suck the leader of the Western World's dick and *not* confide to a friend, or to somebody who *pretended* to be a friend. So, for a while, Bill is left with only Buddy's tongue for sexual companionship. At least, Buddy won't lick and tell. And if I know my president, while Buddy is pleasuring him, Clinton will fantasize that it's a female dog.

President Clinton's Private Confession

The following is an exclusive transcript of a closed-door, se-cretly-taped prayer breakfast that Bill Clinton hosted for a group of religious leaders after the impeachment trial failed to remove him from office.

Gentlemen, and lady — I guess you must be the Episcopalian — thank you for being here. It's too bad Reverend Moon isn't among you, so he could perform a mass impeachment of all the senators who swore under oath that they would be impartial. But seriously, this morning I want to begin with an epiphany I had, one that truly humbled me. Strangely enough, it happened while I was watching the *Roseanne Show*. I'd never seen it before, but she was interviewing Paula Jones and, as my mother used to say, curiosity got the best of me.

Ms. Jones was telling Roseanne about the first time she saw me in that hotel. She was working at the courtesy booth for the governors' conference. She described me as funny-looking, the way my hair was styled, being overweight, how my suit was out of fashion and didn't fit. So, she was sitting at the registration desk with her girl-friend, pointing at me and giggling. Somehow, I perceived her through the filter of arrogance that people with power develop, and I assumed she was giving me a come-hither look. That simple misperception is what triggered this whole long ordeal. I took her willingness for granted.

It was different with Monica Lewinsky. I mean, she flashed the strap of her thong underwear — it made my heart go *thump* — and, you know, I'm a prisoner in the White House, I can't go to a motel, but Monica appeared like a gift from Heaven, and I succumbed to temptation. I was fully cognizant that this was a very delicate situation — I even asked for *permission* to kiss her — yet I blocked out my foresight. Way back in college, when I tried to avoid military service, I was already thinking ahead to campaigning for president, but now I found myself ignoring the likelihood that Monica would not keep our relationship a secret.

I certainly didn't consider the possibility that she would become so seriously involved with me. It was embarrassing to hear the tape that Linda Tripp made, where Monica told her what she had said to me on the phone: "I love you, Butthead." I remember thinking when it happened, "Hey, I'm the president of the United States, you can't call me Butthead." However, I immediately decided to treat the situation with humor. But she hung up before I could say, "I love you, Beavis."

Surprisingly, I was *not* embarrassed about the infamous cigar incident. I felt that it had been an act of restraint from *actual* intercourse. Kind of tender and playful. Now, if it had been a Cuban cigar, *that* would have been illegal. But this was not the sort of intimacy that I would have felt comfortable performing with the First Lady. Hillary and I are really close but, as I'm sure you understand, no cigar.

For her, the most revealing thing in *The Starr Report* is Monica's fantasy about our being together more often when I'm out of office, where she quotes me as saying, "I might be alone in three years." Hillary was furious, not only because it had provided a young intern with false encouragement, but also because it implied that Hillary and I don't have sex, and she felt it divulged our agreement that if we were to separate, it would not occur before we left the White House.

For me, the most revealing section — in that same section of the report — is Monica's testimony that I jokingly said, "Well, what are we going to do when I'm 75 and I have to pee 25 times a day?" True, I did say that, but I wasn't joking. It was my fear of old age that kept drawing me to Monica. She was my direct link to youth. So I was being literal about peeing 25 times a day when I'm 75. Hell, I drink at least eight glasses of water a day *now* — just like I'm supposed to, for my health — but then I have to *pee* at least eight times a day. Ironically, I've read that if you have to pee more than eight times in 24 hours, it's a symptom of an overactive bladder.

Indeed, irony has permeated this scandal beginning to end. It was ironic that my sexual appetite helped put me in office — the Gennifer Flowers allegation originally placed me in the media spotlight — and it was my sexual appetite that almost tossed me out of that same office. And it's ironic that although Kathleen Willey *enjoyed* our brief encounter, to prove it we would have had to resort to testimony by her confidant, Linda Tripp.

Now, there are things that I've done as president of which I'm *truly* ashamed. Even before my inauguration, I made it a point to stop in Arkansas to oversee the execution of a mentally retarded prisoner. At his last meal, he said he'd wait to have his dessert, a slice of pecan pie, until after the execution; that's how much he understood what was going on. I'm ashamed of *under*protecting the rights of gays and *over*protecting children from the Internet. I'm ashamed of being *against* medical marijuana and *for* requiring a urine test as a prerequisite to obtaining a driver's license. I'm ashamed of bombing Iraq, Afghanistan and Sudan. I'm ashamed of *in*creasing the military budget and *de*creasing the welfare budget. I'm ashamed of dropping cluster bombs and continuing to plant land mines.

But the Republicans didn't dare attack me for any of those positions because they are *their* positions too.

But I'll tell you how I survived this past year, how I maintained such high approval ratings, while Newt Gingrich and Bob Livingston fell by the wayside. How I managed, in short, to remain president. It was partly the state of the economy, and it was partly the state of the culture. Pornography is a twenty-billion-dollar-a-year business in this country. Steven Spielberg told me that's more than Hollywood's entire domestic box-office receipts. Because that's what the American public *wants*. And the TV networks exploit that fact. Harry Thomasen told me it's why sweeps weeks are always so raunchy. So, then, what I did wasn't considered such a big deal after all.

Mainly, though, I have survived because, one sunny afternoon, Monica was positioning herself on the carpet under my desk in the Oval Office while I was on the phone with Benjamin Netanyahu. I was telling him about that time Monica was performing oral sex on me while Yassir Arafat was waiting in the Rose Garden for our appointment. I *didn't* tell Netanyahu that she was just about to perform the same act on me while I was on the phone with *him*. Anyway, at that point, Monica found a big old dusty Mason jar under my desk. There was a label on the side which read, "Property of Ronald Reagan."

That Mason jar was filled with Teflon, and I have rubbed it on myself every day since.

I began my talk this morning with an epiphany, and I'd like to end with another. This epiphany also occurred while I was watching television — *Larry King Live* — and, once again, Paula Jones was the guest. At one point she said, "I've never voted in my life." I was astounded. Then she said, "I'm so apolitical, it's unreal." And I realized what an incredibly great country America really is, that somebody who was just a plain citizen, who was never even *interested* in politics — somebody who had never even *voted* for a president — had nearly succeeded in toppling one.

Well, this has been a catharsis for me. I just want to say once more how much I appreciate your presence here. And finally I would like to share with you a little witticism that Hillary came up with last night, an idea for what my epitaph should be: "Here lies Bill Clinton, but that depends on what you mean by lies." Isn't she wonderful?

Oh, and one more thing. Now listen carefully. I did *not* have sexual assault with that woman, Ms. Broaddrick. I'll be honest with you, it may have been *rough* sex, but it was totally consensual.

That, I can guarantee. God bless you.

THE WORLD PORNOGRAPHY CONFERENCE

Where will it end, the pornographication of the news, and when did it begin? Was it during the Clarence Thomas hearings, when porn star Long Dong Silver and the notion of a pubic hair on a Coca-Cola can made the front page of the *New York Times*? Or was it before that, when certain porn flicks — *Deep Throat, Behind the Green Door, The Devil in Miss Jones* — entered our pop-culture awareness?

I think that the main moment of transition occurred when reporters Bob Woodward and Carl Bernstein of the *Washington Post* were investigating the Watergate scandal and named their source "Deep Throat." Recently, NPR commentator Daniel Schorr referred to that journalistic baptism as "recycling the title of a movie." He didn't even mention that it was a *porn* movie.

Deep Throat has become such a mainstream reference that you don't even have to *know* that the Linda Lovelace character's clitoris was imbedded deep in her throat, so that giving head to a man was her only way of achieving orgasm. That's the kind of stuff that was being discussed at the World Pornography Conference, co-sponsored by Cal State Northridge's Center for Sex Research and the Free Speech Coalition, a trade association of the adult entertainment industry. Held at the upscale, family-friendly Sheraton Universal Hotel in Universal City, California, it was attended by several hundred college professors, students and porn stars.

At the luncheon, a lifetime achievement award was presented to attorney Stanley Fleishmanm, who has fought many battles for 1st Amendment rights. The keynote speech, "In Defense of Pornography," was given by Nadine Strossen, president of the national ACLU. "Freedom of sexual expression," she said, "is an essential element of human rights in general."

I mean, this event was positively reeking with raunch and respectabilty. There were intellectual hard-ons all over the place. However, conference chairman James Elias was careful to point out, "We're not endorsing pornography any more than if we held a conference on the news media or serial killers."

There were 58 panels, and after a while I began to get confused as to who were the porn stars and who were the professors. I thought Patti Britton was a vivacious porn star — she talked about the use of romance to justify being sexual — but she's a Ph.D. who has studied the influence of gender on the content and approach of porn videos.

On the other hand, I thought John Stagliano was a Ph.D. — he talked about the epistemology of porn films — but he is the producer of the *Buttman* series. Whereas, Annie Sprinkle is a porn star who *also* lectures at art colleges. Just for the purpose of this conference, she obtained a mail-order Ph.D. for $125.

My favorite panel was "The Money Shot in Pornography Movies." Former porn star William Margold referred to come shots as "the single most important element" in porn films. He has performed in 500 sex scenes on camera and referred to "the thrill of being able to see my own orgasm on the big screen." He said that porn is "a facial (ejaculating on a woman's face)-driven industry, vicarious revenge on the cheerleader who rejected you."

Margold's presentation was titled "Get Up, Get In, Get Out, Get Off — On Cue." It reminded me of another session where porn star Christi Lake — who had opened a "sex warehouse" in South Africa where a protester complained, "You make me think dirty thoughts" — was trying to show a video to the audience but was having troubles with the VCR. She was instructed to "Eject and start over again," advice that Margold could well have been given by a dissatisfied director.

At home that evening, I decided to watch a video that I'd picked up at the porn conference. There on my TV screen, a half-naked couple — the man wearing a Bill Clinton mask, the woman wearing a Monica Lewinsky mask — are sprawled on the carpet in a replica of the Oval Office. He is masturbating while using his cigar on her as an organic dildo. Oh, I thought, this video must be from that new breed of creative porn directors who were praised so highly at the conference.

But then I took a closer look. Hey, wait a minute. Those aren't masks. And that actually *is* the Oval Office. In fact, this is *not* a porn flick. Suddenly I realize that I've been watching the *news*. And here comes the come shot now. Clinton's tapioca splatter lands right on Monica's blue cocktail dress. They laugh. She hands him back the glistening cigar, and he lights it, just starting to inhale when he remembers that Yassir Arafat is waiting patiently in the Rose Garden for their scheduled meeting, wondering why the delay.

Well, because the president and his intern have been jerking *him* off, that's why. Arafat was part of a disembodied threesome and he didn't even know it. But the question remains: Will the chief executive's powerful come shot indelibly stain his presidency? I can hardly wait for tomorrow's news.

THE LOVE SONG OF TIMOTHY LEARY

Prologue:

During an interview with Timothy Leary several months before his death from prostate cancer in 1996, I brought up the subject of G. Gordon Liddy's raid on Leary's home in 1966.

"He was a government agent entering our bedroom at midnight," Leary said. "We had every right to shoot him. But I've never owned a weapon in my life. I have never had and never will have a gun around."

"But when you escaped from prison [in 1970], you said, 'Arm yourselves and shoot to live. To shoot a genocidal robot policeman in the defense of life is a sacred act.'"

"Yeah! I also said 'I'm armed and dangerous.' I got that directly from [black militant] Angela Davis. I thought it was just funny to say that."

"I thought it was the party line from the Weather Underground [the radical New Left organization that helped him escape, funded by the LSD-dealing International Brotherhood of Love]."

"Well, yeah, I had a lot of arguments with [Weather Underground leader] Bernadine Dohrn."

"They had their own rhetoric. She even praised Charles Manson."

"The Weather Underground was amusing. They were brilliant, brilliant, Jewish, Chicago kids. They had class and dash and flash and smash. Bernadine was praising Manson for sticking a fork in a victim's stomach. She was just being naughty."

· ■ ■ ■ ·

Although it was recently "revealed" that Tim Leary had once been a rat — a police informant — G. Gordon Liddy once actually *ate* a rat. Literally. He acknowledged in his autobiography, *Will*, that the reason he did this was because he had wanted to get over his fear of eating rats. It worked, too. The fearless Liddy was an assistant district attorney of Dutchess County in upstate New York when he led a raid on Leary's borrowed mansion in Millbrook.

Leary said that Liddy represented "forces opposed to human evolution."

Liddy, justifying his action, reported, "The word was that the panties were dropping as fast as the acid."

During the arrest, Leary told Liddy, "The time will come when there will be a statue of me erected in Millbrook."

"The closest you'll get to that," Liddy replied, "is to be burned in effigy."

Liddy had made a shrewd career move, though. Arresting Leary was a giant step up his professional ladder, to the FBI, to the DEA, to Richard Nixon's infamous Plumbers (their job was to plug leaks in the White House) and, after serving time in prison, he started his own counter-terrorist company, played a role on *Miami Vice*, held hands with Betty White on *Password*, starred in *Nowhere Man* (as a man who fakes his own death to throw cops off the trail so he can make a huge drug score), and finally Liddy got his own talk show. Yet another typical American success story.

The essential difference between Leary and Liddy was that Leary wanted people to use LSD as a vehicle for turning themselves on to a higher consciousness, whereas Liddy wanted to put LSD on the steering wheel of columnist Jack Anderson's car, thereby making a political assassination look like an automobile accident.

Liddy's case against Leary didn't stick, but a byproduct was Leary's notoriety, which eventually resulted in his going to prison — a 10-year sentence for possessing a tiny amount of marijuana —

two roaches — belonging to his daughter, Susan, but for which he took full responsibility.

He escaped after serving seven months, hiding out in a series of safe-houses, then leaving the country with a false passport. He ended up in Algeria, sheltered at first by the somewhat paranoid Black Panther leader, Eldridge Cleaver, himself a fugitive. Then Leary and his wife, Rosemary, were kidnapped at gunpoint by the Panthers and placed under house arrest by Cleaver. They managed to escape and went to Switzerland. There, after the Swiss government imprisoned him for a month at the behest of President Nixon's attorney general, John Mitchell, they refused to extradite Leary to the states. Nixon had labeled him "the most dangerous man in America."

Tim and Rosemary separated, and Joanna Harcourt-Smith conveniently showed up as a guru groupie. Tim and Joanna went to Afghanistan, where, in January 1973, one month after they met, he was arrested by American agents — kidnapped, really, since the Afghans had no extradition treaty with the U.S. — and taken back to the states, accompanied by Joanna.

His bail was set at five million dollars, the largest in U.S. history. The judge stated, "If he is allowed to travel freely, he will speak publicly and spread his ideas." Facing a total of 95 years, Leary was put in solitary confinement at Folsom Prison, right next to Charles Manson. The two "hole-mates" couldn't see each other but they could talk. Manson couldn't understand how Leary gave people acid without trying to control them [as was the CIA's original intention].

"They took you off the streets," Manson explained, "so that I could continue with your work."

At Leary's trial in April 1974, his defense team argued unsuccessfully that when he escaped, he had been in a state of "involuntary intoxication" due to flashback effects of LSD. He was transferred from Folsom to Vacaville Prison.

One morning in May, just before dawn, Leary was quietly taken from Vacaville to a private cell in the Federal Correctional Institution. A state prison official said that Leary's move had been voluntary, initiated by the FBI, and he speculated that Leary was "giving testimony about the drug culture." Panic spread from the drug culture to the radical-politics culture. There was fear that Leary would snitch on the people who had arranged for his original escape.

In September, an *ad hoc* group, People Investigating Leary's Lies (PILL), issued a statement: "We condemn the terrible pressures brought to bear by the government on people in the prisons of this country. We also denounce Timothy Leary for turning state's evidence and marking innocent people for jail in order to get out of jail himself."

PILL held a press conference in Berkeley. It was organized by Yippie-turned-Yuppie Jerry Rubin and *Berkeley Barb* editor Ken Kelley, under the assumption that, as a result of Leary's testimony, the federal government was planning to file criminal charges against radical attorney Michael Kennedy for allegedly helping the Weather Underground to orchestrate Leary's escape from prison. Sitting on the dais were: Rubin; Kelley; Leary's former colleague, Ram Dass; poet Allen Ginsberg; and Leary's son, Jack. One by one, they accused Leary of telling preposterous lies to a federal Grand Jury in Chicago about a non-existent hippie Mafia.

Ginsberg and Ram Dass had not been informed about the nature of the press conference and were both surprised to learn that it had been called in the name of People Investigating Leary's Lies. Ginsberg said, "Is this a hotel room in Russia where we turn against our friends? *None of you* have *ever* believed a word the police have said to you, but now you want to believe them, because it's easier than continuing to care about this man in prison."

When Jack Leary began reading a statement denouncing his father, it struck me as so distasteful that I impulsively bypassed my role as a reporter.

"Judge not," I blurted out, "lest ye be stoned!"

Somebody came to the bitter PILL press conference wearing a kangaroo head and costume with boxing gloves to protest symbolically the kangaroo-court nature of the press conference. I knew it was my old friend, physician Gene Schoenfeld (whose "Dr. Hip" column was syndicated in the underground press) because he had called me the previous day to ask if I wanted to wear a kangaroo costume too. Since I was planning to attend as a journalist, I declined his invitation.

Schoenfeld had stashed in the pouch of his kangaroo costume a whipped-cream pie covered by Saran Wrap. He hopped into the room, past scores of media people, preparing to smush the pie in Rubin's face. However, he was unable to remove the plastic wrapping with the boxing gloves on his hands. Kelley grabbed him and pulled off the *papier mache* kangaroo head.

Rubin proclaimed the press conference "a political victory" because it stopped action on indictments that were supposed to have come down as a result of Leary's rollover. Stew Albert, co-editor with Judy Gumbo Albert of *The Sixties Papers*, explaining Rubin's tactic at the PILL press conference, observes: "Public-relations oriented prosecutors might have been influenced not to indict because they envisioned a future trial where even Leary's kid and many others who knew him would take the stand to say he was a liar. All very ugly indeed."

PILL's strategy was to discredit Leary so that the Grand Jury wouldn't bring indictments based on his word alone. FBI memos indicate they were *trying* to make a case against attorney Kennedy, but Leary's information could not be corroborated, since Rosemary was still on the run, and she had to remain so for many years in order to avoid testifying. In the early '90s, when she turned herself in, Leary declared at her hearing that it was all his fault, and the judge let her off with parole. Ultimately, Rosemary forgave him, they became close again, and almost remarried. She continues to honor him with an annual get-together for their circle of friends.

Was anyone else hurt by Leary's testimony? A central figure in underground-overground contacts was targeted by the FBI, and an agent managed to become his roommate, eventually setting up his group to spend several years in prison for planning terrorist activities. In Los Angeles, Joanna set up Leary's former attorney, George Chula, on a cocaine bust. He spent three months in jail. She also fingered him for slipping a chunk of hashish to Leary in prison, and his license was suspended for one month. She tried to sweet-talk lawyer Tony Serra into smuggling hashish to Leary, but he refused.

Joanna led a half-dozen FBI agents to the home of Michael Horowitz, Leary's archivist, where they seized his archives, then succeeded in turning their action into a propaganda victory. By June 1974, Joanna had already been working with the Orange County district attorney's office and investigators from the Drug Enforcement Administration (DEA). Her companion, Dennis Martino, was also an informant for the DEA. He had been spying on Leary's lawyers since 1973, and was responsible for over 30 drug busts in Santa Cruz alone. He died mysteriously, from an overdose of natural causes.

Either Joanna was an undercover agent from the beginning, or she had become one in order to free her "perfect love" from prison. While Tim was in jail, Joanna's mission was to gather information connecting the drug subculture with the political subculture. She conned her way into what she referred to as "the pecking order." She said Tim had given her a list of men to seduce, including Senator Ted Kennedy. When Allen Ginsberg suggested to Leary that Joanna was a double agent, Leary repeated the charge to her.

"Ginsberg just hates women," she responded.

Joanna's mother, the mistress of an ambassador, had decorated the apartment of Henry Kissinger, whose parents were supposed to have fled Nazi Germany, though they somehow managed to bring all their antique furniture with them. Joanna had socialized with Kissinger during the Pentagon Papers trial, and Daniel Ellsberg's co-defendant, Tony Russo, was now one of her targets. Russo recalls: "There was that time Joanna took us all over to her place, and it was a set-up. She brought out the dope and, as soon as everybody had lit up, the cops were at the front door, and [Ken] Kesey and I bounded out the back window and we were gone."

Despite Joanna's efforts, the FBI was so dissatisfied with Leary's testimony that he was put in prison out on the "main line" (general population) under the name "Charles Thrush" — a songbird, get it? — as a blatant attempt to label him a snitch and get him murdered by prisoners, or at least to scare him into giving the FBI the answers they wanted. He continued to reside behind bars for two years with neighbors he described as "singing waiters in the Rathouse Cafe." He was released in 1976, only after the political climate was changed by Nixon's downfall and Jerry Brown had replaced Ronald Reagan as governor of California.

·▪█▪·

So, the new revelation about snitching is neither new nor revelatory. In fact, Leary devoted an entire chapter of his 1983 autobiography, *Flashbacks*, to a detailed, behind-the-scenes account of what transpired in prison. For example, he describes Joanna's visit with the news that federal agents had approached her, wanting to make a deal with him.

"My next step," he wrote, "was to contact San Quentin Sammy, a lifer who I knew was connected to militant leftist groups. We met on the athletic field. I asked him if he could get a letter out of the prison to the Weathermen. He agreed. That night in the mess hall I handed him a magazine in which I had hidden an unaddressed envelope containing words of warning and reassurance. A week later Sammy slipped me a note. The message was simple. 'We understand. Be careful.' It was signed with a Chinese character *Huan* (Dispersion), the *I Ching* hexagram which had been thrown by the Weathermen in the hideout after my escape."

The government has released selected portions of Leary's file, clearly chosen to hurt his reputation, meanwhile hindering the release of his complete file, according to researchers who have made Freedom of Information Act requests. Late in June 1999, a celebrity true-crime Web site called "The Smoking Gun" — dedicated to digging out old government documents — made public an old file on Leary that had just been released by the FBI. The story was picked up from cyberspace by Associated Press and quickly spread across the nation and Europe, in print, on radio and TV.

The newsweeklies treated it with snide cuteness. *U.S. News & World Report*: "The good doctor's famous injunction was to 'turn on, tune in, drop out.' He never talked about dropping a dime." *Time*: "The late counterculture icon of the '60s was an FBI informer. Put that in your pipe and smoke it." *Newsweek*: "The '60s LSD guru was an FBI snitch. Revised motto: Tune in, turn on, turn in."

Why did the "news" about Leary three years after his death generate such a flurry? Ken Kesey, author of *One Flew Over the Cuckoo's Nest* and leader of the Merry Pranksters, believes that "Tim's power still exists, and that power goes against a very established and stiff-necked grain.

"Tim and I talked about our similar predicaments: the cops had us both by the shorthairs a time or two. They wanted me to speak out against acid after the FBI snagged me in 1966. I did the Acid Test Graduation, telling people we had to go beyond LSD. All that evening I yammered doublespeak, knowing the crowd could tell I was ripped — as Hunter Thompson put it — to the tits on 600 mikes. It was tricky business. Tim knew he had to make the same sort of rollover when he was in the belly of the beast. He also knew he wasn't telling the feds anything they didn't already know. And he figured it the same way I did: our true allies and comrades would understand.

"I have no need to associate with doubters. When the priests in the Star Chamber promise to stop pouring hot lead in your ear if you'll confess to being in league with Satan, you do what you have to do. Those citizens who think you are being a traitorous coward have never had hot lead poured in their ears. Tim Leary was a great warrior, funny and wise and clever and, above all, courageous. I judge myself blessed to have battled alongside a revolutionary like this blue-eyed battler. Those who want to gnaw on his bones never knew his heart."

Leary was the godfather of actress Winona Ryder, the daughter of archivist Horowitz. She attests, "He stood up bravely for individual freedom of speech and behavior, and deserves to be remembered for that." Novelist Tom Robbins calls him "the Galileo of our age."

·■■■·

Altogether, Timothy Leary spent time in 39 jails and prisons over a period of eight years, including several prisons that G. Gordon Liddy was in. Who could have predicted that — 16 years after the original arrest in Millbrook — Leary would end up traveling around with Liddy in a series of debates on campuses across the country? I decided to attend the debate in Berkeley in April, 1982. My friend, Julius, wouldn't go with me.

"Liddy is Hitler," he said. "Would you pay to see Hitler?"

Our friend, Lee, answered, *"I'd* pay to see Hitler." Then he turned to me. "Wouldn't *you* pay to see Hitler?"

"Well, first I'd try to get a free backstage pass."

"Sure," Lee said. "You could tell the security guard, 'It's okay, I'm with the *bund*.'"

In cowboy movies, you could tell the good guy from the bad guy because the good guy wore a white hat and the bad guy wore a black hat. But on the stage of the Berkeley Community Theater, they weren't wearing hats, so you had to tell by their shoes and socks. Leary was wearing white socks under white sneakers, slacks and a salmon mauve sweater. Liddy was wearing black socks under black shoes, a suit and tie.

Their body language contrasted sharply. Leary was practically dancing along the inner borders of a jigsaw puzzle laid out invisibly on the stage. Liddy just stood there, microphone in his right hand, never removing the left hand from his pocket. He exuded a programmed casualness betrayed by the quivering vein in his temple.

Leary had once written an article in *Ramparts*, "The Day I Was Busted by G. Gordon Liddy." He described how he and his wife were "rousted out of bed. I stood up and looked into the wild eyes of G. Gordon Liddy." Now Leary was telling this audience what a wonderful opportunity they had to confront Liddy "eye to eye."

Liddy had once written an article in *True*, "How I Caught Timothy Leary With His Pants Down" He stated that Leary "was just one more problem of the sick '60s, to be dealt with by someone else — like an outbreak of plague in Bombay." Now Liddy was telling this audience that he disagreed with Leary 180 degrees on issues, "but there are people I agree with 100% but can't stand their rotten personality. Tim is as engaging as the night I arrested him."

Leary warned the audience that Liddy was a lawyer — "trained in the adversary process, not to seek truth. I was trained as a scientist — looking for truth, delighted to be proved wrong." He confessed that "Liddy is the Moriarty to my Sherlock Holmes — the adversary I always wanted — he is the Darth Vader to my Mr. Spock."

"As long as it's not *Doctor* Spock," said Liddy. He argued that "the rights of the state transcend those of the individual." Not that he was without compassion. "I feel sorry," he admitted, "for anybody who uses drugs for aphrodisiacal purposes."

"Gordon doesn't know anything about drugs," countered Leary. "It's probably his only weakness." He looked directly at Liddy. "It's my duty to turn you on," he said, "and I'm going to do it before these debates are over." Then he made a unique offer: "I'll eat a rat if you'll eat a hashish cookie."

Liddy declined the offer. One can carry *machismo* only so far, and then, somewhere, the line must be drawn.

And so it came to pass that, while Leary and Liddy were on tour, the Psychedelic Liberation Front (PLF) found out their itinerary and considered feeding hashish cookies to rats and releasing them — one by one, in Liddy's room at the various motels he stayed at while he was debating Leary — in the hope that sooner or later Nature would take its course, and one night Liddy would feel in the mood for a midnight snack, *catch* the rat that had been left in his room, eat it and, by extension, the hashish cookie that the rat had eaten, and then Liddy would think that he got stoned from eating the rat. However, this would have been a violation of the ethics of dosing.

Epilogue:

My interview with Leary concluded:

"Consider, Paul, death with dignity, dying with elegance. It's wonderful to see it happening. I talk about orchestrating, managing and directing my death as a celebration of a wonderful life! That has touched a lot of people. They say, 'My father went through this whole thing. He wanted to die.' Amazing."

"So the response has been that people are glad to know that they aren't the only ones who are thinking about death?"

"Yeah. People are thinking about dying with class, but were afraid to talk about it."

"What do you want your epitaph to be?"

"What do *you* think? You write it."

"Here lies Timothy Leary. A pioneer of inner space. And an Irish leprechaun to the end."

"Irish leprechaun! You're being racist! Can't I be a Jewish leprechaun? What is this Irish leprechaun shit?"

"Okay. Here lies Timothy Leary, a pioneer of inner space, and a Jewish leprechaun to the end."

The Sexual Misadventures of Female Comedians

Female stand-up comics were originally a rarity, but pioneers like Moms Mabley, Totie Fields, Phyllis Diller and Joan Rivers paved the way for such performers as Roseanne, Elaine Boosler, Paula Poundstone and Ellen DeGeneres.

Ultimately, the Comedy Store in Hollywood opened the Belly Room just for women comedians. However, this put two principled feminists at odds: Lotus Weinstock served as emcee because of the showcasing opportunity for her sister comics, whereas Shelley Bonus boycotted — all right, girlcotted — the room because it perpetuated segregation.

Here are highlights from the true confessions of female comics over the past couple of years at the UnCabaret's Sex Show, with founder and hostess Beth Lapides providing the mortar between the bricks. It's sort of like eavesdropping in the Girls' Locker Room....

Judy Toll

I am a huge whore, and I'm also a really huge hypochondriac, so it's such a drag because I've actually been tested for AIDS more times than I've had sex. The last time that I had any real sexual activity was in March, and it was on the way home from my girlfriend's wedding. I was so depressed because I was engaged, and then she got engaged after me, and then mine fell apart and she got

317

married. It was *so* depressing that on the way home I stopped off at my ex-fiancee's house and accidentally blew him.

Since I have really no sexual activity, I have discovered something that came into my life a few days ago and has changed my life forever, and it's my new favorite porno video. Oh, my God, it's all Pendleton Camp marines jerking off one after the next, with this sleazy gay porno film director in the background who has somehow convinced them that if they do this he's gonna put them in porno movies with beautiful women. And they just do it. I can't get enough of it. And the weird thing is, none of them has any expression the whole time. I guess they're so young they can just do it like that and have *no*...

He plays a porno video for them — so that's playing in the background and you hear "Ooh! Ooh!" — but you just focus on the marines, that's all. So they're all watching the porno video — maybe that's the first one they've ever seen — and they're just doing their thing, and then when they come, nothing changes in their expression. Except for one guy, who goes, "Ah, here it comes, baby, ah, you fuckin' bitch, *you fuckin' bitch!*" One guy and that's it. He's kinda my boyfriend.

Beth Lapides

I actually read two things this week. One, I read in *Vogue* that sleep is the sex of the '90s, and I had ten hours two nights ago, so I am *high*. And I can't believe it took them until 1997 to figure that out.

And then I read in the *L.A. Weekly* that sex is the new religion. But if sex is the new religion and sleep is the new sex, then would that make sleep the new religion? Or religion the new sleep?

Julia Sweeney

I don't know if I happened upon it or whatever, but at the age of three I knew how to masturbate. So I would say, "Mom, I can do this *thing* that makes your whole *body* shake! And then I would show her what I could do. And I'd go, "Oooh!" And then my mother would go — this fucked-up Irish Catholic—"I don't think you should do the thing that shall remain nameless."

When I was five, I remember in first grade, on weekends I would masturbate — I didn't call it that, I didn't know what I was doing then — and I would come like twelve times in an hour. I'd just go *bam! bam!* And it was so much fun, and I kept trying to teach people how to do it. This was the greatest thing, and I couldn't understand why everyone just didn't spend their weekends masturbating.

And then finally my mother sent me to a *doctor*, and they called it "hanging." My mom would say, "She's hanging again," because I would kind of hang on like a doorknob, and it was so intense and so much *fun* and it was really *great*. And then the doctor would say, "You're too young to be hanging on things." I never got what he was talking about. I never really felt like it was bad, even though they kind of were telling me that. I just continued and continued.

Then I got into high school, and suddenly the nun got up and said, "You shouldn't masturbate." And of course I didn't know *what* she was talking about. I did not correlate what I was doing. When I masturbated, I thought, "Oh, I'm running down the street and somebody's running after me." My fantasy was like, "Oh, my paper's due tomorrow." I didn't even know it *had* anything to do with sex. I didn't know at all.

So the nuns would get up and say, "Masturbation is terrible, and it's a sin," and I would say, "Yes, it *is*." Of course, they didn't describe what it was, it was just masturbating. And I just thought, "Masturbation is terrible and you shouldn't do it." And I thought that until I was seventeen. And then I read *Our Bodies, Our Selves,* and I had this moment where I went, "Oh, my God, I have been masturbating my entire life."

Then I thought, like, "I'm supposed to be aroused sexually and then I'm supposed to come?" I couldn't figure out how that came together. No, you start thinking, "Oh, no, tomorrow in class I have to turn in my assignment. Then you come."

So it took a very long time for me to have a psychological meeting of the idea of being sexually aroused and coming at the same time. Of course, now, I actually do. Once I connected with the idea, they *connected*, believe me. But when I would read stuff about women not being able to come, my whole thing is trying *not* to come. It's a good problem.

Beth Lapides

Yoga is a very sexy way to work out. I think that anyone who pretends that yoga's not about sex is just lying to you, and if they're going, like, "It's very spiritual," well, as if spirituality and sex are not totally connected.

Also in yoga, there are women who wear leotards without any underpants on — which is very yogic, apparently — except I can totally see their asshole. And I guess that's cool.

Sabrina Matthews

I recommend engaging in recreational lesbianism. Don't worry particularly that you're gonna hurt some lesbian. Probably you're not. Because we all have a straight woman at some point in our lives. It's something we have to do. When we sign the contract, they say, "Paragraph 4-E, this woman's gonna come along, she's gonna be *curious*, and, you know, you're gonna be first in line at the buffet that Sunday if you do her."

But, on the other hand, if you *are* curious, and you're a woman, and you meet a lesbian and you sort of come on to her and she says, "Oh, I've already *had* my straight woman," don't be offended because — one, that's our quota, and then we're done. Really, ask any lesbian. It sounds very funny, but I'm not making this shit up.

When I moved to San Francisco, it was such a mind-fuck it wasn't even true. Everything was freaky to me, like there were leather-clad women with tattoos. I called up this friend of mine who had moved to San Francisco a little bit earlier, thinking, "Okay, this will be my sort of oasis, this will be someone who can help me transfer into this clearly, really open, sexual what-I-may-one-day-interpret-as-a-paradise, but today it's just really freaky and terrifying, and I'd rather just drink in the corner at the bar."

I called her up, and I had to leave a message on her answering machine. She called me back like ten minutes later. She said, "I'm really sorry I couldn't take your call, but I recently got my nipples pierced, and I was changing my nipple ring, and the pain was so intense that the endorphin rush made me pass out, and I couldn't take your call."

Beth Lapides

I hear a lot of people talk about their sexuality in terms of Catholicism and guilt and everything, but you don't hear that many people talk about their sexuality in terms of their Judaism. And there's a reason. I think in a way my sexuality *is* connected to Judaism in a big way.

For instance, I have a dildo, and it's black, and we keep it in a drawer with the *yarmalkes* (black skull caps). We use them equally as much. Also, I think my sexuality blossomed on the *bar mitzvah* circuit, quite frankly. I went from one *bar mitzvah* party to another.

And — this a weird beginning sexual experience — I was at an all-girls' summer camp, and we had socials with the boys' summer camp, and I snuck off with a boy from the dance into the woods or the tennis court or wherever you might go. I remember that he was feeling me up — that'd be second base — and he was going, "Yeah, the Jewish girls are the best." Suddenly, I did not feel sexy. I was like, "Take your hand off my breast." That's so weird. Isn't that like saying black men have the biggest dicks?

Margaret Cho

I was living with this guy, and one night he was fucking me up the ass, and I'm laying there, and fortunately there was an open copy of *Mother Jones* on the floor, and it was open to an article on capital punishment. So I'm reading, and I get to the bottom of the page and it says, "Continued on page 67," and I'm like, is it *rude* to go to the back of the magazine and finish the article or should I wait for him? I realized I must err on the side of caution. So I'm waiting, and he's taking forever. And I'm like, okay, I *get* it, wrap it up — June, July, August — let's go!

There's a certain penis style that really bothers me. You know, when it's a grow-er, not a show-er. It just starts off like really small, you don't think it's gonna be any kind of big deal, it's just sort of there, and it's kind of like a frog on a lily pad, you know, it's adorable, it kind of looks like a corsage, and then out of nowhere it just kind of like *expands* and becomes like a huge elephant-trunk thing. What is that? That's too much, I don't want all of that. I want half of that. Could I put half of that *back*? That's too much for me. I can't eat all that, frankly. I know my limits, and when I go to Subway, I do not get the foot-long, I get the six-incher.

Beth Lapides

People have come up with *kinky* sex because it's memorable. That's the thing about kinky sex, you *remember* it. Regular sex — how many times have you had sex where nothing particular happened and it wasn't a one-night-stand — and you actually remember it? You just have a vague memory of some *sex*, right?

But when you do something kinky, it's like *yes*, the mango sex. And forever, we'll always remember the mango sex. Try it, but try it with a sheet you can throw away, because there's nothing stickier than mango sex. It wasn't even that good, but we remembered it. And that's the key — the remembering, the remembering.

Ellen Cleghorne

I do give a good blow job. I really, really do, and I wish that you could like get a grade, or some type of certificate. It's so wrong, if you're so good at something — and I realized I was really good at it. I guess I was 20-21, I was giving this guy a blow job, and he said, "You do this so well. What are you gonna do with the rest of your life?" And I said, "Well, I can't do *this*." Stupid *me* — I had to get a real profession, so I started training to be an actress — but I could've just kept *blowing*. I could've just kept sucking dicks.

And I asked my gay friends — this is why it's so good for a woman to have gay friends — because men give each other head on a regular basis when you're gay, so they have more experience. So I asked my gay friend, "How do you do it without gagging?" He goes way down in his throat. So he told me this exercise. These are things you can't learn on morning TV. They teach you shit like planting tomatoes. I don't fucking plant tomatoes! I wanna know, how do I get it down a little further without gagging on my dinner?

Beth Lapides

We don't role-play — I don't have that kind of energy — if you need to role-play with the person you're with, that's just gonna require a lot of effort. But if we *did* role-play, who would we be?

Maybe we would be the ringmaster and the clown. And then that sounded so good, I think we're gonna try it.

What would be our safety word if we were into that? Your safety word has to be something that you would never, ever say — like in S&M — and I realized the only thing that I would never, ever say under any circumstances is, "I think I've lost too much weight, and I'm actually too thin now." That's my safety word. My biggest sex fantasy is *(whispering)*, "We're making love, and I realize I'm out of debt."

Moon Zappa

I had an awful make-out session recently. I met this guy who was repellant, and I thought, well, maybe that's what marriage is like. But I made out with him, and he had this tongue that poked. It was just like a poking rock-hard tongue, but it also had flaps underneath, like a car-wash. He also deposited a lot of saliva in your mouth during a kiss, so it was like the rock-hard poking the flat dry — kind of like a cat's tongue — the flaps, and then the saliva. But I said no. When you're not attracted, you're not attracted.

I had an affair with this guy who said, "You never initiate." So he wanted me to initiate, and I thought, "You know what? Yeah, yeah." So I set the stage, and basically I blindfolded him, had him lie down, and I started to give him a hand job, but what he didn't know was, I went in the kitchen and I got a butcher knife, and then I jerked him off with one hand, and fucking *stabbed the air* with the other hand, and he never knew. I realize I'm not gonna have sex with any of you here in the room.

Beth Lapides

I had this boyfriend, and he was just hard *all* the time. I used to call him Ever-Ready. So we would have sex all the time, and then one day he goes, "I don't think I can have sex any more, because, you know, I've had sex so much in my life, I was thinking my come could probably fill a huge garbage can. A *huge* one, you know, one of those big ones, that's how much I've come in my life. And I just thought, maybe I should give it a rest." And he did. He stopped. He says, "You know what? Enough!" I hope he's back at it, because he was good.

Merrill Markoe

On the topic of faked orgasms, if sex fraud were a crime, I'd be in jail for the rest of my life. Sometimes, if I think a guy is very good, I fake *multiple* orgasms. Here's what I don't get. So many guys don't seem to know where anything is on a woman. Guys who can assemble a refrigerator for you, guys who can take your computer apart and put it back together again, guys who can fix your dishwasher, have no idea where anything is on a woman.

Why can't we just give everyone, when you meet them, some sort of a manual, like you would get when you buy a Cuisinart? And it would just have a small map, and it would show them where they're going, because of lot of times they're close, but it's like they got on the Hollywood Freeway and they got off at Lankershim and they meant to get off at Highland. So close but yet so far away.

The last guy I had an affair with, his whole approach was like the female sex organ was a plate of spaghetti. But the harder they're trying, the more orgasms I fake, because you want to encourage them. As if a *guy* would ever do that. As if a woman were searching and searching for a guy's penis and couldn't find it, a guy would go, "Look how hard she's trying. I gotta give her points for that."

I have come to think of orgasms as the thing that I have really quickly while the guy gets up to look in the refrigerator and see if there's anything to drink. My definition of bad sex is contained in the question, "How many times should you let a guy slam your head into the bed-board behind you before you call a halt to the proceedings?" And the answer is *two*. The first time could've been an accident.

My best piece of sexual advice: If you're a guy, and you've been attempting to arouse a woman and you are working very hard and it's going very slowly and it seems to be taking more than half an hour, rest assured that you do not know what you are doing, and, for God's sake, don't do it harder.

Driving While Stoned

I don't have a driver's license. I've never even driven a car. In fact, I don't know *how* to drive. I simply never learned. Maybe it's because I was brought up in Astoria, only 20 minutes away from Times Square by subway. And when I grew up, I moved to the Lower East Side, where there were subways and buses and cabs. And walking. I used to walk all around the city. That was my only exercise.

Then I moved to the West Coast and bought a used Volkswagen convertible for $500, but I still didn't learn to drive. I could operate the glove compartment, and that was it. I had planned to take driving lessons, but there were always other priorities. I lived with a couple of friends from the Merry Pranksters, Hassler and Poopsie, and they drove me places. Poopsie told Ken Kesey that I was very dependent.

"Yeah," Kesey replied, "but he knows a lot of independent people."

My job has been to check the street signs and roll the joints, so that the driver can keep both hands on the steering wheel — except, of course, when shifting a gear or tuning the radio or taking a toke. This is not exactly a Gallup Poll, but in my own decades of experience as a professional passenger, I have always felt safer driving with a stoner than with a boozer.

A friend who has been in both camps makes this comparison: "I would drive while swigging away on a bottle of gin, getting drunker and drunker, having less and less control over the car, and marveling at my own deteriorating state. But I had no problem controlling the car when I smoked marijuana. What I really loved was to ride my motorcycle down Lexington Avenue at 3 in the morning, and time all the lights."

It's always reassuring, though, to have such personal observations underscored by official research.

In Australia, in October 1998, the largest study ever done linking road accidents with drugs and alcohol found that drivers with cannabis in their blood were no more at risk than those who were drug-free.

Indeed, the findings by a pharmacology team from the University of Adelaide and Transport SA showed that drivers who had smoked marijuana were marginally less likely to have an accident than those who were drug-free.

A spokesperson for the study, Dr. Jason White, said that the difference was not enough to be statistically significant, but could be explained by anecdotal evidence that marijuana smokers were more cautious and drove more slowly because of altered time perception.

The study of 2,500 accidents, which matched the blood-alcohol levels of injured drivers with details from police reports found that drug-free drivers caused the accidents they were involved in in 53.5% of the cases; injured drivers with a blood-alcohol concentration of more than 0.05% were culpable in nearly 90% of the accidents that they were involved in.

Drivers with cannabis in their blood were less likely to cause an accident, with a culpability rate of 50.6%. The study has policy implications for those who argue that drug detection should be a new focus for road safety. Dr. White said that the study showed the importance of concentrating efforts on alcohol rather than other drugs.

In March 1999, a study at the University of Toronto found that people who smoke moderate amounts of marijuana are not much more dangerous behind the wheel than completely sober drivers, concluding that the hazards of smoking marijuana had been overrated, and that those who smoke pot and drive should not be demonized.

Canadian researcher Alison Smiley compared several studies that looked into how serious the impairment was from marijuana compared to alcohol, which clearly affects driving ability.

"Both substances impair performance," she stated. "However, the more cautious behavior of subjects who received marijuana decreases the drug's impact on performance. Their behavior is more appropriate to their impairment, whereas subjects who received alcohol tend to drive in a more risky manner."

She pointed out that earlier studies into the effects of marijuana on driving ability gave volunteers "fairly hefty doses" and put them behind the wheel immediately afterward.

Reporting her findings in *Health Effects of Cannabis*, published by Toronto's Center for Addiction and Mental Health, she said that such studies may have exaggerated the effects of the drug.

"There's an assumption," she wrote, "that because marijuana is illegal, it must increase the risk of an accident. We should try to just stick to the facts."

In October 1996, Bill Clinton, in his weekly radio address, urged stronger measures to reduce teenage drug use and driving under the influence of drugs.

That same day, he asked the Director of National Drug Control Policy and the Secretary of Transportation to present recommendations within 90 days that would meet those goals. The president specifically requested that they consider drug-testing for minors applying for drivers' licenses.

Their recommendations called for a federally-funded, $16 million, two-year demonstration program to devise and test "essential core elements of pre-driver licensure drug-testing" — which, the task force felt, would send an important message to American youth that drugs and driving don't mix.

If states were to develop drug-testing programs for young people prior to their obtaining a drivers license," they warned, "states should be sensitive to upholding constitutional standards under the 4th Amendment (reasonable 'search' in the procurement of the individual's blood, breath, urine or other specimen), and under the equal protection clause and the due process clause...."

"First-time driver's license applicants under 18 must be tested. The states may choose to test others as well. For example, states could test all first-time applicants, regardless of age (this would increase costs only slightly, since most first-time applicants are teenagers, and it would reduce litigation risks based on charges of age discrimination)."

So now I may *never* be able to get a driver's license — even if I first learn how to drive — just because the government wants to avoid a lawsuit over age discrimination from some teenaged pot-smoker who can't get a driver's license. Is this creeping fascism or what? On the other hand, I'll remain, inadvertently, ecologically ahead of my time.

A Tale of
Two Conspiracies

In *A Dictionary of Euphemisms: How Not to Say What You Mean* (Oxford University Press), R.W. Holder explains that a euphemism is "the language of evasion, of hypocrisy, of prudery, and of deceit." *Gap* is a euphemism for "vagina." *Honk*: "to feel the genitals of a male." *I hear what you say* means "I do not agree with you." *Restore order*: "to invade and conquer a country." *Look at the garden*: "to urinate outdoors." *States' rights*: "the continuation of discrimination against blacks."

States' rights was the rationale for Alabama Governor George Wallace to block school doors in an attempt to prevent African-Americans from getting an equal education. But one person's racist is another person's populist. When Wallace, presidential candidate of the American Independent Party, was shot by Arthur Bremer during the 1972 campaign, he dropped out of the race — paralyzed from the waist down, confined to a wheelchair — and 25 million votes were shunted toward Richard Nixon's so-called mandate.

Could this have been the ultimate dirty trick orchestrated — or at least exploited — by the Committee to Re-Elect the President? Conspiracy researcher R. Frank Salant investigated the role of E. Howard Hunt, the White House Plumber and CIA operative for 21 years. Immediately following the incident, Nixon confidant Charles Colson phoned Hunt, instructing him to go to Bremer's apartment.

Although Hunt insisted that he immediately countermanded Colson's order, declaring that such an operation would involve a high degree of risk and possible embarrassment for the Nixon administration, he also reassured investigators that even if he had complied with Colson's order, he would only have been "looking for evidence," an expression which did not make the cut in *A Dictionary of Euphemisms.* According to Salant, "This is a most important statement, because in my experience as a researcher, the phrase 'looking for evidence' in clandestine jargon actually means to *plant* evidence."

And suddenly Bremer, who never kept a diary, had now written a diary, which Salant read carefully and, having read all of Hunt's writings, found "a disturbing sense of similarity in both writing styles. Was Hunt the mystery man who made off with Bremer's notebook? Did Hunt forge Bremer's diary?" Other questions: Why did FBI Director L. Patrick Gray order the FBI to call off its investigation of the Wallace shooting? Why wasn't the source of Bremer's mysterious finances investigated? What happened to the $400,000 that Nixon aide H.R. Haldeman approved for the purpose of defeating Wallace?

Salant claims, "The ballistics evidence alone proves there was a conspiracy. Although the Maryland police report points to Bremer as the 'lone assailant,' it is worthwhile noting that at Bremer's trial, an FBI agent gave testimony which indicated that some of the bullets found at the scene of the crime and in the victims' bodies would not match with Bremer's gun."

Several years ago, George Wallace wrote to President Clinton asking him to reopen the federal investigation of the attempted assassination. Wallace said he didn't believe that Bremer had acted alone. A White House spokesperson said that Clinton received the letter and was "taking it under advisement." A euphemism for *ignoring.* In 1993, I wrote to Clinton, asking, specifically, "Why *not* reopen the investigation?" Over a year later, I received a reply from George Stephanopoulos:

> "As Senior Advisor to the President, I am grateful for the perspective that your letter has given me. Comments and suggestions from concerned citizens like you should prove useful to me in performing my job. President Clinton and I appreciate the opportunity to hear your views, and I thank you again for taking the time to write on this important issue."

Yeah, as they say, right.

■ ■ █ ■ ■

Peter McWilliams, the publisher (Prelude Press) and best-selling author of *Ain't Nobody's Business If You Do: The Absurdity of Consensual Crimes in a Free Society*, has AIDS and cancer. Under California's Proposition 215, doctors have legally prescribed marijuana to relieve nausea and increase appetite. Otherwise, if he vomits up his lunch, the antiviral pills he takes to stay alive are also regurgitated.

McWilliams hired Todd McCormick (also allowed by law to take his medicine) to write a book about the varieties of medical marijuana, giving him an advance of $150,000 to conduct his research. McCormick was arrested by federal authorities for growing 4,000 marijuana plants.

In 1997, McWilliams flew to Detroit for a family reunion. He was arrested at the airport for possession of seven joints. Somebody smelled them. The prosecutor in this case had legally changed his name to Luke Skywalker in 1977, when he was in his twenties and got inspired by *Star Wars*. That's still the name he uses. In court, he is Luke Skywalker, and he perceives each new defendant as Darth Vader. May the farce be with you.

In July 1998, McWilliams was arrested by DEA agents in Los Angeles, charged with being the ringleader of a conspiracy to cultivate and distribute medical marijuana. Because he is not allowed to leave the state, his trial in Detroit has been postponed.

McWilliams spent a month behind bars in Los Angeles until his $250,000 bond could be raised. As a condition of his pre-trial release, he cannot smoke pot. If one of his urine tests were to indicate that he *did* smoke pot, it would be back to jail, while his mother and brother would lose their homes, since they borrowed money on their homes to bail him out.

Since he will not be allowed to use a medical-marijuana defense — nor will the just-published *How to Grow Medical Marijuana* be permitted as evidence — he has pleaded guilty in the hope of lenient sentencing.

Meanwhile, his viral count continues to multiply, putting his health in ever-increasing danger. He is in a state of physical and emotional debilitation. He has lost 30 pounds. When he went to court to request the right to smoke his medicine, he was brought in seated in a wheelchair.

Judge George King asked the federal prosecutor, "If Mr. McWilliams can only use marijuana in inhaled form, and other methods were ineffective (they are), would the government consider that irrelevant?"

The prosecutor fidgeted. "It is still irrelevant under the current state of law. There are no exceptions."

Q. "And if there's nausea, that's just the way it goes?"

A. *"It sounds terrible, the way the court says it. As human beings, we're sympathetic to Mr. McWilliams' plight. As officers of the court, we're sworn to uphold the law that has clearly made use and possession illegal. We are sensitive to the fact that his health has deteriorated. But we are not the legislators."*

In March 1999, Judge King denied McWilliams' request. "We do not mean to express indifference to the defendant's situation," he stated, "(but) we are not empowered to grant (him) what amounts to a license to violate federal law." Thus, the federal government is ignoring the mandate of the people who voted Proposition 215 into law.

[Todd McCormick is currently serving five years in federal prison. Peter McWilliams was scheduled to be sentenced in August, but he died on June 14th, 2000, choking on his own vomit, in effect being murdered by the federal government which forbade him to smoke his medicine to avoid nausea.]

States' rights. It's not just for racists any more.

The Tabloidization of America

In an interview for *On Campus*, a weekly entertainment magazine distributed at colleges and universities, Bill Maher of ABC's *Politically Incorrect* states, "People always say to me, 'I get my news from your show.' And I say, 'You shouldn't.' It's frightening. You know how they have those polls, like a *Time* magazine/CBS poll? I've actually seen, like, and NBC/*National Enquirer* poll. That's how close tabloid life has encroached upon the so-called legitimate news-source life. We joke in the office that we're going to see 'An NBC News/*Hustler* poll has revealed...'"

In the aftermath of reporting on so much scandal and horror with equal fervor, the respectable journalistic community has — inevitably, it seems — surrendered its professional standards and is now bringing total tabloidization to the newspapers of America. Here are a couple of recent examples.

In Bed With the Fed

TV news junkies and Wall Street insiders alike may have been surprised when NBC correspondent Andrea Mitchell, the wife of Federal Reserve Chairman Alan Greenspan, told Barbara Walters that Viagra had saved their marriage. But they were in total shock when the veteran reporter revealed how their private sex life had inadvertently affected the stock market.

When Greenspan began having problems with arousal, Andrea persuaded him to get a prescription for those little blue pills. "What a difference that made," she confessed to Barbara. "Alan and I made love all through the night. It was just fantastic."

But the next day, as shareholders in Pfizer Pharmaceuticals watched the value of their stocks almost double, the market in general slumped after Greenspan was overheard warning a friend: "There are imbalances in our expansion that, unless redressed, will bring this long run of strong growth and low inflation to a close."

Word spread quickly, and investors interpreted his statement as a sign that inflation was resurgent, and that the stock and bond markets could take a deep plunge as a result.

Andrea was flabbergasted. "But my husband was not referring to the state of the economy," she insisted. "He was talking about erectile dysfunction."

Tragedy Has Happy Ending

There exists no map for the road to a career in show business, and nobody knows that better than Gretchen Miller. She thought she would remain a popular history teacher at Columbine High School in Littleton, Colorado, until the day she retired. But then came that bloody massacre by two students, armed with deadly weapons and a deranged attitude.

As the frightening sounds of bullets and bombs reverberated through the halls, she barricaded the door to her classroom with a desk and several chairs, turned out the lights, then huddled in a corner with her twenty-three students, leading them in prayer. "Oh, Lord," she pleaded, "help us survive this nightmare, and protect all those in this building from this horrible evil."

Five weeks later, Gretchen was fired. "I was absolutely stunned," she says. "Because I prayed with the children in a public school, I was accused of violating the separation of church and state." A spokesperson for the school explained that they didn't want any trouble from the American Civil Liberties Union.

However, the resulting publicity landed the talented schoolteacher her own radio talk show. "I'm very excited," she admits. "I only wish that the program wasn't being sponsored by the

Gap. I cringe every time I hear their commercial for black trench coats."

An Interview With Chiquita Banana

When I was growing up, Chiquita Banana first triggered my sense of skepticism. In those days, she was just a poor street hooker with curvature of the spine, a yellow complexion and false eyelashes. She would do her little dance and beckon me, singing, "I'm Chiquita Banana, and I've come to say, bananas have to ripen in a certain way.... So you should never put bananas — in the refrigerator. No, no, no, no!"

"That's bullshit," I told her. "You absolutely *can* put bananas in the refrigerator. But your pimp just wants people to leave them out in the open to rot, so then they throw the rotten bananas away and buy a bunch of fresh bananas."

These days, Chiquita Banana is a very expensive call girl. She lives in a lavishly-furnished, postmodern duplex condo. It seems her pimp was recently awarded a settlement of $10 million in a lawsuit. The *Cincinnati Enquirer* had published a series detailing inhumane labor conditions and environmental crimes by Chiquita's pimp, and the paper was sued — not because they reported anything that was untrue, but only because they intercepted internal voice mail in obtaining their documentation.

I began our interview on that note.

Q. "Chiquita, let me ask, which do you think is worse — the invasion of your pimp's privacy or his running a business that involves third-world slavery, deforestation, poisonous residues, intimidation by thugs, bribery..."

A. *"I'm sorry, Paul, but the attorneys won't allow any discussion about that subject. I mean, even though our suit was settled with the* Cincinnati Enquirer, *we're still under investigation by the government."*

Q. "Okay. When Honduras was severely struck by Hurricane Mitch, international environmentalist activists reported that the death and devastation were made worse by deforestation and destruction of animal habitats to make way for banana plantations..."

A. *"Excuse me, in the first place, Hurricane Mitch was certainly not our fault. And I'll have you know that we sent aid to Honduras."*

Q. "No, Chiquita, what I'm saying is that it was the policies of your pimp that led to much of the destruction. And he didn't just send aid to Honduras. When Bill Clinton ran against Bob Dole back in 1996, your pimp sent huge bribes — oops, I mean mega-contributions — to *both* of them. And it worked. You got favors from the government. Clinton's people went to Geneva for World Trade Organization authority to impose tariffs on European products, and this was done on your pimp's behalf."

A. *"Paul, you've changed. Why are you so hostile? You know something, I'll bet it was you who was behind that Internet hoax, warning everybody about bananas from Costa Rica being infected with flesh-eating bacteria. That false information went around the world. We were saddled with a challenging public-relations problem."*

Q. "No, it wasn't me, I swear. And I'm not hostile, I'm just disappointed that you would lend your image to this trade dispute over bananas between the United States and Europe. The U.S. is fighting to end preferential treatment for Caribbean bananas in Europe. Caribbean nations are watching this battle in total fear, because it would desolate their tiny economies, and banana farmers would have no choice but to cultivate marijuana instead — they're already making that switch — and then their marijuana fields become the target of American eradication projects."

A. *"You know what? I'm gonna roll a joint, and we're gonna smoke it, I'm gonna put on some music, I'm gonna light some incense, and you're gonna mellow out, and* then *we'll continue talking...."*

[A half-hour later]

Q. "I'm so zonked. This sure is powerful weed."

A. *"Bananas aren't the only thing we grow, sweetie-pie. In fact, marijuana is a much more lucrative crop, did you know that?"*

Q. "I'm not surprised. But try to see this from the *poor* banana farmers' point of view. America provides weapons, machinery and manpower to destroy their little pot farms, and yet America is also trying to deprive them of the European market for bananas. Don't you think that that kind of unfair competition interferes in the internal affairs of other countries?"

A. *I'm so stoned I don't know* what *the fuck you're talking about, honey. Why don't you just interfere with* my *internal affairs?"*

[An hour later]

Q. "Wow, you went around the world like *you* were false information."

A. *"Well, I think you conducted a very* probing *interview."*

Q. "Look, all I want you to do is at least *acknowledge* your symbolic contribution to your pimp's undue influence, which trickles down to farmers who need to be able to put bread on the table for their children to eat. It's that simple."

A. *(Singing) "I'm Maria Marijuana and I've come to say, marijuana has to ripen in a certain way.... So you should never put marijuana — in the glove compartment. No, no, no no!"*

Rapture, Shmapture

The Second Coming is history. Now it seems like it was just another publicity stunt. You may recall how Billy Graham and Larry King were discussing Jesus Christ, and Billy Graham mentioned that there are four hundred individuals in Los Angeles alone who all claim to *be* Jesus. Then Larry King asked him if he thought the *real* Second Coming would occur in his lifetime. Without a moment's hesitation, he said, "Yes."

And, as if Jesus Christ simply wanted to reward the aging evangelist's faith, he decided to return to earth. Of course, the great event was covered by CNN. Don King immediately signed him up to do the media circuit. Jesus wanted to reach all kinds of people, and that's exactly what Don King would accomplish. Everything he had done for Mike Tyson was just a dress rehearsal for this.

"Christ," he said, "you're gonna charm everybody's ass off."

Jesus went on *Good Morning, America*. Diane Sawyer said, "Wow, you're a real celebrity, huh?" And Jesus replied, "Fan is short for fanatic, hype is short for hyperbole, and Mel Gibson is short for a leading man."

Jesus went on the *Howard Stern* show. Howard said, "Hey, c'mon, you banged Mary Magdalene, right? You can tell me. Nobody's listening to this." And Jesus replied, "Bang not lest ye be banged."

Jesus went on the *Oprah Winfrey Show*. Oprah said, "How do you feel about posting the Ten Commandments in schools?" And Jesus replied, "I have believed *passionately* in the separation of church and state before there ever was a First Amendment. I think they should post the Bill of Rights in schools."

Jesus went on the *Late Show*. David Letterman said, "Why don't you tell us about one of your Stupid Lord Tricks?" And Jesus replied, "Whenever the president has a press conference — no matter what political party he has belonged to — they always stand in front of the banner that says THE WHITE HOUSE and underneath it says WASHINGTON, D.C. Well, I know when he's telling a lie, and if he is, by sheer will power I can make him move to his left so that behind him it says, THE WHITE WASHING."

Jesus had a healing competition with Pat Robertson. Jesus did a product endorsement for Birkenstock sandals. Jesus appeared on the cover of *Vanity Fair*, "nailed" to a crucifix. When you looked closely, you could see that he had a bellybutton ring, and on his arm a tattoo of an arrow going through a heart with the word *Mom*.

Jesus finally got his own weekly series on CBS, called *Savior Time*. On the premiere, he devoted the entire program to the Nielsen families, and earned 100% of the audience share. His popularity continued until the night that the Fox network presented co-ed nude mud wrestling, and the ratings plummeted downhill after that. Ultimately the show was cancelled. The headline on *Variety* read: "J.C. Dies — Overexposure."

And so now there are four hundred and one individuals in Los Angeles alone who claim to be Jesus.

See You in
the Funny Papers

Maybe it's because I've developed an MTV attention span in the face of profound change, but I find it difficult to concentrate on newspaper editorials while I savor the wit and insight in Garry Trudeau's *Doonesbury*.

Comic strips have long served as a vehicle for cultural and political propaganda, on the left (*Pogo*) and — much more frequently — on the right (*Steve Canyon*). A *Buz Sawyer* strip once backed a naval campaign for more funds for anti-submarine warfare; Buz and the U.S. Navy took on a Soviet submarine which had been nestling off our shores. A few months later, back in real life, Congress voted extra money for anti-submarine warfare programs.

When Steve Canyon learned that the "RX-71 program" had been cut back to save funds, he commented to his coffee cup: "I guess it won't really matter! If the Russians send a few Roman candles at us some cloudy night, we'll make a formal protest in the United Nations — if we can only find the pieces of the building!" The U.S. Senate later voted 74-13 approving an extra $332,000,000 — an appropriation strongly opposed by the Johnson Administration — for development of the Air Force's RS-70 reconnaissance-strike bomber.

During the Vietnam war, Canyon arranged a police escort for a group of peace marchers. A predictably bearded demonstrator says, "A police escort for *us?*" Canyon: "Of course! I *told* you there is an angry mob up ahead waiting to harm you. As citizens of the United

343

States you are entitled to freedom of speech and peaceful assembly! Now all you need to do is to prove that you *are* citizens! Otherwise the police do not have to protect your parade — and with an angry mob up ahead they cannot, for your *own* protection, allow your parade to go on!"

The bearded guy: "What is *proof?*" Canyon: "Your passport! Your birth certificate! Baptismal certificate!" Bearded guy: "No one carries a passport *INSIDE* the U.S.!" Canyon: "As you know, the Constitution states that citizens are entitled to free speech and free assembly! The police will protect all paraders so entitled! No draft cards or Social Security cards — you do not have to be a *citizen* to obtain either! Line starts here!"

A reader of the *Chicago Sun-Times* wanted to know when Steve Canyon had "replaced the United States Supreme Court as interpreter of the Constitution." The right of the people peaceably to assemble "applies to all people, not just to citizens." I wrote directly to Canyon's creator, Milton Caniff, who replied: "*Of course* it was unconstitutional to stop the impending riot and bloodshed. Colonel Canyon never said it wasn't. He stated that the Chief of Police *thought* it was legal to require the people on both sides to show proof of citizenship."

During World War II, President Roosevelt personally complimented Ham Fisher, creator of *Joe Palooka*, for helping to make the pre-war draft more acceptable to the public. And the British Ministry of Information kept Fisher apprised of General Montgomery's progress in the Battle of Tunisia so that the real battle and Palooka's participation in it could reach a mutual, simultaneous climax. Jules Feiffer's reaction: "Seemingly, publishers' only objection to World War III is the loss in newspaper circulation it might mean for them. 'Oops, there goes New York and Washington. How many papers does that leave me?' "

Feiffer told me, "I get terribly annoyed on those rare occasions when I happen to come across one of the several dedicated Cold War adventure strips like *Terry and the Pirates*. The official policy on syndicated strips is that they are to be non-editorial in nature. Walt Kelly in *Pogo* attacked McCarthyism in 1954 and editors protested that this *was* editorial comment. I have finally discovered the distinction. So long as a cartoon does not waver from official government policy — or unofficial Pentagon fantasy — it is not considered editorial in nature."

But that was in 1960. Comic strips now reflect the evolution of the Cold War into the War on Drugs and the co-evolution of the military-industrial complex into the prison-industrial complex.

In 1999, a *Rex Morgan, M.D.* strip depicted a police officer searching a van while the driver stands outside. "A box full of marijuana!" says the cop. "No wonder you were nervous!" The driver, with shaved head and earring, responds: "Hey, you don't have a warrant to search my van!" The cop: "It's called 'probable cause' ...I smelled pot the second you opened the door!" He points his gun at the driver and says, "Now turn around... and put your hands on your head!"

This year, when Whitney Houston was found carrying a baggie of marijuana in a Hawaiian airport, the incident made its way into *The Boondocks*, a comic strip revolving around an African-American kid, Huey. "I think she was stupid," he says. His classmate, a little white girl, asks, "Do you think she'll be doing remixes with Dre and Snoop?" Huey: "Yeeesh! I pray one of them learns how to 'Just say no' ..."

Huey's grandfather at home: "What upsets me is when I think about the impressionable *fans*. They see their favorite singer do something, they're gonna think it's *cool*. Me, I'm just about seventy. I *know* right from wrong. But what about the *young* folks? The people that might see her using these drugs and want to emulate that? Huh? What about Whitney Houston's thirty- and forty-year-old fans who don't know no better? Personally, I blame Bobby Brown..."

Pot often turns up in editorial cartoons. For example, syndicated editorial cartoonist Ed Fischer quotes a news report: "Teen sex, alcohol use down, marijuana use up." Then he shows a teacher saying, "Before we take the roll, are there any questions?" A student stands up, raises his hand and says, "I have a question teacher... was I here yesterday?"

When medical marijuana was in the news, it inspired editorial cartoons in newspapers across the country.

The *Springfield News:* At the Rite Pharmacy, a druggist handing a filled prescription to a customer suggests, "This dynamite Jamaican reefer should be taken four times a day with Grand Funk Railroad." "However," he warns, "some patients will experience the munchies."

The *Richmond Times-Dispatch:* A doctor is telling a patient, "Sorry, but I can't prescribe marijuana for chronic dandruff..."

The patient — who has a beard and pony-tail and is wearing a Jimi Hendrix T-shirt: "Uh, skin rashes?... Hemorrhoids?..."

The *Commercial Appeal:* A doctor is sitting at his desk, saying on the phone, "Take two joints and call me in the morning!" Coincidentally, in the *New York Daily News,* another doctor is sitting at a different desk and saying on the phone, "Smoke two joints and call me in the morning..."

The *Times Union:* A couple of tokers are sitting on a sofa with their feet on a coffee table and watching the test pattern on TV. One says, "Pass me that medicinal delivery system, will ya?" The other passes the joint, saying, "Smoking pot just isn't what it used to be..."

The *San Diego Union:* A man in a cafe is looking at a newspaper with the headline "Medical Marijuana." A bystander says, "Why legalize pot? Everyone knows it's a chemical crutch..." Nearby, a woman is placing her order: "Triple-shot cappuccino, please."

The *Los Angeles Times:* A billboard features Joe Camel smoking. In tiny letters at the bottom of the sign: "Some General Surgeon Said It's okay to Get Cancer for Medicinal Purposes."

A workman explains to a passerby, "It's okay, man. It's pot."

Medical marijuana has also been working as a perfect metaphor in editorial cartoons.

The *Asbury Park Press:* A stoned Uncle Sam is smoking a huge joint labeled "Stock Market." The caption: "Recreational *and* medicinal."

The *Rochester Post-Bulletin:* A gleeful man in mid-air is holding on to a street sign pole — Wall Street, of course — as others dance in the street, tossing money in the air. One observer says to his friend, "Look, Louie — what we're seeing is probably ample proof that marijuana does help people deal with their anxieties."

And finally, the *New Jersey Record*: In Bill Clinton's office, a chart indicates that available Medicare funds are decreasing. A doctor passes him a smoking joint, advising, "Try some marijuana..."
Amen.

Kenneth Starr
Meets
JonBenet Ramsey

Kenneth Starr has accepted an invitation from the Boulder, Colorado, Chamber of Commerce to serve as an independent prosecutor in the JonBenet Ramsey murder case.

"I am just as surprised as you are," he announced at a press conference. "Actually, I thought I had retired from this business, but I just couldn't refuse. You know, I worked for a while investigating pedophiles, and I came to realize that a grown man who is capable of having sex with young children is also capable of killing them. It's simply a matter of degree."

"Sir," a reporter from the *San Francisco Chronicle* asked, "are you saying that you believe a pedophile was responsible for JonBenet's death?"

"It's too early to tell."

"But," a reporter from the *New York Times* asked, "since DNA — so far, unidentified DNA — was found on Ms. Ramsey's underpants, wouldn't it be a foregone conclusion that the murderer was a pedophile?"

"Not necessarily. It could be two separate individuals. Now, this is purely hypothetical, of course, but, say, the father could be a pedophile and the mother could be a murderer."

"Judge," a *Los Angeles Times* reporter said, "you issued that extremely graphic Starr Report after the Clinton investigation. Will you issue a similar report about JonBenet?"

349

"I can't answer that yet. I just don't want to have a premature ejaculation at this stage of the game."

The *Washington Post* correspondent followed up, sarcastically, "Well, will there be any leaks, like there were to the White House press corps?"

"I'm sorry, I don' t accept the premise of your question. Next?"

And a gossip columnist for the *National Enquirer* stood up. "What was the result of your original investigation of pedophiles?"

"Oh, that. Well, after six months, it turned out that every member of our pedophiles chat room was an undercover officer posing as a pedophile."

"Sir —"

"Thank you all. I look forward to our next meeting."

Psychedelic Relics at the Cannabis Cup

The fact that the flight to Amsterdam is scheduled to depart at 4:20 balances on the cusp between appropriate coincidence and good omen, because 420 has become a number representing celebration in the marijuana subculture. Some say it's the police code for a pot bust. Others say it's the number of ingredients in the herb. Who knows, maybe it's from that nursery rhyme about 4 and 20 blackbirds. In any case, during the weeklong 12th annual Cannabis Cup, sponsored by *High Times* magazine, there will be huge partying at 4:20 every afternoon, and also at 4:20 every morning, with live music, from blues to reggae, at Melkweg, a night club several yards away from police headquarters. The emcee will be an invigorating stand-up comic from San Francisco, Ngaio Bealum, whose parents were both in the Black Panther Party. "You know," he says, "when we were kids, we didn't have bongs. We just had to fill our mouths with water and suck real slowly." He describes smoking pot while drinking coffee as "the poor man's 8-ball."

Usually you can spot the folks at LAX who are traveling to the Cup, but I'm surprised to overhear a retired 62-year-old grandmother say to her 49-year-old companion, "I was so stoned I couldn't get off the toilet." The two women will be staying at a youth hostel. They're looking forward to checking out the coffee shops, which are open until 1 a.m. In 1976, the Health Ministry of Holland decriminalized marijuana, and 20 years later licenses were given out to the coffee shops, the same ones that had already been selling pot and hash. Customers can choose from an actual menu, then sit down at a table and smoke their purchase. They can also buy coffee. Cup attendees are given "passports" to see who will be the first to have their passport stamped by all the coffee shops where they sampled their goods. The winner: a group of seven college students from Buffalo. However, there's a mix-up about the tour bus, so that the grandma I met at LAX has to schlep around from coffee shop to coffee shop by streetcar, unaware that one coffee shop, the Green House, offers "an energy drink after smoking too much all day." She complains, "This is like the march to Bataan. I've had my first bad high here."

This event is a non-stop orgy of pot-smoking. In the funky Quentin Hotel lobby, a gigantic painting of Keith Richards watches over the guests as they sit at wooden tables, cheerfully chatting while they smoke their joints and drink their hot chocolate. Joints are shared with cab drivers. The pot-smoking continues at the opening banquet. *High Times* editor and Cannabis Cup founder Steve Hager refers to marijuana as "our sacrament." He labels pot-smokers "the most repressed minority group on the planet." This year, as a countercultural version of *Roots*, icons of the Beat Generation — Jack Kerouac, Neal Cassady, Allen Ginsberg and William Burroughs — will be honored. Hager asserts that "Beat culture is the bedrock and foundation that provides a continuity of tradition as counterculture continues to evolve." He demands respect for "the elders of our tribe" and requests a moment of silence for recently deceased Beat patriarch Paul Bowles. Even the pot-smoking is temporarily halted.

At the PAX meeting-house, we're gathered in a ballroom with a bar, a stage, rows of chairs, and some tables at the back. On stage, Neal Cassady's widow, Carolyn, and their son, John, are paying tribute to Cassady. Seated at one of the tables are three psychedelic relics — Robert Anton Wilson, John Sinclair and Stephen Gaskin, each sporting a white beard and mustache — there to honor a different Beat icon every day. While passing around a joint, they recall the specific years that they started smoking pot.

Wilson is the author of 32 books. The latest is an encyclopedia of conspiracy, *Everything Is Under Control*. Wilson does six drafts of everything he writes, alternating between straight and stoned, the final draft always while stoned. On stage, John Cassady is gesturing toward his mother. "This is the gal that started the Beat Generation," he says proudly. Wilson smiles and mutters, "I thought it was Burroughs, but what the hell." Wilson started smoking pot in 1955.

Sinclair was chairman of the White Panthers in Detroit and manager of a hard-rock band, the MC [Motor City] 5. The cover of his book, *Guitar Army*, features a photo of him smoking what had been a cigarette but which was morphed into a joint because he didn't want to send the wrong message to kids. When a Dutch TV correspondent questions him about his cigarette-smoking, he replies with a snarl, "It's none of your business." Sinclair started smoking pot in 1963.

Gaskin was founder of The Farm, an intentional community in Tennessee that left San Francisco in a convoy a few decades ago. He is challenging Ralph Nader for the Green Party presidential nomination. At the upcoming debate, he plans to delineate and praise Nader's accomplishments, then add, "But I can bring out the hippie vote." His platform includes "health care for all" and decriminalization of marijuana in such a way that it will "not fall into the hands of tobacco manufacturers." In Gaskin's administration, there will be mandatory drug testing to find out who has the *good* stuff. His Secret Service agents will be urine tested to be sure that they have a high enough THC level. But what if he wins? "First I'd shit, and then I would kick ass." Gaskin started smoking pot in 1962.

His wife, Ina May, president of the Midwives Association of North America, predicts that she would be "an unruly First Lady." She would turn the Lincoln Bedroom into a birth center for the poor. She would grow hemp in the Rose Garden, all meals at the White House would be vegetarian and she'd teach a Secret Service agent to braid his hair. When asked if she has intern concerns, she replies, "No, we'll do the blow jobs in every room." Her husband will be left to explain to the media, "I can't control her. You try."

The Cannabis Cup has become a big event in Amsterdam. In 1993, there were 52 attendees. This year, 2,000. But there is disgruntled discussion about previous awards possibly having been fixed. Originally, there were celebrity judges, and the various seed companies courted them. Later on, *anybody* attending the Cup could be a judge, and that resulted in equal-opportunity bribery. But this year the coffee-shop owners are the judges, and the 16 brand name entries have been coded, so that it will be a blind competition. "We truly don't know who's gonna win," Hager promises. The only complaint is that coffee-shop owners are expected to smoke too much cannabis.

For many, the first joint they smoke automatically becomes the winner, because everything after that one is cumulative. There is no surcease of euphoria, no time to savor one strain of marijuana or anticipate the next. This is not like tea-tasting, where the tea is spit out between tastes. At least, in the Aromatherapy booth, coffee beans are whiffed between each new fragrance, to neutralize the olfactory sense. Nevertheless, there is a winning strain of marijuana at the Cup: Super Silver Haze. But three coffee shops have been disqualified for collusion. It is the ultimate irony of this whole affair that an herb which promotes a sense of cooperation keeps being inhaled in such an aura of competition.

Ah, but I am jaded. Indeed, my cannabis cup runneth over. An issue of *High Times* once included in a questionnaire, "Is it possible to smoke too much pot?" And a reader responded, "I don't understand the question."

Predictions
for 2000

- Wearing clumps of elephant dung on women's breasts will become a fashion statement.

- Starbucks will begin selling coffee enemas, and customers will eagerly anticipate their Anal Latte each morning.

- George W. Bush will replace Dan Quayle as the generic icon of dumbness for comedians fond of resorting to easy-reference jokes.

- Al Gore will carry on a torrid affair with his personality adviser, Naomi Wolf, in order to prove that he is really an alpha male. He will also claim that he invented gravity.

- Reform Party candidate Pat Buchanan will be revealed as having been a participant in the early testing of Viagra, and, although he failed to obtain an erection, his right arm stiffened and went straight up.

- Since Donald Trump is germophobic and doesn't like to shake hands with strangers, he will conduct his entire presidential campaign wearing latex gloves.

- The Clinton Administration will revise its policy on gays in the military by changing their slogan to "Don't ask, don't tell, don't commit a hate crime."

- The prison-industrial complex will go public, and stocks will rise so high and so quickly that the market will finally crash and there will be a deep depression, except for inmates, who will celebrate in their cells.

- Campaign finance reform will finally be realized when a law is passed requiring all political contributions to remain anonymous.

- America will have free trade with China, but as a compromise measure, slave laborers will not be allowed to listen to pirated CDs.

- The Berlin Wall will be reconstructed along the Mexican border.

- Fidel Castro will lead a crusade for term limits.

- The United States and Russia will launch nuclear missiles at each other simultaneously, but computer problems caused by pacifist hackers will result in total failure.

- There will be a new rating for movies — PS, for Predictable Screenplay.

- Ricky Martin will convert to Judaism. He will then be circumcised on pay-per-view TV.

- MTV's Tom Green will get beaten up by muggers who aren't even aware that he's a professional asshole.

- The makers of crush video will get around the law by killing mice on camera with poison and mousetraps instead of spike heels.

- As new information comes out, the *San Jose Mercury News* will apologize for apologizing about their series on the CIA and cocaine.

- The new edition of the *Dictionary of Euphemisms* will include "lewinsky" as a euphemism for blow job and "genetic material" as a euphemism for semen.

- Inspired by Milo Minderbinder, an entrepreneurial hustler in the late Joseph Heller's novel, *Catch-22*, the Monsanto Company will market genetically engineered chocolate-covered cotton.

- The first successful cloning of a human being will take place, but the clone will be unhappy because he can't live a normal life, and he will sue the scientific team that brought him into being. The case will be dismissed as a frivolous lawsuit.

- AT&T will provide realistic toy cell phones to mentally ill homeless people who talk to themselves, so that passersby will think they're having business discussions.

- Intel will announce a new line of condoms with microchips so intricate that they have the ability to tell if an orgasm is being faked.

- Medical technology, always ahead of medical ethics, will enable a poverty-stricken, unwed, teenage girl, who is pregnant but lives in a state that does not permit abortion, to undergo a fetal transplant of her fetus from her womb to the womb of a wealthy, married, 40-something woman, who has never had an abortion, and is so pro-choice that she will then fly to a state which *does* permit abortion and have the surgery done there, without a single law having been broken in the process.

- In a moment of weakness, Pope John Paul will blurt out to a shocked crowd in Vatican Square, "After all, I'm not infallible, you know."

- Evangelist/sinner Oral Roberts will impregnate his housekeeper and she will have the child, who will be named Anal Roberts.

- A horde of angry apes will ransack the Board of Education in Kansas for not allowing evolution to be taught.

- An antidote for anthrax will be developed just in time for a terrorist attack.

- Dr. Jack Kevorkian will attempt to commit suicide by hanging himself in his cell, but prison guards will save his life at the last moment.

- John Kelly, director of the National Weather Service, will be charged with sexual harassment when he names a tornado Pussy.

- There will be a global competition for the best rationalization by a cult when the world doesn't end on the day they prophesized it would.

Be There Then

The city of Weimar, the Goethe Institute and the European liter-ary magazine Lettre Internationale *co-sponsored an essay contest in conjunction with Weimar's role as Europe's cultural capital for 1999. According to the* New York Times, *the organizers "invited some 900 philosophers, historians, scientists, artists and assorted luminaries from around the world to propose topics."*

After considering more than 113 replies, the judges chose not one but two questions for the world's Thinkers to ponder: "Liberating the Future from the Past?" and "Liberating the Past from the Fu-ture?"

The Weimar contest asked participants for a maximum of 10,500 words on these pressing issues. After some reflection, The Nation *decided there must be metaphysicians out there who could do the job in about 500 words, so they invited a number of them to take up the challenge, also asking them to be philosophical about their in-ability to offer a first prize to match Weimar's $28,000. But, as Goethe said on his deathbed, "More light!" What follows is my en-try.*

If life is choice, then I have chosen not to choose. Not to choose between Bill Clinton and Paula Jones. Not to choose between Ger-

many and Scientology. Not to choose between paper and plastic —
but do you have hemp? — I mean, choiceless awareness ain't a totally rigid process. Preferences are allowed. So, why should I
choose between Liberating the Future from the Past and Liberating
the Past from the Future? Instead, I choose to ponder the liberation
of the Past and the Future from each other.

Permit me to start with an epiphany. In the summer of 1984, I
was the comedy counselor at Winnarainbow, Wavy Gravy's circus
and performing arts camp. One morning I accompanied Wavy as he
made his rounds inspecting the tepees to decide which was best.
When we opened the flap of one particular tepee, we gasped with
delight. We knew we were entering the winner. The kids had created a veritable shrine on the ground.

Beautiful shells and stones and twigs and pieces of jewelry were
carefully arranged in semicircular rows that became smaller and
smaller, so that your eyes were led inevitably to the center, where,
on a miniature throne, sat a personal computer. I've always been an
unintentional Luddite — I have yet to program a VCR or drive a car
— but this moment served as an omen. I was witness to the marriage of nature and technology. I decided on the spot to buy a computer.

At first, I only used it for word processing, but I began to understand how time was in effect being compressed. Without my computer it would've taken me three more years to complete a book
manuscript. The concept of a first draft became obsolete, since I was
able to edit as I wrote. And because I didn't have to retype a whole
page every time I had to make a correction, I could surrender to per-
fectionist impulses that I might otherwise have rationalized away.

Then along came the Internet. Tim Berners-Lee, inventor of the
World Wide Web has observed, "To be overloaded by the existence
of so much on the Web is like being overloaded by the mass of a
beautiful countryside. You don't have to visit it, but it's nice to
know it's there. Especially the variety and freedom."

It's the essence of democracy that you can choose between a site
about the struggle for freedom in Burma or an online conference
where someone asks about vegetable dildos and received a fast,

pragmatic response: "Sticking acidic fruit up one's butt or vagina would probably smart."

It used to take a couple of decades for truth to work its way up from graffiti to alternative press to mainstream media, but now the acceleration from underground to cyberspace is instantaneous.

And it used to be, as Steve Allen said, that satire was tragedy plus time, but now, between fax machines and e-mail and talk radio, there is widespread instant irreverence. For example, while the David Koresh compound in Waco was still burning, there were already jokes being spread about the tragedy. Sample: "How many sects of Branch Davidians are there?" Answer: "Two — orthodox and extra crispy."

And Carl Havermist's recipe for Messiah Flambé: "Obtain one Lamb o' God. Garnish with approximately 90 vegetables, and seal up tightly with Alcohol, Tobacco and Firearms. Allow them to stew in their own juice for 51 days, then sear quickly using a wood fire. Serves one media circus."

During the hearings, Attorney General Janet Reno said she had considered spraying something that would put the cult members to sleep for ten hours so that agents could take control of the facility, but this was beyond current technology. Senator Barney Frank suggested, "Try pumping in C-Span."

It used to take a couple of decades for truth to work its way up

In 1966 I published an article in *The Realist*, "The Cybernetic Revolution" by Robert Anton Wilson, in which he wrote: "If the structure allows for feedback from the environment and alteration of behavior in accordance with the feedback, you have a cybernetic system. The essence of cybernetics is just that: an information flow that allows for self-correction."

As if to illustrate his point, Wilson wrote an article for *The Realist* in 1994, "My Life After Death," in which he described the feedback resulting from a false Internet report of his own demise in an obituary supposedly copied from the *Los Angeles Times*. With conspiracy theories flying left and right on the electronic bulletin board, it turned out to be an interactive delight. In other words, let a thousand Matt Drudges bloom.

If communication is indeed a path to the liberation of the Past and the Future from each other, then that leaves us with nothing but the Present to ponder.

There is only now. And that's already gone. Oops.

YOU WILL ALSO WANT TO READ:

☐ **94101 NATURAL LAW or Don't Put a Rubber on Your Willy,** *by Robert Anton Wilson.* A continuing episode in the critique of natural rights theories started by L.A. Rollins' *The Myth of Natural Rights*, Wilson lets fly at Murray Rothbard, George Smith, Samuel Konkin, and other purveyors of the "claim that some sort of metaphysical entity called a 'right' resides in a human being like a 'ghost' residing in a haunted house." An entertaining, informative and well thought out book that should be read by anyone who has ever been attracted to *any* ideology. *1987, 5½ x 8½, 72 pp, soft cover.* **$7.95.**

☐ **94067 THE MYTH OF NATURAL RIGHTS, *by L.A. Rollins.*** Once you've read this book, you'll be able to put those imaginary protectors of freedom back in the museums whence they came. In this seminal work, L.A. Rollins effectively demolishes the "bleeding heart libertarians" who promote these rights, including Ayn Rand, Murray Rothbard, Tibor Machan, Samuel Konkin and others. Rollins dissects the arguments for natural rights, cutting through the faulty logic to the core of libertarian dogma. An important book for libertarians who take their ideas seriously. *1983, 5½ x 8½, 50 pp, soft cover.* **$7.95.**

☐ **85182 PSYCHEDELIC SHAMANISM, The Cultivation, Preparation and Shamanic Use of Psychotropic Plants,** *by Jim DeKorne.* From the author of *The Hydroponic Hot House* comes the boldest exploration of psychedelic plants since Terence McKenna's *Food of the Gods.* DeKorne is a "psychonaut" exploring the "imaginal realms" through personal experimentation and scholarly research. He guides the reader through the history and lore of psychotropic plants, with advice on how to handle the eerie "entities" one encounters in "hyperspace." Plants and combinations covered include: Belladonna Alkaloids; D-Lysergic Acid Amide; Mescaline; Ayahuasca; Smokable DMT from Plants; Psilocybin; and more. *1994, 8½ x 11, 163 pp, illustrated, soft cover.* **$19.95.**

☐ **85212 THE POLITICS OF CONSCIOUSNESS,** *by Steve Kubby, with a Foreword by Terence McKenna.* The War on Drugs is really a war on freedom of thought. Our fundamental right to the pursuit of happiness includes the innate right to explore inner space without government interference. Author Steve Kubby explains how the authorities have short-circuited democracy through illegal, unconstitutional sanctions on the use of psychoactive plants and substances... and voices a fiercely patriotic rallying cry for a campaign of liberation that will enable us to recapture our freedom to think as we choose. This is a compelling, brutally honest book that is unlike anything ever published before. *1995, 8½ x 11, 160 pp, illustrated, soft cover.* **$18.95.**

☐ **85203 STONED FREE, How to Get High Without Drugs,** *by Patrick Wells and Douglas Rushkoff.* Now you can just say "NO!" to drugs... and get high anyway! This book enumerates many drugless consciousness-altering techniques, both timeless and recent in origin, that anyone can make use of. Meditation, breathing techniques, high-tech highs, sleep and dream manipulation, and numerous other methods are examined in detail. Avoid incarceration, save money, and skip the wear and tear on your body, while getting higher than a kite. *1995, 5½ x 8½, 157 pp, illustrated, soft cover.* **$14.95.**

☐ **94283 HARD CORE; Marginalized by Choice,** *by P.J. Nebergall. Hard Core: Marginalized by Choice* is a photo-journalistic odyssey into the Punk world that permeates our current intercultural milieu. P.J. Nebergall has placed the modern Punk phenomenon in its proper historical perspective by conducting hundreds of interviews and photo shoots with rebellious and disenchanted youngsters in both Great Britain and the United States. His text and photographs provide a penetrating glimpse into the philosophical musings and neotribal disfiguration fashion trends of today's disenfranchised youth. The author points out that there is no reason to fear the unstructured nihilism from the Punks we encounter. *1997, 5½ x 8½, 112 pp, several photographs, soft cover.* **$8.95.**

☐ **94293 LOOMPANICS UNLIMITED CONQUERS THE UNIVERSE, Articles and Features from the Best Book Catalog in the World,** *Edited by Michael Hoy.* Loompanics Unlimited has expanded the domain throughout the galaxies with 44 articles, stories, and essays in a mind-boggling compilation that will have every entity in space screaming in delight! Some of the most gifted writers on Earth have contributed to this compendium of literary masterfulness. We have also enlisted the aid of some of the planet's finest illustrators. The force was definitely with this talented group of creative troopers. Hey... we couldn't have conquered the universe without them! *1998, 8½ x 11, 224 pp, illustrated, soft cover.* **$13.95.**

☐ **94268 LOOMPANICS UNLIMITED LIVE! IN LAS VEGAS, Articles and Features from the Best Book Catalog in the World,** *Edited by Michael Hoy.* Every three years or so, Loompanics Unlimited lights up the desert landscape of American letters by compiling a collection of articles and stories, culled from the catalogs and supplements that we've published during that time. Since we've specialized in providing controversial and unusual works for over twenty years, it should come as no surprise to anyone that many of the selections in this book are both shocking and exhilarating. *1996, 8½ x 11, 255 pp, illustrated, soft cover.* **$14.95.**

☐ **94207 LOOMPANICS' GOLDEN RECORDS, Articles and Features from the Best Book Catalog in the World,** *Edited by Michael Hoy.* This collection will blow your thinking wide open! Essays on anarchy, hemp, housing and more promise to entertain, educate and illuminate even the most jaded reader. It contains more than 40 of the best and most imaginative pieces Loompanics has ever published, including work by Bob Black, Jim Hogshire, Michael Newton, James B. DeKorne, and many others. *Loompanics' Golden Records* also features artwork by some of America's most talented artists, such as Mark Zingarelli, Nick Bougas, and Ace Backwords. *1993, 8½ x 11, 200 pp, illustrated, soft cover.* **$10.95.**

☐ **94146 LOOMPANICS' GREATEST HITS, Articles and Features from the Best Book Catalog in the World,** *Edited by Michael Hoy.* A collection of articles and essays, cartoons and rants, gleaned from the pages of the Loompanics Unlimited book catalog. For over a decade, the Loompanics Catalog has served as a kiosk for writers from the far left, the far right and the *far out* — including Robert Anton Wilson, Bob Black, Kurt Saxon, Robert Shea and many, many others. A compendium of counterculture thought, this provocative book contains more than 75 features in all. *1990, 8½ x 11, 300 pp, illustrated, soft cover.* **$14.95.**

We offer the very finest in controversial and unusual books! — A complete catalog is sent **FREE** *with every book order. If you would like to order the catalog separately, please see our ad on the next page.*

SDTM2

LOOMPANICS UNLIMITED
PO BOX 1197
PORT TOWNSEND, WA 98368

Please send me the books I have checked above. I am enclosing $ _____ which includes $4.95 for shipping and handling of orders up to $25.00. Add $1.00 for each additional $25.00 ordered *Washington residents please include 7.9% for sales tax.*

NAME_____

ADDRESS _____

CITY_____

STATE/ZIP _____

We accept Visa, Discover, and MasterCard.
To place a credit card order *only,* call 1-800-380-2230,
24 hours a day, 7 days a week.
Check out our Web site: www.loompanics.com